The Complete I...

USENET A...

AAMOF	As a matter of fact		Member of the opposite sex
AFAIK	As far as I know	MOTSS	Member of the same sex
BTW	By the way	MUD	Multiple-User Dimension (or Dungeon)
CFV	Call For Votes		
CU	See you	NRN	No response necessary
DIIK	Damned if I know	OTOH	On the other hand
EOT	End of thread	PMJI	Pardon my jumping in
FOAF	Friend of a friend	RFD	Request for Discussion
FOTCL	Falling off the chair laughing	ROTF	Rolling on the floor
FTF	Face-to-face	ROTFL	Rolling on the floor laughing
FYA	For your amusement	ROTFLOL	Rolling on the floor laughing out loud
FYI	For your information		
HHOJ	Ha ha only joking	RSN	Real soon now (read: never)
HHOK	Ha ha only kidding	RTFM	Read the foolish manual
HHOS	Ha ha only serious	SO	Significant other
IMHO	In my humble opinion	TIA	Thanks in advance
IMO	In my opinion	TPTB	The powers that be
IOW	In other words	TTFN	Ta-ta for now
IYFEG	Insert your favorite ethnic group	WRT	With respect to
LOL	Laughing out loud	YMMV	Your mileage may vary
MEGO	My eyes glaze over		

Some USENET Smileys to Remember

Smiley	Meaning
:-)	Ha ha, just kidding
:-D	(Laughing) That's hilarious; I break myself up
;-)	(Winking) Nudge, nudge, wink, wink; I'm flirting
:-(	I'm unhappy
;-(	I'm crying
:-I	I'm indifferent; well whatever, never mind
:-#	My lips are sealed
:-/	I'm skeptical
:->	I'm being sarcastic
:-V	I'm shouting
;^)	I'm smirking
%-)	I've been staring at this screen for too long!

alpha books

Command Summary for Selecting a Newsgroup in rn and trn

Press	To do this	Press	To do this
g *newsgroup*	Go to (or subscribe to) *newsgroup*.	-	Go to the last group that was displayed.
u	Unsubscribe to the current newsgroup.	/*pattern*	Search forward for the first group with a name that includes *pattern*.
n	Go to the next group with unread articles.	/	Search forward again using the previous pattern.
N	Go to the next group.		
p	Go to the previous group with unread articles.	?*pattern*	Search backward for the first group with a name that includes *pattern*.
P	Go to the previous group.	?	Search backward again using the previous pattern.
^	Go to the first group with unread articles.		
1	Go to the first group.	l *pattern*	List all unsubscribed groups with a name that includes *pattern*.
$	Go to the last group.	L	List the contents of .**newsrc**.

tear here

Command Summary for Selecting an Article in rn and trn

Press	To do this	Press	To do this
y	Start reading articles in the selected newsgroup.	j	Junk this article (for example, mark it as read).
=	Display a list of Subject lines.	c	Catch up (for example, mark all articles as read).
n	Go to the next unread article.	k	Kill the current subject.
Ctrl+N	Go to the next unread article with the same subject.	/pattern	Search forward for the first Subject line that includes *pattern*.
N	Go to the next article.	/	Search forward again using the previous pattern.
p	Go back to the previous unread article.		
Ctrl+P	Go back to the previous unread article with the same subject.	?pattern	Search backward for the first Subject line that includes *pattern*.
P	Go back to the previous article.	?	Search backward again using the previous pattern.
^	Go to the first unread article.		
$	Go to the last article.	q	Quit the current newsgroup.

Command Summary for Reading an Article in rn and trn

Press	To do this	Press	To do this
Spacebar	Display the next page.	v	Redisplay the article, including the header.
d	Display the next half page.	Ctrl+X	Use rot13 to decode the article.
b	Display the previous page.	g *pattern*	Search for text that contains *pattern*.
q	Go to the end of the article.	G	Search again for text that contains the previous pattern.
Ctrl+R	Redisplay the article.		

Command Summary for All tin Lists

Press	To do this	Press	To do this
j	Move the highlight down one line.	/	Search forward for the first item with a name that includes a specified pattern.
k	Move the highlight up one line.		
Spacebar	Display the next page.	?	Search backward for the first item with a name that includes a specified pattern.
b	Display the previous page.		
$	Highlight the last item in the list.	r	Toggle the list between all items and those with unread articles.
<*n*>	Read the item with the id number *n*.		
Tab	Read the next unread item.		

Command Summary for the Newsgroup Selection List in tin

Press	To do this	Press	To do this
N	Highlight the next group with unread articles.	S	Subscribe to all groups that match a specified pattern.
g	Highlight (or subscribe to) a specified group.		
u	Unsubscribe to the highlighted group.	Enter	Read the highlighted group.
s	Subscribe to the highlighted group.	d	Toggle Group Selection list descriptions on and off.
U	Unsubscribe to all groups that match a specified pattern.		

The Complete IDIOT'S GUIDE TO USENET Newsgroups

by Paul McFedries

alpha books

A Division of Macmillan Computer Publishing
A Prentice Hall Macmillan Company
201 W. 103rd Street, Indianapolis, Indiana 46290 USA

This book is dedicated to those people who are dedicated readers of book dedications.

©1995 by Alpha Books

All rights reserved. No part of this book shall be reproduced, stored in a retrieval system, or transmitted by any means, electronic, mechanical, photocopying, recording, or otherwise, without written permission from the publisher. No patent liability is assumed with respect to the use of the information contained herein. While every precaution has been taken in the preparation of this book, the publisher and author assume no responsibility for errors or omissions. Neither is any liability assumed for damages resulting from the use of the information contained herein. For information, address Alpha Books, 201 West 103rd Street, Indianapolis, IN 46290.

International Standard Book Number: 1-56761-592-2

Library of Congress Catalog Card Number: 94-073042

98 97 96 95   8 7 6 5 4 3 2 1

Interpretation of the printing code: the rightmost double-digit number is the year of the book's first printing; the rightmost single-digit number is the number of the book's printing. For example, a printing code of 95-1 shows that this copy of the book was printed during the first printing of the book in 1995.

Screen reproductions in this book were created by means of the program Collage Complete from Inner Media, Inc., Hollis, NH.

Printed in the United States of America

Publisher
Marie Butler-Knight

Managing Editor
Elizabeth Keaffaber

Acquisitions Manager
Barry Pruett

Product Development Manager
Faithe Wempen

Development Editor
Heather Stith

Production Editor
Kelly Oliver

Manuscript Editors
Barry Childs-Helton, Anne Owen

Book Designer
Barbara Kordesh

Cover Designer
Scott Cook

Illustrator
Judd Winick

Indexer
Brad Herriman

Production Team
Gary Adair, Angela Calvert, Dan Caparo, Brad Chinn, Kim Cofer, Dave Eason, Jennifer Eberhardt, Rob Falco, David Garratt, Erika Millen, Angel Perez, Beth Rago, Bobbi Satterfield, Karen Walsh, Robert Wolf

Special thanks to Discovery Computing, Inc., Chris Denny, Brad Miser, and C. Herbert Feltner for ensuring the technical accuracy of this book.

Contents

Part 1: The USENET Nitty-Gritty   1

1 The Least You Need to Know   3

What Is USENET? 3
What Are Newsgroups? 4
What About These Article Thingies? 4
Netiquette? What's That? 5
What's a Flame? 6
What's a Smiley? 6
Can I Read Articles Without a Newsreader? 6
Can I Post Articles Without a Newsreader? 7
Is There Any Way to Get Only the Articles I Need? 7

2 So Just What the Heck Is USENET, Anyway?   9

The Internet: A Quick Review 10
Understanding the USENET Thing 13
Getting a Grip on Articles 16

3 Learning Netiquette: Minding Your USENET Ps and Qs   23

Netiquette for USENET Neophytes 24
A Primer on Posting Politeness 26
Avoiding Follow-up Faux Pas 30

4 Jargon, Acronyms, Smileys, and More   33

The Essential English-USENET Phrase Book 34
Flaming: Can't We All Just Get Along? 38
An Initial Look at USENET Acronyms 40
USENET Hieroglyphics: Smileys 43
USENET Miscellany 45

5 Useful USENET Tidbits   47

How to Gopher the News 48
Posting By Mail to Ensure You Get Your Two Cents In 50
Filtering the News Down to a Dull Roar 52
Getting Pictures from USENET Groups 54
Do It Yourself: Creating a Newsgroup 57

Part 2: Start Spreading the News: A Guide to Popular Newsreaders   63

6 Venerable UNIX Newsreaders: rn and trn   65

    rn and trn: The Lowdown on the Hi-Fi 66
    Cranking Up rn and trn 66
    How to Tame a Wild .newsrc File 69
    Selecting a Newsgroup 71
    Selecting an Article 74
    Selecting a Thread in trn 75
    Reading the News 76
    Posting an Original Article 79

7 A UNIX Newcomer: tin   81

    Breaking the tin Ice 82
    Selecting a Newsgroup 84
    Selecting an Article 89
    Reading an Article 91
    Posting an Original Article 93

8 Blowing Your Own Horn with Trumpet   95

    Getting Your Hands on Trumpet 96
    Before You Start Playing with Trumpet 97
    Starting Trumpet with a Flourish 97
    Subscribing and Unsubscribing in Trumpet 101
    Reading News with Trumpet 102
    Archiving an Article 105
    Following Up an Article 107
    Posting an Original Article 109

9 Pulling News Out of Thin Air: Working with AIR News   111

    Walking on AIR News 112
    Filling the Newsgroup Browser Window 113
    Finding a Newsgroup Needle in the Browser Haystack 114
    AIR Traffic Control: Subscribing and Unsubscribing 115
    Reading the News 118
    Saving and Printing an Article 119
    Following Up an Article 120
    Airing Your Views: Posting an Original Article 120
    Some AIR News Options 121

10 Surveying Netscape's USENET Landscape — 123

Surf's Up: Getting Started with Netscape's Newsreader 124
Handling Subscriptions in Netscape 126
Reading Articles 128
Saving an Article 131
Retorting: How to Follow Up an Article 131
Delurking: How to Post an Original Article 133

11 Newswatcher: The Mac Newsreader of Choice — 135

Where to Get NewsWatcher 136
Getting NewsWatcher Ready for Action 136
Finding a Newsgroup Needle in the
   Full Group List Haystack 137
Selecting Groups to Read 138
Reading Articles 139
Saving and Printing an Article 140
Following Up an Article 140
Posting an Original Article 141
Setting NewsWatcher Preferences 141

12 Checking Out the CompuServe Connection — 143

A Word About Internet Prejudice 144
Finding the USENET Newsgroups on CompuServe 144
Setting CompuServe's USENET Options 146
Subscribing and Unsubscribing in CompuServe 147
Reading the News 150
Saving an Article 152
Writing a Rejoinder: How to Follow Up an Article 152
Posting an Original Article 153

13 Chatting in Friendly Confines of America Online — 155

A Word About Internet Prejudice 156
Finding America Online's Newsgroups Area 156
Subscribing and Unsubscribing in America Online 157
Reading Articles 161
Saving and Printing an Article 162
Talking Back: Following Up an Article 162
Posting an Original Article 163

14 Doing the USENET Thing on Delphi — 165

Registering for Delphi's Internet Services 166
Getting Delphi's Newsreader Off to a Flying Start 166
Adding Newsgroups to Your Personal Favorites List 169
Reading Articles in Delphi 170
Saving an Article to Your Personal Workspace 172
How to Create a Signature File in Delphi 172
Following Up an Article 173
Posting an Original Article 174
Removing Newsgroups from Your
  Personal Favorites List 175

Part 3: All the News That's Fit to Surf — 177

15 Getting Star-Struck in the Entertainment Newsgroups — 179

Browsing the Boob-Tube Groups 179
Movie Newsgroups for Cinemaniacs 183
Reading About Reading: Books, 'Zines, and Comics 185
Hanging Out with Groupies, Roadies,
  and Other Music Fans 187
Boldly Going: The Science Fiction Newsgroups 191

16 Getting Advice in the Business and Consumer Newsgroups — 193

General Business Biz 194
Conversing on Consumer Concerns 194
Not Just IRAs: Investment Advice 195
Checking Out the USENET Classifieds 198
Job-Hunting on the Net 198

17 From Antiques to Videos: The Hobby Newsgroups — 201

Audio, Video, and Radio 201
Conversing with Collectors 205
An Online Banquet: Food and Cooking Newsgroups 207
Chatting in the Crafts Groups 209
Parleying in the Pet Newsgroups 210
Transportation Tête-à-Têtes 212
A Hodgepodge of Hobbies 215

18 Newsgroups for the Games People Play — 217

Computer Games 217
Multi-Player Games 220
Fantasy and Role-Playing Games 222
Board Games 224
Video and Arcade Games 225
Play-by-Mail Games 227
A Grab Bag of Game Groups 227

19 Left Versus Right: The Politics Newsgroups — 229

Keeping Abreast of Current Events 230
Freedom and Civil Liberties 234
Skirmishes Between Conservatives and Liberals 236
Trading Old War Stories in the War
   and History Groups 238
Miscellaneous Political Stuff 240

20 Psychology, Sex, and More: The Social Newsgroups — 241

Psychology and Support Groups 242
Pillow Talk: Sex and Sexuality Newsgroups 244
Traveling the World in the soc.culture.* Groups 245
Heavy Thinking in the Philosophy Forums 245
USENET's Religious Round Tables 246
Confabs on Kids and Education 249
A Selection of Social Newsgroups 251

21 Monday Morning Quarterbacking in the Sports Newsgroups — 253

Groups for Baseball Buffs 253
Hoops, There It Is: The Basketball Groups 255
Huddling in the Football Newsgroups 256
Hockey Night in USENET 258
Other Sports Groups 259

22 Geek Heaven: The Computer Newsgroups — 267

Artificial Intelligence 268
Discussions About Data Communications 269
Multimedia Madness Online 271
USENET's Software Newsgroups 272

Operating Systems 276
Computer Systems' User Groups 280

23 Talking with Tall-Forehead Types in the Science Groups 285

Dissecting the Biology Newsgroups 286
Conversations with Chemists 287
Groups for Geology and Other Earth Sciences 288
USENET's Medical Science Newsgroups 289
Mathematical Mystery Tours 292
USENET's Forums for Physicists 294
Newsgroups for the Social Sciences 296
The Space and Astronomy Groups 298
More Science Stuff 299

24 News About the Net: Internet-Related Newsgroups 301

Random Internet Interactions 302
Newsgroups for Specific Internet Services 305
USENET-Related Newsgroups 307

Index 311

Introduction

The Information Superhighway (or the National Information Infrastructure or the Infobahn or the I-Way—whatever its current name *du jour*) doesn't exist yet, and it isn't likely to appear for many years to come. But we live in a wired world, so many people aren't content to twiddle their thumbs and diddle their mice until the revolution comes. Instead, they've flocked by the millions to the closest thing we have to a digital expressway: the Internet.

Unfortunately, the Internet (or the Net, for short) is complicated; it's complicated to get on the Net, use the Net software, and find what you're looking for on the Net. In short, the Internet makes most of us feel like complete idiots.

The problem, I think, is the sheer size of the Internet. Once you've chosen from among the dozens of access providers, settled on which of the umpteen Internet services you want to use, and selected the appropriate software to get at these services, you're still faced with the daunting task of sifting through the mountainloads of Internet info that's available. To call the wealth and scope of all this data breathtaking is to indulge in big-time understatement.

So what's the solution? For my money, the best way to tackle any large project is to break it up into smaller chunks. If the Internet is too big to take in at a glance, then just reduce your field of view. If the sheer variety of Internet services is causing your brain to cramp, then just concentrate on one service at a time.

Welcome to The Complete Idiot's Guide to USENET Newsgroups!

That, in a nutshell, is what this book is all about. In *The Complete Idiot's Guide to USENET Newsgroups*, we'll look only at the subset of the Internet that's known as USENET. I'll explain what USENET is, how you can access it, and why you should care. Our goal will be to learn the basics of USENET with a minimum of fuss and bother. No long-winded technical treatises; no obscure Internet jargon; no networking mumbo-jumbo. You'll get just the USENET facts you need to know, not everything there is to know. My main assumption will be that you have a busy life—that all you really want is to get what you need out of USENET and then move on to more important things.

To keep things simple, I'm going to make two other assumptions. First, I'll assume you have some sort of Internet connection already established, and have at least a passing familiarity with the major Internet services. (Although Chapter 2 contains some Internet basics, this should be considered a quick review, not a true tutorial. If you're totally in the dark about the Internet, I'd suggest picking up a copy of *The Complete Idiot's Guide to the Internet* by Peter Kent.)

My second assumption will be that you're reasonably comfortable operating your computer. *The Complete Idiot's Guide to USENET Newsgroups* won't tell you how to turn on your machine, wield a mouse, or reset your computer with a well-aimed kick. For this kind of info, check out *The Complete Idiot's Guide to PCs* by Joe Kraynak, or *The Complete Idiot's Guide to Windows* by some geek named Paul McFedries.

What's in It for You?

Since most of us pay through the nose for our time spent online, I've set up this book so you can get whatever information you need quickly—and then get back to your session. I encourage you *not* to read the book cover-to-cover, and memorizing stuff should be avoided at all costs. To get you started, here's a brief overview of the book's structure:

Part 1: The USENET Nitty-Gritty

The book leads off with five chapters that give you the basics of USENET. Chapter 1, "The Least You Need to Know," takes you through a list of frequently asked USENET questions. Chapter 2, "So Just What the Heck Is USENET, Anyway?," gives you the lowdown on USENET, and explains fundamental USENET concepts such as newsgroups, articles, and posting. For the Miss Manners fans in the crowd, Chapter 3, "Learning Netiquette: Minding Your USENET Ps and Qs," shows you the various do's and don'ts that are the cornerstone of polite USENET society. Chapter 4, "Jargon, Acronyms, Smileys, and More," translates some common words, acronyms, and symbols into plain English. Finally, Chapter 5, "Useful USENET Tidbits," gives you a smorgasbord of handy tricks and techniques designed to make your life online a little more bearable.

Part 2: Start Spreading the News: A Guide to Popular Newsreaders

In USENET parlance, a *newsreader* is the software you use to read and respond to articles, and to post articles of your own. Although it's possible to peruse USENET news without a newsreader (Chapter 5 shows you how it's done), newsreader software really makes things easy. Part 2 takes you through ten of today's most popular newsreaders: rn, trn, tin, Trumpet, AIR News, NetScape, NewsWatcher, and the newsreaders available through CompuServe, America Online, and Delphi.

Part 3: All the News That's Fit to Surf

As you'll see, USENET is divided into various *newsgroups* that cater to particular interests and hobbies. If dogs are your thing, you'll find a dogs newsgroup with all sorts of interesting canine lore. Addicted to crossword puzzles? There's a puzzle newsgroup that should satisfy your cravings. In fact, there are thousands of newsgroups covering everything from alien visitors to zoology. How do you manage this torrent of info? Well for starters, the chapters in Part 3 take you through many of the most often-read newsgroups. We'll look at the groups that cater to entertainment (Chapter 15), business (Chapter 16), politics (Chapter 19), and lots more.

The Complete Idiot's Guide to USENET Newsgroups also includes a handy tear-out reference card that gives you easy access to important (or just plain handy) USENET stuff.

Features of This Book

The Complete Idiot's Guide to USENET Newsgroups is designed so you can get the information you need fast, and then get on with your life. To that end, I'll use certain conventions throughout the book. For example, if you ever need to type something, it will appear like this:

type this

Some USENET software packages use particular *key combinations* to access their features. I'll be writing these key combinations by separating the two keys with a plus sign (+). For example, I may say something like "press **Ctrl+P** to post an article." The "Ctrl+P" part means you hold down the **Ctrl** key, tap the **P** key, and then release **Ctrl**. (Don't worry: you are in no way required to memorize these keyboard contortions to become a competent USENET user.) Speaking of keyboards, you should note as well that I'll often tell you to do a certain thing and then "press **Enter**." If you're using a terminal that doesn't have an Enter key, press the **Return** key instead.

Also, look for the following icons that'll help you learn just what you need to know:

This icon defines geeky computer terms in plain English.

There are always dangerous ways to do things on a computer—and this icon will tell you how to avoid them.

These boxes contain notes and technical info about USENET that are (hopefully!) interesting and useful.

If you rearrange the letters in "complete idiot," you end up with "de cool tip time," and that's just what this icon means. It presents you with handy tips that show you easier ways to get things done in USENET.

Acknowledgments (Faves, Raves, and Assorted Thumbs Up)

Writing books is endlessly fascinating for me because what begins as just a few thoughts ends up as a physical, tangible thing that gets sent out (hopefully) to the far-flung corners of the world. Of course, the trip from thought to thing is a long one, and lots of people get their fingers in a book's pie before it's ready to ship. This book was no exception. It began with Acquisitions Manager Barry Pruett asking me to write the darn thing. Then I hashed out an outline with my good buddy Faithe Wempen, Alpha Books' Product Development Manager. Then the Development Editor Heather Stith made sure I towed the line and met my deadlines. (This is important because I often agree with what Douglas Adams has said: "I like deadlines; I especially like the sound they make as they go whooshing by.") Then Copy Editors Barry Childs-Helton and Anne Owen made sure my prose was pristine (and wasn't infested with too many Canadianisms). Next, DCI, Chris Denny, Brad Miser and C. Herbert Feltner made sure what I said happens really does happen. Finally, Production Editor Kelly Oliver made sure everything was where it was supposed to be. I extend big-time thanks to all of you for your competence and sheer niceness. (There must be something in the Indiana water, because all the Hoosiers I've ever met are just the nicest people on the face of the planet.) Before I forget, I'd also like to thank Ted Alspach for helping me on the NewsWatcher chapter, and all the too-numerous-to-mention Netizens who provided advice, suggestions, criticism, and comic relief.

Part 1
The USENET Nitty-Gritty

One factor that separates the wheat from the chaff in USENET is how prepared a person is for the ordeal to come. People who just wade in without picking up some background info (or boning up on the few USENET fundamentals) never seem to stick around very long. They just rummage around for a bit, sniffing here and there for online truffles and other goodies. They never find them, of course, because they haven't done their homework in advance, so they just give up and are never heard from again.

The chapters here in Part 1 are designed to help you avoid such a fate. I'll take you through everything you need to know to get the most out of USENET. We'll begin with the basics (Chapters 1 and 2), and work our way up to things like online etiquette (Chapter 3), understanding USENET jargon (Chapter 4), and some goodies that'll help you tackle USENET in your own way (Chapter 5).

Chapter 1

The Least You Need to Know

As you'll soon find out, much of what you see on USENET takes the form of commentary, criticism, and the cut-and-thrust of contentious debate. But the majority of USENET interaction is just basic Q&A: someone will ask a question, and some other kind soul (or souls) will provide an answer. Questions play such a big part on USENET that there are files called "Frequently Asked Questions lists." These files simply list all the questions people have asked repeatedly over the years (and that the veterans have become sick of answering). You'll find out more about these things in Chapter 3, "Learning Netiquette: Minding Your USENET Ps and Qs." For now, however, this chapter presents you with a Frequently Asked Questions list for *The Complete Idiot's Guide to USENET Newsgroups*.

What Is USENET?

The simplest, nontechnical definition of USENET is that it's a collection of discussion topics. For example, there's a Grateful Dead topic where Deadheads from around the world discuss concerts, upcoming events, lyrics, and whatever other Dead-related stuff comes to mind. Each of these topics (there are thousands) are open to all comers, and they don't cost you anything (outside of whatever exorbitant rates you're paying for your Internet connection, of course).

These topics are broken down into seven main *hierarchies*: **comp** (computer hardware and software), **misc** (miscellaneous stuff that doesn't really fit anywhere else), **news** (USENET-related topics), **rec** (entertainment, hobbies, sports, and more), **sci** (science and technology), **soc** (sex, culture, religion, and politics), and **talk** (debates about controversial political and cultural topics). A large **alt** hierarchy covers topics that don't fit into the main seven, and a number of smaller hierarchies cover specialized interests (such as the **biz** hierarchy that's used for product announcements and advertising).

For a more detailed look at USENET, see Chapter 2, "So Just What the Heck Is USENET, Anyway?"

What Are Newsgroups?

Newsgroup is the official designation for each of the USENET discussion topics (they're often called simply *groups*, for short). There are, as I write this, over 8,000 newsgroups (with more popping up every day), and they cover everything from the pleasures of antiques to the mysteries of Zima.

Each newsgroup name identifies the topic it covers. The name always begins with the hierarchy in which the group resides, followed by a dot, followed by the topic itself. So, for example, the newsgroup **rec.antiques** is in the **rec** hierarchy and it contains discussions about antiques. Topics that are more specific will often add more dots and words to the name. For example. **alt.tv.simpsons** is a newsgroup in the **alt** hierarchy. Its main topic is TV, but it focuses in on the show *The Simpsons*. For more newsgroup know-how, check out Chapter 2, "So Just What the Heck Is USENET, Anyway?"

What About These Article Thingies?

An *article* is an individual message in a newsgroup. Whoever has something to say in a group composes an article, and then uses newsreader software to *post* the article to the group. Others can then read the article and (if they like) post *follow-up* articles that comment on or criticize the original message. Others may do the same; you can easily end up with a dozen articles related to the same topic. A bunch of related articles is called a *thread*.

Each article you'll see has three sections: a *header* that gives the vital statistics of the article—who sent it, when, the subject of the article; a *body* that contains the message itself; and an optional *signature* that tells the reader more about the person who sent the article.

There are more article facts in Chapter 2, "So Just What the Heck Is USENET, Anyway?"

Netiquette? What's That?

USENET is a huge, unwieldy mass that has (like the Internet as a whole) no central "powers that be" who can dictate content or standards. This is, for the most part, a good thing; it means there's no censorship, and no one can wield authority arbitrarily. To prevent this organized chaos from degenerating into mere anarchy, however, a set of guidelines has been put together over the years. These guidelines are known collectively as *netiquette* (*network etiquette*), and they offer suggestions on the proper way to interact with USENET and its denizens. You can think of netiquette as a sort Emily Post/Miss Manners guide to USENET behavior. To give you a taste of what I mean, here are some netiquette highlights to consider:

➤ Read the newsgroups **news.announce.newusers** and **news.newusers.questions** if you're new to USENET.

➤ Read the Frequently Asked Questions list for a newsgroup before posting your own articles.

➤ Don't post to a newsgroup until you've read its articles for a while and developed a feel for the group's style and conventions.

➤ Use article Subject lines that explain what your article is about.

➤ Make sure you post your article to the appropriate newsgroup.

➤ Don't send an article to multiple groups unless it's truly necessary.

➤ Don't SHOUT by writing your articles entirely in uppercase letters.

➤ Don't use a regular newsgroup to post test messages. Use one of the **test** groups, instead (e.g., **misc.test**).

➤ Don't advertise products or services in the regular newsgroups. Use the groups in the **biz** hierarchy, instead.

To sink your teeth into more netiquette niceties, go to Chapter 3, "Learning Netiquette: Minding Your USENET Ps and Qs."

What's a Flame?

The vast majority of USENET correspondence is civil and courteous, but with millions of participants from all over the world, it's inevitable that some folks will rub each other the wrong way. When this happens, the combatants may exchange emotionally charged, caustic, often obscene messages called *flames*. When enough of these messages change hands, an out-and-out *flame war* develops. These usually burn themselves out after a while, and then the rest of us can get back to more interesting things.

There are lots more flame facts in Chapter 4, "Jargon, Acronyms, Smileys, and More."

What's a Smiley?

One of the problems with written communication (especially for people who don't express themselves in writing very well, or for whom English is not their native tongue) is that it's easy to be misunderstood. In face-to-face conversation, a smile, wink, or change in voice inflection alerts the other person that you're being humorous, wry, sarcastic, or whatever. This is a lot harder to accomplish in an article, so several *smileys* (or *emoticons*) have been developed over the years. Smileys are symbol combinations designed to let everyone know your current feelings. For example, to let people know you're being humorous, you'd use the following smiley: :-). (To get the full effect, tilt your head to the left.) Other smileys can let people know you're sad :-(or winking ;-). You'll find lots more in Chapter 4, "Jargon, Acronyms, Smileys, and More."

Can I Read Articles Without a Newsreader?

A *newsreader* is software that lets you subscribe to newsgroups, read their articles, and post your own articles. If you don't have access to a newsreader, you can still read the news by using the Gopher service. Here are a couple of sites you can try:

➤ Gopher to **gopher.bham.ac.uk** and select the **Usenet News Reader** item from the main menu.

➤ Gopher to **gopher.msu.edu**, select **News & Weather**, and then select **Usenet News**.

For more details, burrow your way to Chapter 5, "Useful USENET Tidbits."

Can I Post Articles Without a Newsreader?

If all you do is read USENET news (this is called *lurking*), you're only having half the fun you could. To get the most out of USENET, post your own articles so other people get the benefit of your vast wisdom and experience. What do you do if you don't have a newsreader? No sweat. You can still post articles via e-mail. Just send your article to *newsgroup*@cs.utexas.edu, where *newsgroup* is the name of the group in which you want the article to appear. Make sure you replace the dots in the group name with dashes (e.g., **alt-zima** instead of **alt.zima**). This procedure (and how to use e-mail to post articles anonymously) is explained in Chapter 5, "Useful USENET Tidbits."

Is There Any Way to Get Only the Articles I Need?

With over 8,000 newsgroups generating over 60,000 messages a day, there's just too much USENET info for us mere mortals to digest. If you have some specific interests, how can you make sure you read every article that's related to those interests? The only reasonable method I know of is to subscribe to the Stanford Netnews Filtering Service. "Subscribing" means you tell the service to keep its eagle eyes peeled for certain words or phrases. When these show up in an article, the service automatically mails the article to you. The mechanics for subscribing are outlined in Chapter 5, "Useful USENET Tidbits."

Chapter 2

So Just What the Heck Is USENET, Anyway?

In This Chapter

➤ A few Internet basics
➤ Getting the big USENET picture
➤ Understanding USENET newsgroups
➤ Learning about articles, posting, and such
➤ Lots of useful background info for USENET newcomers

Are you new to the Internet (or to USENET, in particular) and feeling more than a little overwhelmed at the sheer monstrosity, the unabashed gargantuanness (to coin a word), of it all? Or have you been poking around in various Net nooks and crannies for a little while, and now you feel a bit confused by the overwhelming variety of resources available? Perhaps you're simply wondering just what in blue blazes you've gotten yourself into this time.

Ah, not to worry. These feelings are a perfectly normal reaction to the size and scope of the Internet. Believe me, *everybody* is overwhelmed at first, and *nobody*—not even the most grizzled of Net veterans—is capable of grasping the thing in its entirety.

So what's a body to do? Well, as I mentioned in the Introduction, you need to knock the Internet down to size by concentrating on one thing at a time. This book examines the most popular part of the Internet: USENET. In this chapter, we tackle some basic USENET concepts so you'll have a least some idea of what you're doing out there in cyberspace.

The Internet: A Quick Review

First off, let's get the boring definition of the Internet out of the way. *The Internet* is (yawn) a worldwide collection of networks that can communicate with each other over high-speed phone lines, fiber-optic cables, or (sometimes) satellite links. In turn, each of these networks is a collection of two or more computers (usually dozens or hundreds) connected via specialized cables so they can share resources such as files and printers. These networks are typically owned by universities, corporations, research labs, and businesses that enable private individuals and small companies to hook themselves up to the Internet (the latter are called *access providers*).

> **Cyberspace** is the place you "go to" when you reach out beyond your own computer (usually via modem) and interact with information or people on other computer systems.

This prosaic definition doesn't even begin to describe the Internet as it exists today. It doesn't come close to capturing the diversity and utility of this most complex of human creations, nor does it explain why it holds such fascination for hackers and computer neophytes alike. Here, then, is an attempt to redefine the Internet as it *really* is:

The Internet is a means of communication. Many people use the Internet solely for exchanging electronic mail (e-mail) messages with friends, colleagues, or even total strangers. The main attraction here is that e-mail is ridiculously cheap. Outside of your normal Internet connection fees, it costs precisely nothing to send an e-mail message, whether the recipient is on the other side of town or on the other side of the planet. It's also fast (even the longest missive takes only a few seconds to send), and it's just about universal because every major e-mail system in the world has built-in electronic "bridges" (called *gateways*) that allow their users to send messages to and receive messages from the Internet.

Chapter 2 ➤ *So Just What the Heck Is USENET, Anyway?*

The Internet is an information resource. Now *that's* an understatement. The various computers that make up the Internet are brimful-to-bursting with documents and other resources that cover just about any topic imaginable. Whether it's rocket science, stock market quotes, or just the latest soap opera updates, the Internet has something to say about it. (The problem, of course, is *finding* the information you need. The Net is so vast that looking for a particular document is often like looking for the proverbial needle in a digital haystack.)

The Internet is a storehouse. One thing computers do real well is store stuff. Be it documents, graphics, sounds, or software, the millions of Net computers are repositories of massive numbers of files and programs. And to make our lives that much easier, the Internet has a number of built-in resources (described later in this section) that let you retrieve these files with only a few keystrokes or mouse clicks.

The Internet is a community. For me, the truly astonishing thing about the Net is that behind everything you see—messages, documents, software—there stands the person (or persons) responsible for it. Untold numbers of Internet enthusiasts have spent countless hours assembling information, writing software, and answering questions. Amazingly, all this toiling in obscurity somehow managed to create a massive structure that works surprisingly well, *without* the need for any semblance of central authority or governing body. Having said that, however, I don't want to be accused of viewing the Net through rose-colored glasses. Any endeavor that boasts millions of participants is bound to attract its fair share of bozos and bellyachers. Hey, that's life. But overall, the Net denizens you'll encounter will be surprisingly helpful and generous, and are only too willing to engage in random acts of senseless kindness. USENET is the best place to get a real sense of the Internet community in action, because it allows diverse users to "converse" on a multitude of topics.

Throughout this book, I'll be pointing out how you can obtain more info on various USENET topics and discussions. Just to make sure we're always on the same page, let's review some of the available services you can use to interact with other parts of the Internet:

FTP   Short for *File Transfer Protocol*, FTP is the most common way to bring files from a particular Net locale onto your computer.

11

Typical FTP instructions will include a *host name* (the Internet name of the computer storing the file; e.g., **ftp.microsoft.com**), the *directory* (the file's storage location inside the computer; e.g., **/pub/software**), and the name of the file itself.

Gopher   A *Gopher* is a system that displays Internet documents and services as menu options. You just select a menu choice; the Gopher will either display a document or transfer you to a different Gopher system. Gopher descriptions always include an *address* (the Internet location of the Gopher system) and one or more menu options to select.

World Wide Web   Throughout this book you'll catch me saying things like, "To find out more about proper Net etiquette, see Chapter 3, 'Learning Netiquette: Minding Your USENET Ps and Qs.'" These instructions let you jump easily from your current position to another part of the book to get more info. This is, essentially, the way the *World Wide Web* works. Each document in the Web (as it's usually called) serves two purposes: it contains information that is useful in and of itself, and it contains specially marked words or phrases that serve as "links" to other Web documents. If you select the link, the Web loads the other document automatically. The descriptions of World Wide Web documents are called *uniform resource locators (*URLs), and they look something like this:

   http://www.internic.net/infoguide.html

Telnet   This is a program that lets you log in to another computer on the Internet and use its resources as though they existed on your machine. For example, you can often telnet to a computer to use its newsreader software. Of course, not every computer will let just anyone barge in unannounced. In many cases, you'll need to have an account on that machine, and you'll be required to enter your user ID and password to log in. Still, there are plenty of computers that are happy to allow guests. For example, there are a number of online libraries you can telnet to and use their electronic card catalogues. Telnet descriptions require only the Internet address of the computer and, in some cases, a specific user ID.

Mailing Lists This is a system that sends out regular e-mail messages related to a specific topic. For example, if home beer-making is your thing, then you'd definitely want to subscribe to the Homebrew mailing list to get things like recipes, how-to articles, beer festival announcements, and more. You usually *subscribe* by sending an e-mail message to the list's subscription address.

Understanding the USENET Thing

Okay, so much for the Internet as a whole. Now let's turn our attention to the real subject of this book: USENET. USENET is, in essence, a collection of topics available for discussion. These discussion groups (or *newsgroups*, as they're normally called) are open to all and sundry, and they won't cost you a dime (aside from the usual connection charges, of course).

Will you find anything interesting in these discussion groups? Well, let's put it this way: with around 8,000 (that's right, eight *thousand*) groups to choose from, if you can't find anything that strikes your fancy, you'd better check your pulse. And if a particular topic that really turns your crank doesn't have its own group, it's even possible to create your own. The next few sections explain USENET in a little more detail so you can hit the ground running in the book's remaining chapters.

> USENET began its life back in 1979 at Duke University. A couple of resident computer whizzes (James Elliot and Tom Truscott) needed some way to easily share research, knowledge, and smart-aleck opinions among the Duke students and faculty. So, in true hacker fashion, they built a program that would do just that. Eventually other universities joined in, and the thing just mushroomed. Today, it's estimated that over 7 million people participate in USENET, sending a whopping 60,000 messages a day.

Getting the USENET Patois Down Pat

For a beginner, one of the most intimidating things about the Internet is its aggressive use of jargon and colorful idioms. The USENET

Part 1 ➤ *The USENET Nitty-Gritty*

vernacular is particularly rich, and I'll be devoting an entire chapter to it (see Chapter 4, "Jargon, Acronyms, Smileys, and More"). For starters, though, let's look at some basic USENET lingo:

Hierarchy   USENET divides its discussion groups into several classifications, or *hierarchies*. There are seven so-called *mainstream* hierarchies:

comp	Computer hardware and software.
misc	Miscellaneous stuff that doesn't really fit anywhere else.
news	USENET-related topics.
rec	Entertainment, hobbies, sports, and more.
sci	Science and technology.
soc	Sex, culture, religion, and politics.
talk	Debates about controversial political and cultural topics.

Most USENET-equipped Internet service providers will give you access to all the mainstream hierarchies. There's also a huge **alt** (alternative) hierarchy that covers just about anything that either doesn't belong in a mainstream hierarchy or is too whacked-out to be included with the mainstream stuff. There are also tons of smaller hierarchies designed for specific geographic areas. For example, the **ba** hierarchy includes discussion groups for the San Francisco Bay area, the **can** hierarchy is devoted to Canadian topics, and so on.

Newsgroup   *Newsgroup* (or, often, simply *group*) is the official USENET moniker for a discussion topic.

> Why are they called *news*groups? Well, the original Duke University system was designed to share announcements, research findings, and commentary. In other words, people would use this system if they had some "news" to share with their colleagues. The name stuck, and now you'll often hear USENET referred to as *Netnews* or simply as *the news*.

14

Article   An individual message in a newsgroup discussion.

Post   To send an article to a newsgroup. Someone who posts an article is called, of course, a *poster* (but that doesn't mean you can stick pins in them and hang them on the wall).

Newsreader   The software you use to read a newsgroup's articles and to post your own articles.

Figuring Out Newsgroup Names

Newsgroup names aren't too hard to understand, but I'm going to go through the drill to make sure you're comfortable with them. In their basic guise, newsgroup names have three parts: the *hierarchy* to which they belong, followed by a *dot*, followed by the newsgroup's *topic*. For example, check out the following name:

rec.boats

Here, the hierarchy is **rec** (recreation), and the topic is **boats**. (To be hip, you'd pronounce this name as *reck dot boats*.) Sounds simple enough so far. But many newsgroups were too broad for some people, so they started breaking them down into subgroups. For example, the rec.boats people who were into canoeing got sick of speedboat discussions, so they created their own "paddle" newsgroup. Here's how its official name looks:

rec.boats.paddle

You'll see lots of these subgroups in your USENET travels. (For example, there are also newsgroups named **rec.boats.building** and **rec.boats.racing**.) Occasionally, you'll see sub-subgroups such as **soc.culture.african.american**, but these are still rare in most hierarchies (the exception is the **comp** hierarchy, where there are all kinds of these sub-subgroups). One variation on this theme is to tack on extra subgroup names for emphasis. For example, consider the following newsgroup:

alt.tv.dinosaur.barney.die.die.die

This newsgroup, of course, is designed for people who don't exactly like TV's Barney the Dinosaur (to put it mildly).

Part 1 ➤ *The USENET Nitty-Gritty*

Getting a Grip on Articles

Articles, as you can imagine, are the lifeblood of USENET. Happily, USENET places no restrictions on article content (although, as you'll see below, a few newsgroups have *moderators* who decide whether an article is worth posting). Articles can be as long or as short as you like (although extremely long articles are frowned upon because they take so long to retrieve); they can contain whatever thoughts you feel like getting off your chest (within the confines of the newsgroup's subject matter, of course). You're free to be inquiring, informative, interesting, infuriating, or even incompetent. (Having said all that, however, I don't want you to get the impression that USENET is total anarchy. If you want to get along with your fellow newshounds, there are a few guidelines you should follow. Read Chapter 3, "Learning Netiquette: Minding Your USENET Ps and Qs," to get the poop on USENET politesse.) The next few sections explore some basic article-related topics.

Article Anatomy

In order for you to make heads or tails of the articles you read, let's inspect a typical specimen to see what's what. As you can see in the following figure, an article has three main parts: the *header*, the *body*, and the *signature*.

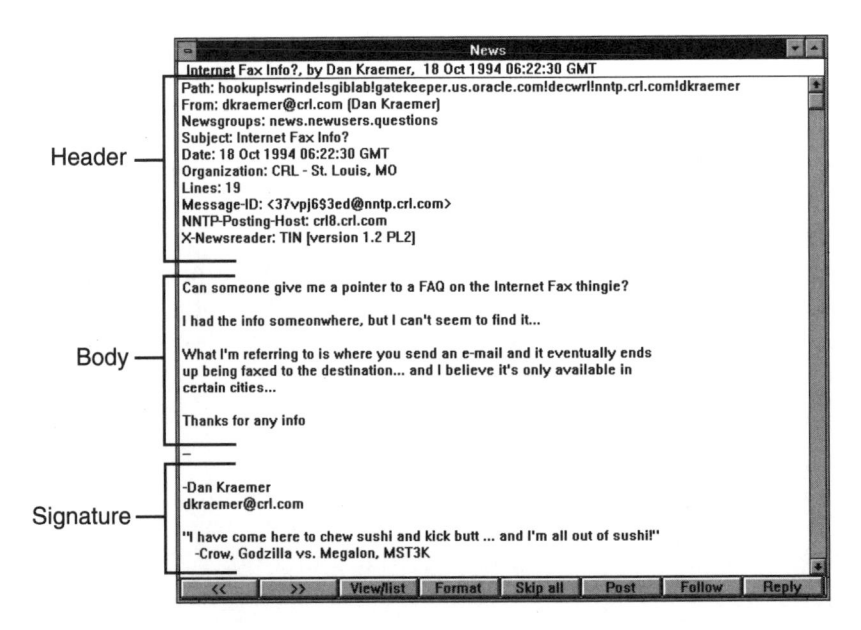

Yer basic newsgroup article.

16

Chapter 2 ➤ *So Just What the Heck Is USENET, Anyway?*

The header contains the article's vital statistics. Most of the stuff in the header is pure gobbledygook, and can be safely ignored by the likes of you and me. Some of the data is useful, though, so let's take a closer look:

From   This is the e-mail address and (usually) the real name of the person who posted the article.

> Most newsreader software has a command that will cut article headers down to size by showing (usually) only the From, Subject, and Date lines.

Subject   This is a one-line description of what the article is all about. When you're doing your own posting, this line is crucial because most USENETers decide whether they'll read an article just by scanning the Subject line. To maximize your readership, make sure the Subject line is detailed enough that it accurately reflects what your article talks about. (I'll talk more about this in Chapter 3, "Learning Netiquette: Minding Your USENET Ps and Qs.")

Date   This is the date and time the article was posted to USENET. The time given is usually Greenwich Mean Time (GMT) which is 5 hours earlier than Eastern Standard Time. (You'll also see GMT referred to as Universal Time, or UT.)

Organization   This optional line contains the name of the company the person who posted the article works for.

Approved   Some newsgroups are *moderated*, which means all the articles go through a single person who then decides whether the article is worth posting. Check out **rec.humor.funny** for an example of a moderated newsgroup.

The body of the article is the message text you want the world to see. As I've said, just about anything goes when writing your articles. However, here are a few things to keep in mind when polishing your prose:

➤ Although it's considered bad USENET taste to complain about someone's spelling and grammar (USENET is, after all, an international network, so not everyone speaks perfect English), it's still human nature to think less of an article that has poor spelling and tortured syntax. So always try to proofread your articles before firing them off to your favorite newsgroup.

17

➤ Keep in mind that your readers are probably working their way through dozens of other articles. Don't ramble on, and try to keep your missives short and to the point. Separating ideas into paragraphs (with a space between them) will also make your article easier to plow through.

➤ Don't try to show off with fancy adjectives and polysyllabic nouns. USENET readers appreciate articles that are clear and unpretentious.

➤ Keep in mind that your article has a potential audience of thousands. While nobody likes to "dumb down" his writing, nobody likes to read something that's way over his head, either. Unless you're posting to a group full of other eggheads (such as some of the **sci** groups, or **rec.org.mensa**), aim your writing at a general audience.

➤ If you're thinking about posting something that may offend someone, think again. Most USENET newcomers forget that there are real, live human beings on the other end of a post, so they just write whatever comes to mind and think no more of it. Ask yourself whether you'd be comfortable reciting your article to someone's face. If you just *have* to send something offensive, some newsreaders let you "rotate" the text so the casual reader can't make out what it says. (I'll explain more about this in the next section.)

➤ Remember, too, that subtlety *almost never* works in print. If you're being humorous or wry, there are things called *smileys* that will let your readers know. Chapter 4, "Jargon, Acronyms, Smileys, and More," gives you lots of examples.

The signature is an addendum that appears at the bottom of the article. Its purpose is to let the folks out there reading your message know a little more about the whiz who posted it. Although signatures are optional, most people use them because they can add a friendly touch. You can put anything you like in your signature, but most people just put their real name, their e-mail address, and maybe a quote or two that fits in with their character. (Some signatures are absurdly elaborate, but most USENET types get offended at any signature that extends for more than four lines.) Your newsreader should let you create a separate signature file so you don't have to type it in yourself every time. In UNIX systems, you should create a text file named **.signature** in your home directory.

"Hey, This Article Contains Nothing but Gibberish!"

When you're perusing articles, you may occasionally come across an article that appears to be a random jumble of letters. No, this isn't some weird Internet derivative of Esperanto, it just means the text has been *encoded* (or *rotated*) by the poster using a scheme called *rot13*. Rot13 encodes words by substituting each letter with the letter that is 13 positions away in the alphabet. So *a* becomes *n*, *b* becomes *o*, and so on. The letters toward the end of the alphabet wrap around to the beginning (*y* becomes *l*, *z* becomes *m*, etc.).

Why the Sam Hill would anyone do such a thing? Well, rot13 articles usually contain a joke or observation that might be offensive to some readers. So, out of courtesy, the poster rotates the text before sending it. And if you're brave enough to want to read the article anyway, most newsreaders have a command that will decode the text automatically.

> How do you encode an article using rot13? Good question. Some of the newer newsreaders (such as Trumpet) have built-in commands that will encode an article for you. In other cases, you need to use the UNIX command **tr** (short for translate) to get the job done. Here's how it works:
>
> ```
> tr '[a-m][n-z][A-M][N-Z]''[n-z][a-m][N-Z][A-M]' File EncodedFile
> ```
>
> Here, *File* is the name of the file containing the text you want to encode, and *EncodedFile* is the name of the file you end up with (i.e., the one containing the encoded text).

It's also common courtesy to use rot13 on articles that contain spoilers such as movie endings and riddle answers. In these cases, you should also add the text "**[Spoiler]**" in the article's Subject line. Similarly, you'd add "**[Offensive to Canadians]**" (or whomever) if you're submitting something in poor taste. One caveat, however: there are two newsgroups—**alt.tasteless** and **alt.tasteless.jokes**—where, by definition, *every* article is offensive. Because it's assumed that everyone who reads these groups knows this, *none* of the articles are encoded with rot13. In other words, enter at your own risk!

Following a Newsgroup "Discussion"

Earlier, I told you that newsgroups were "discussion topics," but that doesn't mean they work like a real-world discussion, in which you have immediate conversational give-and-take. Instead, newsgroup discussions lurch ahead in discrete chunks (articles) and unfold over a relatively long period of time (sometimes even weeks or months).

To get the flavor of a newsgroup discussion, think of the "Letters to the Editor" section of a newspaper. Someone writes an article in the paper, and then later someone else sends in a letter commenting on the content of the article. A few days after that more letters may come in, such as a rebuttal from the original author, or someone else weighing in with their two cents' worth. Eventually, the "discussion" dies out either because the topic has been exhausted, or because everyone loses interest.

Newsgroups work the same way. Someone posts an article, and then the other people who read the group can, if they like, respond to the article by posting a *follow-up* article. Others can then respond to the response, and so on down the line. This entire discussion—from the original article to the last response—is called a *thread*. For example, take a look at the article shown in the following figure.

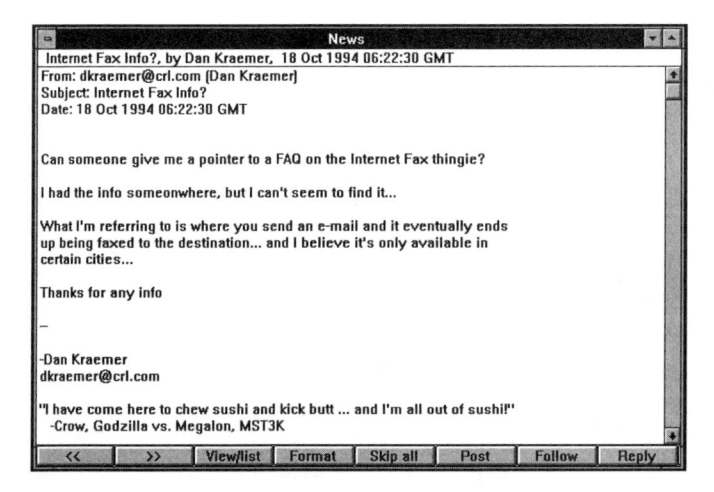

An article posted to the news.newusers.questions group.

Chapter 2 ▸ *So Just What the Heck Is USENET, Anyway?*

Here, the poster is asking for help finding a service that will fax messages via e-mail. In the next figure, some helpful soul has responded with the appropriate instructions. Notice how the original article used the Subject line **Internet Fax Info?**, and the follow-up uses the Subject line **Re: Internet Fax Info?**. The "Re" part tells you this article is a follow-up. (Your newsreader software will add the "Re" to a follow-up automatically.)

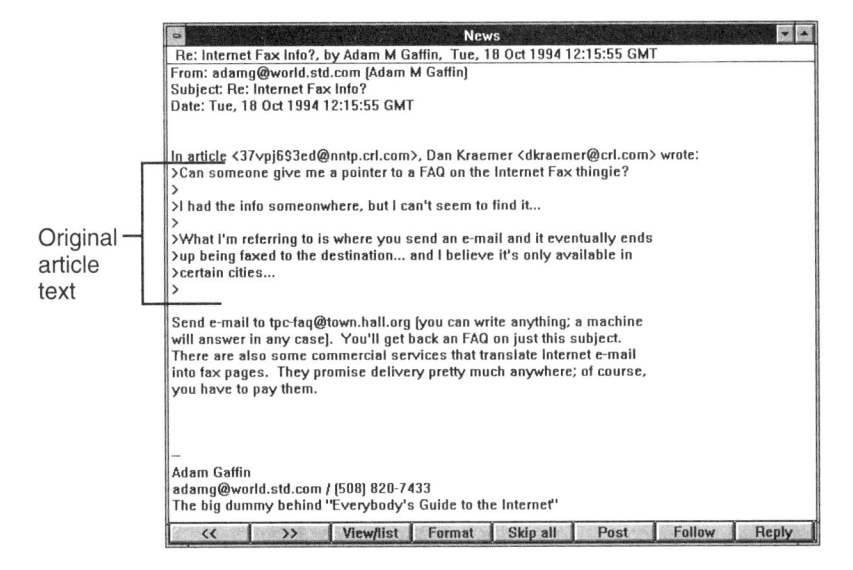

A follow-up article responding to the original query.

There's one other thing to notice about the follow-up article: the author quotes the original article in his response. This is proper USENET etiquette, because it means the readers of the follow-up don't have to go back and re-read the original article to figure out what's going on. Normally, however, it's not good form to quote the entire original article. You only need include enough material (a line or two is usually sufficient) to put your response into context.

The Least You Need to Know

This chapter got you started with USENET by leading you through a few basics. Here are some things to chew on before forging ahead:

- ➤ The Internet is a network of networks, but it's also a means of communication, an information resource, a storehouse, and a community.

- ➤ USENET is a collection of newsgroups, where each newsgroup represents a specific topic of discussion. Each newsgroup is part of a larger hierarchy such as **comp** (computers) and **rec** (recreation).

- ➤ Each newsgroup consists of one or more articles that people have posted to the group. After reading the article with your newsreader, you can post a follow-up article.

- ➤ Newsgroup names consist of the hierarchy in which the group resides, followed by a dot, followed by the topic. Subgroups add more dots and more topics.

- ➤ Every USENET article contains a header, the body text, and a signature.

- ➤ Offensive or spoiler articles are usually encoded using rot13.

Chapter 3

Learning Netiquette: Minding Your USENET Ps and Qs

In This Chapter

- ➤ How to avoid blunders common to USENET newcomers
- ➤ Basic manners for posting and following up
- ➤ Understanding flaming, FAQs, and other USENET f-words
- ➤ A miscellany of USENET do's and don'ts to help keep you on the straight and narrow

The Internet is a wild and woolly frontier populated with free spirits, hackers, libertarians, and non-conformists of every stripe and hue. There's no central organization tying the whole thing together, so you'd think the prevailing ethos would be an anything-goes, dog-eat-dog, free-for-all. And, yes, it's true that there are a few random pockets of anarchy scattered about the Net, but the overwhelming majority of Internet interactions are governed by courtesy and civility.

How can this be? The answer is contained in a set of conventions known collectively as *netiquette* (a combination of *network* and *etiquette*). These prescriptions for politeness are learned early in the careers of most Internauts, and they're enforced by pointing out to wrongdoers the error of their ways, and reminding them of the proper behavior. These remonstrances are usually gentle, but they often can be blunt, caustic, and venomously sarcastic. In other words, you'll want to stay on the good side of the Internet community, and this chapter will help you do just that. Think of this as a finishing school for correct netiquette that will prepare you for your USENET debut.

Netiquette for USENET Neophytes

In USENET lingo, a *newbie* is someone new to the Net. Although the term sounds sort of cute, it's actually an insult that you'll want to avoid at all costs. How do you do that? Easy: just read this chapter and take its lessons to heart, and in everyone's eyes you'll appear like a true Net veteran (which, of course, you will be before long). Most netiquette applies to *all* USENETers, but there are a few guidelines aimed specifically at newcomers. These are covered in the next few sections.

Lurk Before You Leap

You may be sorely tempted to dive right into the USENET deep end and start posting articles left, right, and center. First, however, you should get the lay of the news land by picking out a few interesting-sounding groups and limiting yourself to just reading articles posted by others. This gives you a chance to gauge the tone of the group, the intellectual level of the articles, and the interests of the various group members. Then, once you feel comfortable with the newsgroup (which could take as little as a few weeks, or as long as a few months, depending on how often you're on the Net), you can start posting some original articles and following up articles written by your group colleagues.

> Reading articles without posting any of your own is known as **lurking**.

Introverted types, or those uncomfortable with their writing skills, may decide to become full-time lurkers, never posting their own articles. That's their decision, of course, but it's considered bad form in USENET circles. Why? Well, USENET thrives on participation and the constant thrust-and-parry of post-and-follow-up. Mere rubbernecking adds no value whatsoever to a group, so everyone is expected to post sooner or later. If you're really reluctant, I say feel the fear and do it anyway (to borrow a book title). You'll be amazed at the pride and sense of accomplishment you'll feel when you see your first post appear in a newsgroup.

Chapter 3 ➤ *Learning Netiquette: Minding Your USENET Ps and Qs*

Check Out the Newcomer Newsgroups

The **news** hierarchy contains a couple of dozen newsgroups devoted exclusively to USENET topics. I'll talk about these groups in more detail in Chapter 23, "News About News: The USENET-Related Newsgroups," but for now there are two groups you should read religiously when you're just starting out:

> **news.announce.newusers**   This group posts regular articles (these are called *periodic postings*) that explain USENET concepts to beginners. Some good articles to look for include "What is Usenet?," "Hints on writing style for Usenet," and "A Primer on How to Work With the Usenet Community."

> **news.newusers.questions**   This is the group where USENET rookies ask questions about netiquette, newsreaders, groups, and lots more. In particular, be sure to read the article titled "Welcome to news.newusers.questions," which is posted weekly.

Read the Frequently Asked Questions Lists

In your travels through the **alt** hierarchy, you might come across, say, the newsgroup **alt.buddha.short.fat.guy** (really!). This group could be described as "Buddhism with an attitude," and it can be a lot of fun. So you check it out for a while and, when you decide to post, the first question that comes to mind is "Who the heck was the Buddha, anyway?" That's a good question, but the problem is that most of the other readers of this group probably asked the same question when they were newcomers. You can imagine how thrilled the group regulars are to answer this question for the thousandth time.

To avoid these kinds of annoyingly repetitive queries, most newsgroups have a Frequently Asked Questions list, or *FAQ* (which is pronounced *fack*). Before you even think about posting to a newsgroup for the first time, give the group's FAQ a thorough going-over to see whether your question has come up in the past.

How do you get a FAQ for a group? There are lots of methods you can use, but the following four are the most common:

➤ Check out the newsgroup itself. Some newsgroups post their own FAQs regularly (usually monthly).

25

Part 1 ▶ *The USENET Nitty-Gritty*

> ▶ Look in the **answers** group under each mainstream hierarchy (such as **rec.answers** or **comp.answers**). These groups are set up to hold nothing but FAQ lists for the various groups in the hierarchy. Alternatively, the **news.answers** group contains periodic FAQ postings from most groups.
>
> ▶ Use anonymous FTP to log in to **rtfm.mit.edu** and head for the **/pub/usenet-by-group/news.answers** directory. This directory contains the archived FAQs for every group that has one. (For more info on the MIT USENET archives, see Chapter 5, "Useful USENET Tidbits.")
>
> ▶ Use Gopher to tunnel to **gopher.well.sf.ca.us**, select **The Matrix**, select **Usenet and network mailing lists** and then select **RTFM news.answers FAQ Repository (MIT)**.

By the way, USENET has its own FAQ called "Answers to Frequently Asked Questions About Usenet." It's posted monthly in both **news.announce.newusers** and **news.answers**. If you can't find it there, FTP to **rtfm.mit.edu** and grab the file named **part1** in the **/pub/usenet-by-group/news.answers/USENET-faq** directory.

A Primer on Posting Politeness

Okay, you've had a lengthy lurk in your favorite newsgroups, you've faithfully scoured **news.announce.newusers** and **news.newusers.questions**, and you've studied the appropriate FAQ files. Now you can just plow ahead and start posting willy-nilly, right? Wrong. There's a whole slew of netiquette niceties related to posting—which isn't surprising, since posting is the lifeblood of the USENET system. To get you prepared, the next few sections tell you everything you need to know.

The Three Bs of Posting

An old boss of mine used to call his secrets for successful presentations "the three Bs": be good, be brief, begone. These apply equally well to USENET posting. Being good means checking any facts you use, stating your position or question clearly, and double-checking things like spelling and grammar. Being good can also apply to the tone of your article, as well. The best posts come off sounding level-headed, calm, and confident. Try to avoid expressing excessive petulance, anger, and huffiness. If you really feel that way, take a break; have a shower or go for a walk until you regain your equilibrium.

Being brief is perhaps the most sound advice I can give you. There's nothing worse than waiting forever to retrieve a long article, only to find it's a rambling, incoherent mess. Using succinct (but not cryptic) language, say what you have to say, and then practice the third "B": begone!

AVOID SHOUTING!

USENET messages are just plain old text, so you can't use fancy formatting like italics to emphasize words or phrases. Instead, many people like to use UPPERCASE LETTERS to indicate emphasis. This is fine, but use it sparingly. IF YOU PUT AN ENTIRE ARTICLE IN UPPERCASE, LIKE THIS, IT MAKES IT SEEM LIKE YOU'RE SHOUTING AND PEOPLE WILL WRITE YOU NASTY NOTES TELLING YOU TO TURN DOWN THE VOLUME!

> USENET has several other conventions you can use to add emphasis to words. One of the most common is to *bracket* a word with asterisks. To find out more about these and other conventions, see Chapter 4, "Jargon, Acronyms, Smileys, and More."

on the other hand, you occasionally see usenet articles written entirely in lowercase letters. this, too, is taboo because it makes the text very difficult to read. Just use the normal capitalization practices (uppercase for the beginning of sentences, proper names, etc.), and everyone will be happy.

Don't Use Tabs or Other Text Strangers

As I said earlier, USENET articles are plain text, and that's what most newsreaders expect to see. To avoid problems, build your articles using only the normal alphanumeric characters you can eyeball on your keyboard. (That is, the letters, the numbers, and the special symbols above the top row of numbers such as $, &, and @.) Don't use tabs or any of the so-called *control characters* (characters created by holding down the **Ctrl** key and pressing a letter or number).

Make Your Subject Lines Count

As I mentioned in the last chapter, most USENET readers use the contents of the Subject line to decide whether an article is worth reading. The majority of USENETers *hate* Subject lines that are either ridiculously vague (e.g., "Info required," "HELP!!!"), or absurdly general (e.g., "A Post," "Pets"), and they'll just walk on by without giving the article a second thought. To avoid this, make sure your Subject line is descriptive enough that a quick glance will tell someone what the article is all about.

> Some USENET sites lop off the Subject line at 40 characters, so you should assume this is the maximum length of your Subject text.

Also remember to use the Subject line to warn others of material that may be offensive. In brackets, write "Offensive to *x*," where *x* is the group your article is slamming (such as computer-book authors). Similarly, if your article gives away an ending to a movie, TV show, or book, or if it contains the answer to a riddle, include "Spoiler" in the Subject line so everyone knows what's coming.

Pick Your Groups with Care

If you put together a list of the top USENET pet peeves, "articles posted to inappropriate groups" would be a shoe-in to appear on the list. For whatever reasons, USENET participants always seem to blow a gasket when they come across an article that doesn't fit into their group's theme. So to keep the Net on your good side, think carefully about which newsgroup would welcome your article with open arms. Not only will you avoid some wrathful replies, but you'll be more likely to get a good response to your post.

Here are a few other points to bear in mind when selecting a newsgroup:

> ➤ *Cross-posting* occurs when you send an article to two or more newsgroups. While this is occasionally useful, you should rarely need to cross-post. If you're debating about sending an article to a couple of closely related groups, keep in mind that the same people probably read both groups, so your potential audience won't be any bigger. (And, believe me, nobody likes to read the same article twice!)

➤ If your article only applies to a specific geographic area (if you're selling a car, for example, or if you're discussing a local restaurant), make sure you post to the appropriate newsgroup in a hierarchy that covers your area. For example, Toronto USENETers can post classifieds to the **tor.forsale** group, or want ads to the **tor.jobs** group. If you don't have any local newsgroups, you can post to one of the main groups, but be sure to specify in the Subject line that your article only applies to a certain area (e.g., "Cubic zirconia jewelry for sale: Hoboken, NJ" in **rec.collecting**).

➤ If you want to run a test to see whether your newsreader is posting articles properly, be sure to use one of the **test** newsgroups (such as **misc.test**). Do not—I repeat, *do not*—use any of the regular newsgroups, unless you want your e-mail inbox stuffed with angry complaints. For faster feedback, use a **test** group in your area. (Many access providers have set up their own **test** groups, and you'll find it's best to use them.)

> Many USENET sites have programs that will automatically fire off e-mail messages to you when they receive your test posts. If you'd prefer not to receive these messages, include the word **ignore** in the Subject line of your test article.

➤ If you want to advertise a product on USENET, be *very* careful how you go about it. A while back, a law firm posted an ad for its Green Card service to *every newsgroup*! This created an unbelievable firestorm of controversy, and those poor lawyers are probably still trying to dig themselves out from the avalanche of nasty e-mail messages they received. If you really want to advertise, use the groups in the **biz** hierarchy (e.g., **biz.comp.software**).

Practice Posting Patience

If you post an article and it doesn't show up in the newsgroup five minutes later, don't re-send the article. A posted article goes on quite a journey as it wends its way through the highways and byways of the Internet. As a result, it often takes a day or two before your article appears in the newsgroup. (This is why it's also considered bad USENET form to post articles "announcing" some current news event. By the time the article appears, the event is likely to be old news to most readers, and you'll end up looking just plain silly. If you're aching to discuss it with someone, try the **misc.headlines** group.)

More Snippets of Posting Protocol

Here, in no particular order, are a few more netiquette gems that'll help make sure you always put your best posting foot forward:

➤ If you receive private e-mail correspondence from someone, it's considered impolite to quote from the message without his permission. (You're probably also violating copyright law, because the author of an e-mail message has a copyright on any and all messages he sends.)

➤ If you bolster your argument with a few facts and figures, make sure you cite the appropriate references in your post. This allows the skeptics and "I'm-from-Missouri" types in the crowd to check things out for themselves, and it adds an aura of credibility to your article.

➤ Most people read their news using terminals with 80 columns. To keep your posts looking their best, limit your line lengths to 80 columns. (In fact, you should probably restrict your lines to 70 or 75 columns to allow for the extra characters newsreaders add to quoted articles in follow-ups.)

➤ As I mentioned in the last chapter, keep your signatures down to a dull roar. Believe me, *nobody* is interested in seeing your résumé or your *curriculum vitae* at the end of every article you post. The accepted maximum length for a signature is four lines.

Avoiding Follow-up Faux Pas

One of the best ways to get your USENET feet wet is to respond to an existing article with a follow-up message. You can answer questions, correct errors, or just weigh in with your own opinions on whatever the topic at hand happens to be. Following up has its own netiquette, however, and I've summarized the most important stuff here:

Read any existing follow-ups first. Before diving in, check to see if the article already has any follow-ups. If so, read them to make sure your own follow-up won't just repeat something that's already been said.

Use your newsreader's follow-up command. Don't respond to an article by posting another original article. Instead, use your newsreader's follow-up command to make sure your article becomes part of the appropriate thread.

Quote the original article sparingly. To make sure others know what you're responding to, include the appropriate lines from the original article in your follow-up. You'll need to use some judgment here. Quoting the entire article is wasteful (especially if the article was a long one), and should be avoided at all costs. (Some newsreaders will actually reject an article containing more text from the original than new text.)

Forgive small mistakes. If you see an article with spelling mistakes, incorrect grammar, or minor factual blunders, resist the urge to "flame" the perpetrator. (In USENET lingo, a *flame* is a nasty, caustic message designed to put Internet wrongdoers in their place. I'll talk more about them in the next chapter.) For one thing, the international flavor of USENET just about guarantees a large percentage of participants for whom English is not their primary language. For another, I hope you have better things to do than nitpick every little slip of the keyboard that comes your way.

Avoid "Me, too" or "Thanks" replies. Few USENET experiences are more frustrating than a follow-up that consists only of a brain-dead "Me, too!" or "Thanks for the info" response. (Especially if the dope sending the follow-up has quoted the entire original article. Aaargh!) If you feel the need to send missives of this kind, do it via e-mail.

Reply by e-mail. If you think your follow-up will have interest only to the original author and not the group as a whole, send your response directly to the author's e-mail address.

Use summaries to reduce group clutter. Some posts can elicit many different replies. For example, sending a request for "mother-in-law jokes" to **rec.humor** could get you all kinds of responses from disgruntled hubbies. To avoid cluttering the group with all these follow-ups (especially if there's a chance the replies will have lots of repeats), tell the respondents to send their jokes (or whatever) to you via e-mail, and offer to summarize the results. Then, when all the follow-ups are in, post your own follow-up that includes a summary of the responses you received.

The Least You Need to Know

This chapter gave you a crash course in the USENET social niceties collectively known as netiquette. Here's a summary of the most important do's and don'ts to keep in mind:

Do:

- Read the newsgroups **news.announce.newusers** and **news.newusers.questions** if you're new to USENET.
- Read the FAQ list for a newsgroup before diving in.
- Follow "the three Bs" when posting: be good, be brief, begone.
- Write Subject lines that actually explain what the heck your article is all about.
- Make sure you post your article to the appropriate newsgroup.
- Remember that it may take a day or two for your post to appear in the newsgroup.

Don't:

- Post to a newsgroup until you have a feel for the group's style and conventions.
- SHOUT by writing your posts entirely in uppercase letters.
- Use tabs or control characters in your articles.
- Cross-post your article to multiple groups unless it's absotively, posolutely necessary.
- Use a regular newsgroup to post test messages. Use one of the **test** groups, instead (e.g., **misc.test**).
- Advertise products or services in the regular newsgroups. Use the groups in the **biz** hierarchy, instead.

Chapter 4

Jargon, Acronyms, Smileys, and More

In This Chapter

- ➤ Translating day-to-day jargon
- ➤ Expanding recurrent acronyms
- ➤ Interpreting common smileys
- ➤ Your field guide to USENET flora and fauna

All human communities, large and small, develop unique behavior patterns, arts, beliefs, and institutions. In other words, they develop a culture they can call their own. This is certainly true of the Internet, as well (which isn't surprising, since back in Chapter 2 we defined the Internet partly as a community). "Culture shock," however, is *way* too mild a term for what most people feel when they first get online. I mean, let's face facts: often the Internet—and USENET in particular—can be just plain weird. People on the Net use unfathomable buzzwords unashamedly, unintelligible abbreviations unreservedly, and indecipherable symbols unblushingly. New cybersurfers can be forgiven for thinking the inmates are running the asylum, because, well, they often are!

This chapter is designed to help you overcome the inevitable Internet culture-shock-and-then-some. It introduces you to the jargon, acronyms, and symbols you'll encounter most often in your online travels, particularly those you'll stumble upon in USENET.

> If you're interested in trying to figure out the culture of the Internet, a good place to start is the newsgroup **alt.culture.internet**.

The Essential English-USENET Phrase Book

In our brief journey through USENET territory, we've already encountered a fistful of jargon words and phrases: *hierarchy, newsgroup, newsreader, article, header, body, signature, lurk, thread, post, follow-up*. Fact is, jargon is woven so deeply into the fabric of USENET (and the Internet as a whole) that trying to avoid it would be like trying to avoid air. (There's even a name for Net types who hunt for new jargon and attempt to coin new jargon words: *jargonauts*.) The best approach, then, isn't to rail uselessly against the Net slang gods, but to just "go native" and get into it. To that end, here's a brief selection of some common USENET news-speak, with the appropriate plain-English translations:

> **bandwidth** A measure of how much stuff can be stuffed through a transmission medium such as a phone line or network cable. There's only so much bandwidth to go around at any given time, so you'll see lots of Net paranoia about "wasting bandwidth." In USENET, this means keeping posts as short as possible, quoting a minimum amount of the original article in a follow-up, avoiding unproductive *flame wars* (I'll describe what these are later in this chapter), and so on. Bandwidth is measured in *baud* or *bits per second* (see next page).

Chapter 4 ➤ *Jargon, Acronyms, Smileys, and More*

baud   This is a measure of how much bandwidth a transmission medium has. Its technical definition is "level transitions per second," but nobody knows what that means. Most folks prefer to use *bits per second* (defined below) to describe bandwidth because it's easier to understand. (Many people use the terms *baud* and *bits per second* interchangeably. This is okay in the privacy of your own home, but don't do it while you're online. If you do, the Net's resident techno-pedants will jump down your digital throat in no time flat.)

bits per second (bps)   Another, more common, measure of bandwidth. Here, a *bit* is the fundamental unit of computer information where, for example, it takes eight bits to describe a single character. So a transmission medium with a bandwidth of, say, 8 bps would send data at the pathetically slow rate of one character per second. Bandwidth is more normally measured in *kilobits per second* (Kbps—thousands of bits per second). So, for example, a 14.4Kbps modem can handle 14,400 bits per second. In the high end, bandwidth is measured in megabits per second (Mbps—millions of bits per second).

> You'll often see Net types talking about "T1" or "T3" lines. A *T1* line is a *telephone trunk line* (usually consisting of fiber-optic cables) with a bandwidth of 1.544 Mbps. *T3* lines are *ultra-high bandwidth trunk lines* that can transfer data at a whopping 45.21 Mbps. These two types of lines provide the basic infrastructure of the Internet. Regionally (i.e., within a state or within several adjoining states), networks usually are connected via T1 lines; this is called a *regional backbone*. Each of these regional backbones is then connected to the main Internet backbone—called *NSFNet*—which spans the country with T3 lines.

carpet bomb   To post an ad, chain letter, or get-rich-quick scheme to umpteen different newsgroups. Remember the law firm advertising its Green Card service that I told you about in the last chapter? That was a textbook example of a carpet bomb. This is a major USENET no-no, and usually elicits responses that are both ferocious and voluminous.

catch up A newsreader command that marks all the articles in a newsgroup as having been read. You normally do this when you've checked out the Subject lines in a group, read the ones you found interesting, and then want to ignore the rest. This wipes the newsgroup's slate clean (at least as far as you're concerned; the articles, of course, remain untouched in the newsgroup for others to read), so you'll only see new articles the next time you open the group.

delurk To drop out of lurk mode to post an article or follow-up. (I explained what "lurking" is in Chapter 3.)

expired article An article that no longer appears in a newsgroup because it was deleted by your access provider's system administrator. The volume of USENET news is so huge that the only way most access providers can keep their heads above water is to purge articles after a certain period (usually from two to seven days). The moral of the story is: Check your favorite newsgroups as often as you can. Otherwise, an interesting article could come and go and you'd never know it (especially since 99.99% of all articles aren't archived anywhere).

> Article expiration is the principal cause of one of the biggest frustrations for USENET rookies: the feeling that you've stepped into the middle of a conversation. That's because many of the articles you see at first are either follow-ups to an expired article, or are original posts commenting on some previous state of affairs. The best thing you can do is muddle through and keep reading. After a while, you'll catch on to new threads, and you'll be an old hand before you know it.

flame To post an insulting, emotional, caustic article. See "Flaming: Can't We All Just Get Along?" later in this chapter for a heaping helping of flame facts.

foo, **bar**, and **foobar** These words are used as placeholders in descriptions and instructions. For example, someone might say "To change to the */foo* directory on a UNIX system, use the command *cd/foo*." Here, "foo" acts as a generic placeholder for a directory name. If two placeholders are needed, then both "foo" and "bar" are used, like so: "To FTP two files named *foo* and *bar*, use the *mget* command: *mget foo bar*." "Foobar" is often used as a single placeholder. It's derived from the military acronym FUBAR (bowdlerized version: Fouled Up Beyond All Recognition). Other, more rare, placeholder words are **baz** and **quux** (don't ask).

holy war   A never-ending, unchanging (and *very* boring for the rest of us) argument where the opinions of combatants on both sides of the issue never budge an inch. Common holy war topics include religion, abortion, which operating system is superior, and the optimum way to dispense toilet paper.

kill file   A file used by some newsreaders to reject out of hand any unwanted articles. You specify that you don't want to see posts with certain subjects, certain authors, or certain words and phrases, and the newsreader will automatically mark as read any articles containing the offending material. It's a great way to automatically blow away boring subjects and pontificating bozos.

luser   A portmanteau of "loser" and "user." Someone who hasn't the faintest idea what he's doing, and (more importantly) refuses to do anything about it.

moderator   Overworked, underpaid (read: volunteer) USENETer who reads all submissions to a particular newsgroup and selects only the best (or most relevant) for posting.

net.   A prefix used by Internet types who spend *way* too much time online. These people like to add "net." in front of just about anything even remotely connected to the Internet. For example, a newcomer to the Net becomes a *net.newcomer*; an online session becomes a *net.session*. That kind of thing. A few "net." constructions, however, have achieved mainstream status: net.police (self-appointed netiquette watchdogs who flame offenders), net.gods and net.deities (USENET old-timers who've achieved celebrity status), and net.characters (irritating USENETers who post articles designed only to attract attention to themselves).

newbie   A person who is (or acts) new to the Internet. Because this term is almost always used insultingly, most Net neophytes try to behave in as non-newbie-like a way as possible. The best way to avoid this label is to bone up on netiquette (see Chapter 3, "Learning Netiquette: Minding Your USENET Ps and Qs").

ob-   This prefix means "obligatory." For example, it's traditional that each post to **rec.humor** contain a joke. If someone writes in with some non-joke material, he'll usually finish with an *objoke*, or *obligatory joke*.

sig quote   A quotation added to a signature. Most people choose quotes that reflect their character or their politics.

signal-to-noise ratio   This electronics term is used ironically to compare the amount of good, useful info ("signal") in a newsgroup, with the amount of bad, useless dreck ("noise"). The best groups have a high signal-to-noise ratio, while groups that have lots of flame wars and spamming (see below) rate low on the signal-to-noise ratio totem pole. For example, the group **rec.humor** has a low signal-to-noise ratio because most of the jokes are bad, and many of the posts comment on how bad the jokes are. By contrast, the moderated newsgroup **rec.humor.funny** has a relatively high signal-to-noise ratio because only jokes that are at least mildly amusing make the moderator's cut and appear in the group.

spam   To post irrelevant prattle that has nothing whatsoever to do with the current topic under discussion. Aimless drivel noticeably lacking any point or cohesion.

spewer   A net.character who specializes in spam, trolling, and flame bait (more about that in a minute).

subscribe   In a newsreader, to add a newsgroup to the list of groups you want to read. If you no longer want to read the group (say, because its signal-to-noise ratio has become intolerably low), you *unsubscribe* from the group.

surf   To read USENET news. Also used for the Internet as a whole to denote traveling through cyberspace.

trolling   To post a purposely facetious, flippant, or aggressively dumb article. Its purpose is to dupe the gullible or the self-important into responding with follow-ups that make him look foolish.

Flaming: Can't We All Just Get Along?

With millions of participants from the far-flung corners of the world, it's amazing that USENET discourse is as civil as it is. But, of course, we're all merely human, so disputes are bound to arise. Most of these arguments are handled calmly and courteously, but a few turn downright nasty. An emotionally charged article that contains caustic, rabid rebuttals combined with vicious, personal ridicule is called a *flame*.

Flames are, unfortunately, a fact of USENET life. It's a rare USENET regular who hasn't been shaken to the foundations with anger at something some jerk has posted. The immediate reaction is to crank out a scathing reply laced with sarcasm, vitriol, and insults about the person's ancestry. Then, a couple of keystrokes or mouse clicks later, the flame is on its way, impossible to retrieve. Inevitably, the original poster responds with his own flame, others flame the flamers and, before you can say "There's a fire in the house!," a full-fledged *flame war* has broken out. These are, admittedly, thrilling to watch at first. But it doesn't take long before they degenerate into boring, juvenile name-calling and mindless arguments of the "Did not!," "Did too!" variety. In the end, it's all just low-signal, high-noise, and a major waste of both bandwidth and time.

> When the urge to flame hits, give yourself some time to cool off by going for a walk, having a shower, or just yelling at the top of your lungs for a few minutes. If, after all that, you still have the flame itch in your fingers, do it via e-mail and save the rest of us from having to put up with yet another flame war. Better yet, if your flame prose is particularly inventive and colorful, send it to **alt.flame**, USENET's resident complaints department. Be careful, though: if your flame is lame or uncreative, you may get flamed yourself!

Flaming has become such an integral part of USENET culture that it's developed its own subgenre of colorful lingo and phrases. To get you prepared for the next time the action gets hot in one of your newsgroups, here's a brief primer on flame jargon:

asbestos longjohns   What USENET types put on (metaphorically speaking, of course) before posting an article they expect will get flamed. Other popular flame-retardant garments are *asbestos overcoats* and *asbestos underwear*.

burble   Similar to a flame, except that the burbler is considered to be dumb, incompetent, or ignorant. "Some clueless wonder sent me a burble yesterday. I'm going to flame that luser good."

dictionary flame   An article that attempts to stall or derail an ongoing argument by criticizing the way certain terms are being used. "How can we discuss the violence on 'Ren and Stimpy' when we haven't even defined what a 'Stimpy' is yet?" Also, an article criticizing someone for spelling or grammatical gaffes.

firefighters   People who attempt to put out flame wars before they get out of hand.

flamage   The content of a flame. This words seems to be a portmanteau of the words "flame" and "verbiage."

flame bait   Provocative material in an article that will likely elicit flames in response.

flame warrior   A USENETer who cruises newsgroups looking for flame bait. Someone who tries to start flame wars intentionally.

flamer   A person who flames regularly.

rave   A particularly irritating type of flame in which the writer rambles on *ad nauseam*, even after a flame war has ended.

An Initial Look at USENET Acronyms

For most new users, acronyms are the bugbears and hobgoblins of computer life. They imply a hidden world of meaning that only the cognoscenti and those "in the know" are privy to. The Internet, in particular, is a maddeningly rich source of TLAs (three-letter acronyms) and other ciphers. (In fact, some wag even coined a term for those geeks who insists on converting every multi-word computer term into an acronym: *nymrods*.) To help you survive the inevitable onslaught of Internet acronymy, here's a list of the initials used most commonly in Net discourse:

AAMOF	As a matter of fact.
AFAIK	As far as I know.
BTW	By the way.
CU	See you (as in "see you later").
DIIK	Damned if I know.
EOT	End of thread.
F2F	Face-to-face.

Chapter 4 ➤ *Jargon, Acronyms, Smileys, and More*

FAWOMPT	Frequently argued waste of my precious time.
FAWOMFT	Frequently argued waste of my foolish time (bowdlerized version; substitute your own favorite f-word).
FOAF	Friend of a friend. Used to imply that information was obtained third-hand, or worse.
FOTCL	Falling off the chair laughing.
FTF	Face-to-face.
FYA	For your amusement.
FYI	For your information.
HHOK	Ha ha only kidding.
HHOJ	Ha ha only joking.
HHOS	Ha ha only serious. (Used with ironic jokes and satire that contain some truth.)
IANAL	I am not a lawyer.
IMCO	In my considered opinion.
IMHO	In my humble opinion. (Although, in practice, opinions prefaced by IMHO are rarely humble. See IMNSHO, below.)
IMO	In my opinion.
IMNSHO	In my not so humble opinion. (This reflects most of the opinions one sees on USENET!)
IOW	In other words.
IWBNI	It would be nice if.
IYFEG	Insert your favorite ethnic group. Used in off-color and offensive jokes and stories to avoid insulting any particular ethnic group, race, religion, or sex. You'll sometimes see *<ethnic>*, instead.
KISS	Keep it simple, stupid.
LOL	Laughing out loud.

Part 1 ➤ *The USENET Nitty-Gritty*

MEGO	My eyes glaze over.
MORF	Male or female? Used only occasionally in newsgroups to determine the sex of a poster.
MOTAS	Member of the appropriate sex.
MOTOS	Member of the opposite sex.
MOTSS	Member of the same sex.
MUD	Multiple User Dimension (or Multiple User Dungeon). A text-based, role-playing fantasy adventure game.
NRN	No response necessary.
OIC	Oh, I see.
OS	Operating system.
OTOH	On the other hand.
OTT	Over the top.
PD	Public domain.
PMJI	Pardon my jumping in.
PONA	Person of no account. Used disparagingly to describe someone who doesn't have an Internet account.
ROTF	Rolling on the floor.
ROTFL	Rolling on the floor laughing.
ROTFLOL	Rolling on the floor laughing out loud.
RSN	Real soon now (read: never).
RTFF	Read the fuddled FAQ. (See RTFM, below.)
RTFM	Read the fuchsia manual. (Another bowdlerized version; insert your own f-word.) This is an admonition to users (usually newbies) that they should try to answer a question themselves before posting to a newsgroup. This may seem harsh, but self-reliance is a fundamental characteristic of Internet life. This means reading hardware and software manuals, and checking out newsgroup FAQ lists.

SO	Significant other.
TFS	Thanks for sharing.
TIA	Thanks in advance.
TIC	Tongue in cheek.
TPTB	The powers that be.
TTFN	Ta-ta for now.
TTYL	Talk to you later.
WRT	With respect to.
YABA	Yet another bloody acronym.
YMMV	Your mileage may vary. This acronym means the advice/info/instructions just given may not work for you exactly as described.

If you come across an acronym that's not covered here, there are some Net resources you can turn to. The World Wide Web Acronym Server lets you look up acronyms, or find acronyms whose expansion contains a particular word. Surf to the following page to check it out:

http://curia.ucc.ie/info/net/acronyms/acro.html

Gopher users can head to the Manchester Computing Centre at **info.mcc.ac.uk**. Select **Miscellaneous Items**, then **Acronym dictionary**, and then **Acronym dictionary (keyword search)**.

USENET Hieroglyphics: Smileys

Flame wars ignite for a variety of reasons: derogatory material, the skewering of one sacred cow or another, or just for the heck of it (see *flame warrior*). But one of the most common reasons is someone misinterpreting a wryly humorous, sarcastic, or ironic remark as insulting or offensive. The problem is that the nuances and subtleties of wry humor and sarcasm are difficult to convey in print. *You* know your intent, but someone else (especially someone for whom English isn't his first language) may see things completely differently.

Part 1 ▸ *The USENET Nitty-Gritty*

> Smileys are an easy way to convey meaning in your online writings, but don't lean on them too heavily. Overusing smileys not only means your writing isn't as clear as it could be, but it'll also brand you automatically as a dreaded newbie or as terminally cute.

To help prevent such misunderstandings, and to grease the wheels of Net social interaction, cute little symbols called *smileys* (or, more rarely, *emoticons*) have been developed. The name comes from the following combination of symbols: :-). If you rotate this page clockwise so the left edge points upward, you'll see that this combination looks like a smiling face. You'd use it to indicate to your readers that the previous statement was intended to be humorous or, at least, unserious.

The basic smiley is the one you'll encounter most often, but there are all kinds of others to tilt your head over (some of which are useful, most of which are good and silly). Here's a sampling:

Smiley	Meaning
:-)	Ha ha, just kidding.
:-D	(Laughing) That's hilarious; I break myself up.
;-)	(Winking) Nudge, nudge, wink, wink; I'm flirting.
:-(	I'm unhappy.
;-(	I'm crying.
:-|	I'm indifferent; well whatever, never mind.
:-#	My lips are sealed.
:-/	I'm skeptical.
:->	I'm being sarcastic.
:-V	I'm shouting.
;^)	I'm smirking.
%-)	I've been staring at this screen for too long!

Chapter 4 ➤ *Jargon, Acronyms, Smileys, and More*

USENET Miscellany

To round out our tour of the sights and sounds of USENET, we'll look at a few miscellaneous conventions and symbols that you're sure to stumble upon in your travels:

Adding emphasis in your articles. In Chapter 3, "Learning Netiquette: Minding Your USENET Ps and Qs," I told you that you can add emphasis to your articles by using UPPERCASE letters. Many people interpret uppercase words as shouting, however, so other emphasis conventions are normally used. The most common is to bracket a word or phrase with asterisks, like *this*. You'll occasionally see underscore characters around a word, like _so_, and, rarely, you'll also see words "underlined" with carets (^), as shown here:

```
Why does everyone hate poor Barney the Dinosaur?
                            ^^^^^^^^
```

Conveying mood with non-smileys. As you saw in the last section, smileys are a handy way to make sure your articles aren't misunderstood. However, many people find those little faces to be insufferably cute and so wouldn't be caught dead using them. Instead, they use the following "non-smileys":

Symbol	What it means
<g>	Grinning, smiling
<l>	Laughing
<I>	Irony
<s>	Sighing
<jk>	Just kidding
<>	No comment

Simulating a backspace. In oral conversation, you can achieve an ironic effect by saying one thing, then saying "Oops, I mean," and then saying something else. To simulate this effect in writing, you can use the ^H symbol. Let's look at an example: "Would someone please tell this bozo^H^H^H^Hperson that ads aren't allowed

45

in this newsgroup." You'd read this as "Would someone please tell this bozo—oops, I mean *person*—that ads aren't allowed in this newsgroup." The idea is that you add as many ^Hs as there are letters in the word you're trying to "backspace" out.

Grouping newsgroups with an asterisk (*). You'll often see newsgroup descriptions containing an asterisk (*), such as **rec.***. This is a shorthand way of saying "All the groups in the **rec** hierarchy." Similarly, ***.answers** means "All the group names that end with **.answers**" (e.g., **news.answers**, **sci.answers**).

The Least You Need to Know

This chapter presented you with a field guide to the flora and fauna of USENET. Here's a review of some of the sites we saw along the way:

➤ The Internet is a jargon-lover's heaven, where new phrases and terms are minted with frightening regularity. Fortunately, if you want to talk the talk, there are really only a few "must-know" words. These include *bandwidth, foo, kill file, spam, subscribe,* and *surf*.

➤ A flame is an emotionally charged article that contains caustic, rabid rebuttals combined with vicious, personal ridicule. Exchanging multiple flames with multiple flamers constitutes a flame war.

➤ In general, you should try to avoid flaming because it just wastes bandwidth that could be used for more productive pursuits.

➤ One of the biggest causes of flame wars is the misinterpretation of an otherwise harmless bit of humor or irony. To avoid these misunderstandings, use smileys to make your intentions clear. Just try not to overdo it. If smileys are just too darn cute, use non-smileys such as <g> (grin) or <s> (sigh).

➤ The most common way to add emphasis to words or phrases is to surround them with *asterisks*.

Chapter 5

Useful USENET Tidbits

In This Chapter

- ➤ Reading Netnews via Gopher
- ➤ Posting articles through e-mail
- ➤ Filtering the news down to size
- ➤ Downloading pictures from USENET newsgroups
- ➤ Creating your own newsgroups
- ➤ A bountiful buffet of choice USENET morsels

Our look at USENET so far has been a veritable four-course meal where we've inhaled such stuff as what USENET is, netiquette guidelines, and understanding the inevitable jargon. If you're still feeling a bit hungry, however, this chapter serves up a smorgasbord of USENET snacks. We'll look at how you can read news even if you don't have a newsreader, how to post articles anonymously and via e-mail, how to create your own newsgroups, and lots more. Some of the things we'll look at are, admittedly, a bit on the advanced side. If you're just starting out, you should probably figure out your newsreader (see Part 2) and read a few newsgroups (see Part 3) before tackling some of this stuff.

This chapter assumes you know how to use Internet services such as Gopher and e-mail. If you're not quite up to speed on these topics, may I suggest picking up a copy of Peter Kent's excellent book, *The Complete Idiot's Guide to the Internet*, to learn everything you need to know. I'll also take this opportunity to put in a shameless plug for my own book, *The Complete Idiot's Guide to Internet E-Mail*, available soon in fine bookstores everywhere.

How to Gopher the News

Part 2 of this book, "Start Spreading the News: A Guide to Popular Newsreaders," takes you through the mechanics of using ten of the most popular newsreaders available today. What to do, however, if (for one reason or another) you can't get your mitts on one of these packages? Ah, not to worry; all is not lost. The Net, in its seemingly inexhaustible wisdom, has anticipated your problem and come up with a solution: reading news using Gopher. You won't get any fancy features like kill files and catching up, but it's a heckuva lot better than being newsless.

Your best bet is to use the Gopher from the University of Birmingham in England. Begin by pointing your Gopher software to **gopher.bham.ac.uk**. In the main menu, select **Usenet News Reader**. The menu that appears gives you the following choices:

Mainstream Usenet Groups This option displays a menu of mainstream hierarchies (**Comp Groups**, **Misc Groups**, etc.). Select the hierarchy that contains the group you want to read.

Alternative Usenet Hierarchies This option displays a list of groups in the **alt** hierarchy.

European/UK Groups This item gives you access to newsgroups from Europe and Great Britain. The next menu that appears gives you a selection of hierarchies (e.g., **Scottish Groups**).

Birmingham Usenet Groups This selection displays a list of newsgroups devoted to University of Birmingham issues.

When you've made your choice, a menu appears listing the Subject lines of all the group's threads (the number at the end of each menu item tells you how many articles are in the thread). Select a thread that interests you to display the articles (see below), and then choose the article you want to read.

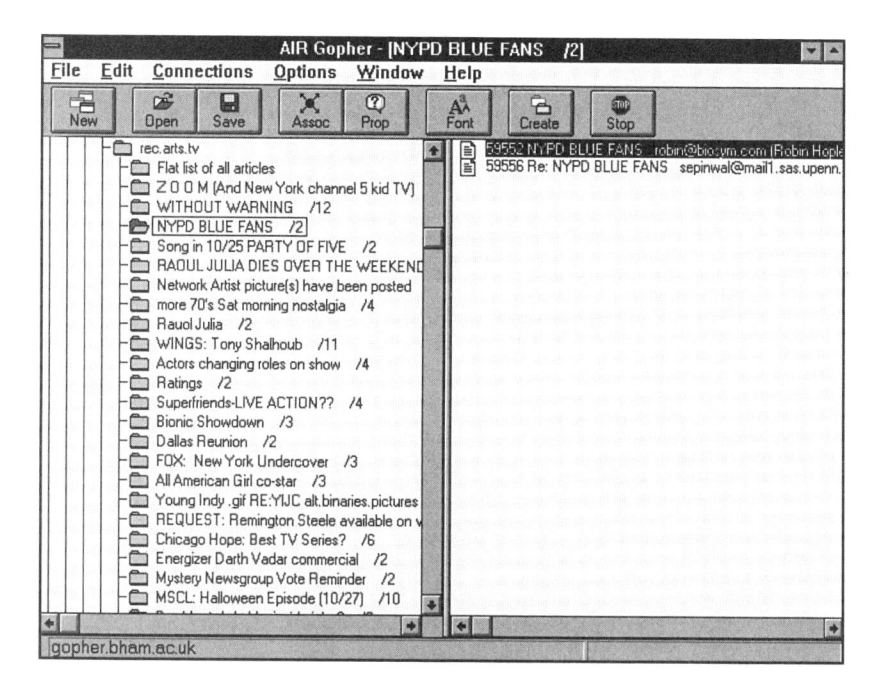

News articles appear as documents in a Gopher menu.

Michigan State University has a Gopher with a slightly less efficient USENET news option. First, tunnel your way to **gopher.msu.edu**. From the main menu, select **News & Weather**, and then select **Usenet News**. The new menu that appears gives you two choices:

News in received order   Select this item to view your news in the order it was received on USENET. This is useful if you only want to read the latest news, right off the press.

News in subject order   Select this item to see the news ordered by Subject line. This is handy for following threads.

In either case, you'll next see a menu of USENET hierarchies. Select the hierarchy that contains the group you want to read, then select the group from the menu that appears. If the group is a subgroup such as **rec.arts.tv**, you'll have to keep burrowing through menu layers (first **rec**, then **rec.arts**, then **rec.arts.tv**, and so on; yes, this *is* a pain). Eventually, you'll see a menu that lists the newsgroup articles. Select an article to read, and you're off to the races.

Part 1 ➤ The USENET Nitty-Gritty

Posting By Mail to Ensure You Get Your Two Cents In

The lack of a nearby newsreader doesn't just mean you can't read the news; it also means you can't post your own articles. And even if you have a newsreader, how do you post to a group that isn't carried by your access provider? To get around these limitations, the world's net.gods have come up with a way to submit articles using the Internet's e-mail system. The next couple of sections show you how to use this system to post both regular and anonymous articles.

Regular E-Mail Posting

Posting articles via e-mail is simplicity itself. In fact, you need to do only three things:

➤ Address the message to *newsgroup*@cs.utexas.edu, where *newsgroup* is the name of the group to which you want to send the article. Make sure, however, that you replace all the periods in the group name with dashes. For example, if you're sending a message to **sci.physics.fusion**, you'd use the e-mail address **sci-physics-fusion@cs.utexas.edu**.

➤ Use the Subject line of the e-mail message to enter the subject of your article.

➤ Use the message body to enter the article body and (optionally) your signature.

That's all there is to it. Just send your message; it will appear in the group like any other post. (It's probably a good idea to try a test post or two before you go off on some e-mail posting rampage. Remember to use one of the dedicated **test** groups, such as **misc.test**.)

Anonymous E-Mail Posting for Clandestine Articles

The vast majority of USENET articles are fully aboveboard and open to all and sundry. There are times, however, when people prefer to post articles and still remain anonymous. For example, someone still "in the closet" might want to post to one of the gay and lesbian newsgroups, or someone who actually *likes* Barney the Dinosaur might want to defend the poor fellow in **alt.barney.dinosaur.die.die.die**.

Chapter 5 ➤ *Useful USENET Tidbits*

For those times when USENETers prefer to travel incognito, an anonymous posting service has been set up (in Finland, of all places). Is it safe? Yeah, probably, but there are always clever crackers who will try to break into systems for the sheer challenge of it. My advice is *caveat emptor* (or should that be *caveat postor*?). If you want to give it a go, here's how it works:

1. Start a new mail message and address it to **anon@anon.penet.fi**.

2. Use the Subject line of the e-mail message to enter the subject of your article.

3. In the first line of the message, enter **X-Anon-To:** *newsgroup*, where *newsgroup* is the name of the newsgroup in which you want the article to appear. For example, if you want to post to **alt.sex.fetish.diapers** (yes, it's a real group), you'd enter the following:

    ```
    X-Anon-To: alt.sex.fetish.diapers
    ```

4. Use the message body to enter the article body. (Make sure, of course, that you don't add a real signature to the end of the article.)

5. Send the message.

The first time you send a message to the service, you'll receive a response telling your anonymous "code name" (it'll be something like *an123456*). This is the only ID that readers of your article will see. If anyone sends an e-mail response to that ID (i.e., to **an123456@anon.penet.fi**), the service will forward it automatically to your mailbox.

The next thing you need to do is set up a password for your anonymous postings. (This is an extra security measure designed to make sure nobody finds out who is behind your code name.) Send an e-mail message to **password@anon.penet.fi** and include only the password you want to use in the message body. When the password has been accepted, you can then post to **anon@anon.penet.fi**. The top of each message should look something like this:

```
X-Anon-To: <put the group name here>
X-Anon-Password: <put your password here>
```

If you'd prefer a catchy nickname instead of those cold letters and numbers in your code name, send an e-mail message to **nick@anon.penet.fi**, and enter the nickname you want to use in the Subject field.

Filtering the News Down to a Dull Roar

The "Usenet Readership Summary Report for Jun 94" says that USENET types are sending an average of over 67,000 messages a day, totaling over 172 megabytes of data! (If you'd like to see this report for yourself, FTP to **rtfm.mit.edu** and look in the **/pub/usenet-by-group/news.lists** directory.) Adjectives such as mountainous, gargantuan, Herculean, even Brobdingnagian, only begin to describe these eye-popping numbers. Clearly, even the most dedicated of USENET junkies can monitor only a tiny percentage of this tidal wave of verbiage.

So how in Hades do you make sure you don't miss anything? For example, you may read **alt.ketchup** faithfully, but what if an interesting ketchup discussion suddenly breaks out in **rec.arts.theatre**? Well, the good folks at Stanford University's Department of Computer Science have come up with a solution. The Stanford Netnews Filtering Service (SNFS) lets you set up a USENET "profile" consisting of one or more keywords (such as "ketchup"). Then, every day, SNFS scours the hoards of news articles and picks out the ones that match your profile. These articles are then e-mailed to you so you can read them at your leisure. Is that handy or what?

Okay, let's see how this thing works. In your mail program, start a new message and address it to **netnews@db.stanford.edu**. In the body of the message, type the following:

subscribe *first-word second-word...*

Here, *first-word* and *second-word* are the words you want SNFS to watch out for (this is your *profile*). For example, typing **subscribe ketchup** tells SNFS to pick out any article that contains the word *ketchup*. Here are some things to keep in mind when selecting your profile:

➤ If you enter multiple words, SNFS only matches articles that contain *all* the words. For example, entering **subscribe ketchup fries** tells SNFS to send only those articles containing the word *ketchup* and the word *fries*. (You can enter as many words as you like.)

➤ If you want SNFS to match articles that *don't* contain a word, preface the word with **not**. For example, to find all articles that contain *ketchup* and *fries*, but not the word *Heinz*, you'd enter the following:

subscribe ketchup fries not heinz

Make sure, by the way, that you always put the **not** portion of the profile at the end of the line.

➤ Don't make your profile too broad. Entering *sex* will match thousands of articles, whereas *sex kinky* would narrow things down a little.

You can also customize your profile by adding one or more of the following commands:

lines   This command tells SNFS how many lines of the article to send. The default is 20, but you can enter any number between 1 and 60.

period   This is the frequency (measured in days) with which SNFS sends you its articles. The default is 1 (i.e., every day), but you can enter whatever number you like.

expire   This is the number of days you want the subscription to remain in effect. The default is 9,999 days.

For example, if you want your subscription to return only 10 lines every 5 days, and to expire in 365 days, your profile would look something like this:

subscribe ketchup fries not heinz

lines 10

period 5

expire 365

When you're done, send the message. In a little while, you'll receive an e-mail reply telling you whether the subscription went through okay.

Part 1 ➤ *The USENET Nitty-Gritty*

> What happens if SNFS sends you only 20 lines of, say, a 50-line article? Well, you have two options: you could use your newsreader to check out the article directly in the newsgroup, or you can have SNFS send you the full article via e-mail. For the latter, send a missive to **netnews@db.stanford.edu**, and enter the following in the message body:
>
> **get** *article*
>
> Here, *article* is the name of the article as given by SNFS (for example, **alt.ketchup.1234**). To get more info on this and other features of SNFS, send an e-mail note to **netnews@db.stanford.edu** with the word **help** in the message body.

Getting Pictures from USENET Groups

Words are the stock in trade of USENET, but there are a couple of dozen newsgroups devoted exclusively to pictures. The names of these groups all begin with **alt.binaries.pictures**, and they include **alt.binaries.pictures.cartoons**, **alt.binaries.pictures.celebrities**, and, of course, all kinds of **alt.binaries.pictures.erotica** groups. (Internet types seem to be nothing if not randy.)

Before you jump in, though, we need to talk briefly about the various file types you'll encounter. We don't have to worry about "file types" with text articles because, for the most part, the world's technogeeks agreed long ago on how to represent yer basic letters and numbers digitally. Pictures, however, are a whole different kettle of fish. To display all those colors on a computer screen, pictures are converted into one of several "binary" formats (this is where the "binaries" part comes from in **alt.binaries.pictures**). Happily, there are only two such formats we need to worry about: GIF files and JPEG files. The difference between these formats is well beyond the scope of this book (and just plain dull, to boot), so we won't concern ourselves with it. Here's everything you need to know:

➤ GIF (Graphics Interchange Format) files end with a **.gif** extension.

➤ JPEG (Joint Photographic Experts Group) files end with **.jpg**.

When you open one of the **alt.binaries.pictures** groups, you'll see lots of article Subject lines that look something like this:

Chapter 5 ➤ *Useful USENET Tidbits*

```
RAPTOR.JPG (1/5)  (The Raptor)
RAPTOR.JPG (2/5)  (The Raptor)
RAPTOR.JPG (3/5)  (The Raptor)
RAPTOR.JPG (4/5)  (The Raptor)
RAPTOR.JPG (5/5)  (The Raptor)
```

Hmmm. Let's see if we can make heads or tails of all this. The first part of the Subject line is the name of the binary file (RAPTOR.JPG, in this case). The second part—the "1/5," "2/5" stuff—tells you which piece of the file you're dealing with. Most picture files are downright huge: usually anywhere from 50 kilobytes to 200 kilobytes in size. That's a lot of info, so the posters typically split the file into various reasonably-sized pieces (anywhere from 2 to 10, depending on the picture). So if you see **1/5** in the Subject line, it means this article is the first part of the picture, and there are a total of five parts. The last part of the line is an optional description of the contents of the picture.

"All I Get Is a Bunch of Characters!"

When you open one of these articles, you'll see mostly what appears to be gibberish: just a bunch of letters, numbers, and symbols. What gives? Well, USENET is designed to handle only text transfers; you can't use it to send binary formats directly. Instead, there are programs (called *uuencoders*) that convert pictures from their natural binary state into pure text: the gobbledygook you see when you try to "read" one of these articles. So, when someone wants to post a picture, they encode it first. The good news is that there are also programs (called *uudecoders*) that can translate these articles back into their appropriate binary format (which I'll talk about later).

Getting, Decoding, and Viewing Pictures

Okay, let's get down to brass tacks and see just how you go about converting pictures from newsgroup mess to computer magnificence:

1. For each article that contains a chunk of the picture, use your newsreader to save the article to a file. (Make sure you give each piece a different file name.)

2. Use a text editor to combine the files together, in order. For each file, you'll need to strip out the header information and any other extraneous data. Most articles will contain a line that looks something like this:

Part 1 ➤ *The USENET Nitty-Gritty*

> If you don't feel like jumping through all these hoops, there are programs that will do all the stripping and combining for you automatically. See the note at the end of this section.

BEGIN — Cut Here — Cut Here

This means you delete everything up to *and including* this line. At the end of each article, you'll see another line that needs to be cut:

END — Cut Here — Cut Here

3. Now use your uudecoder program (see below) to convert the file back to its original binary format.

4. Use your graphics viewing software (see below) to eyeball the picture. The following figure shows the RAPTOR.JPG file, in all its glory.

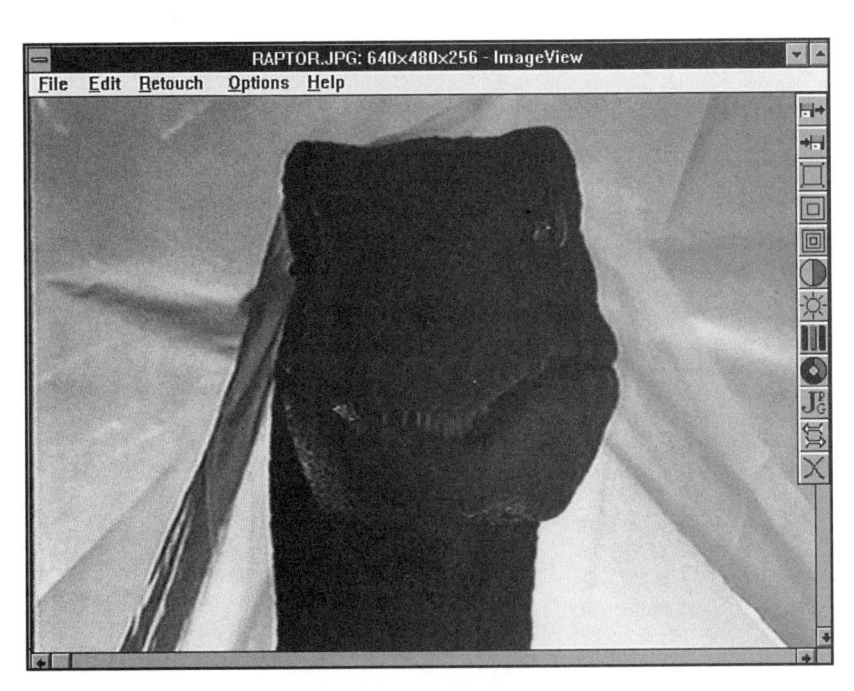

A downloaded, decoded JPEG picture.

Viewing USENET pictures certainly isn't as straightforward as you might have expected. To help out, there's a large FAQ available that contains tons of helpful advice. In fact, it's so large they've divided it into three sections:

```
alt.binaries.pictures FAQ—General etiquette
alt.binaries.pictures FAQ—General info
alt.binaries.pictures FAQ—OS-specific info
```

In particular, if you're looking for software for decoding articles or viewing pictures in GIF and JPEG formats, see the "OS specific info" FAQ. You can also look in the group **alt.binaries.pictures.utilities**, any of the **alt.binaries.pictures** groups that end with **.d** (these are discussion groups; they contain no pictures), or at the FTP site **ftp.cc.utexas.edu**. For the latter, look in the **/gifstuff** directory and then pick out the appropriate subdirectory for your computer. (For example, look in **/gifstuff/ibmpc** for DOS programs, or **/gifstuff/mac** for Macintosh software.)

Do It Yourself: Creating a Newsgroup

As I mentioned back in Chapter 2, there are now over 8,000 newsgroups and new ones get created every day. That's a huge number, but there are still plenty of topics that aren't covered. For example, were you disappointed to find there wasn't a newsgroup for fans of the BeDazzler? Or perhaps you're an ice-hockey aficionado and would like to see a newsgroup devoted to the artistry and balletic grace of the hockey fight. To fill in these holes in the USENET landscape, a procedure has been set up for creating new groups in the **comp**, **misc**, **news**, **rec**, **sci**, **soc**, and **talk** hierarchies. It's pretty involved, and certainly not for the faint of heart, but it *is* possible. The next few sections show you how it's done.

Step 1: The Preliminary Discussion

Creating a newsgroup shouldn't be undertaken lightly. It'll take a good two or three months out of your life, all kinds of regulations must be followed to the letter, and you can also expect lots of flame mail from people who don't agree with your proposal. Why the flamage? All kinds of reasons, unfortunately:

➤ Some new group ideas are inherently controversial (political groups, for example).

➤ Some people are resistant to change. Many readers of a particular group are used to the way things are set up, and don't want to see them altered.

> There's no shortage of nut cases out there. Some folks just seem to live for the sheer thrill of shooting down a proposal in flames (so to speak).

Is there any way to avoid this unpleasantness? Well, there's not much that can be done about the nut cases, but you can avoid wasting a good chunk of your life by sounding out your idea in advance. Post a message to whatever group (or groups) might be affected by your proposal. Let them know what you're thinking and ask for some feedback. If these initial responses are negative, you should probably rethink your idea, or abandon it altogether.

Step 2: The Official Request for Discussion

If, after you've dipped a toe into the group-creation waters, the temperature seems inviting, the next step is to post an official "Request for Discussion" (RFD) to the moderated group **news.announce.newgroups**. The moderator of this newsgroup will review your proposal and, if necessary, ask you to make whatever changes are required to bring the RFD up to snuff. When everything's on the up and up, the moderator posts the RFD and then all the other USENET denizens can follow up with their comments (be they positive, negative, or merely indifferent). Here are some guidelines to follow when creating your RFD:

> **Be sure to *carefully* cross-post the RFD.** The RFD should be cross-posted to **news.groups** as well as any other group that may have an interest in your proposal (within reason, of course). Also, make sure you set the RFD's Followup-To line to **news.groups**. (This ensures that the discussion of your RFD takes place only in **news.groups**, and it saves the moderator from having to do it manually. Every little bit helps!) Once the moderator approves the RFD, he posts it to **news.groups** and cross-posts it to the other groups.

> **Choose an appropriate name for the new group.** Wherever possible, try to follow existing naming conventions. For example, if you're trying to start a BeDazzler group, don't name it **rec.bedazzler**. Something like **rec.crafts.bedazzler** would be better.

Begin the RFD with an "at-a-glance" summary. There's always lots of salesmanship involved in getting a new group off the ground. You not only have to convince people the group itself is a good idea, but you have to sell yourself as a knowledgeable USENETer who knows what the heck you're doing. In particular, you need to make sure your RFD looks good and is laid out clearly. The best RFDs begin with a short summary of the pertinent facts about the new group: the name, whether or not it will be moderated, a short description, and so on. The following figure shows an ideal example of the top of an RFD.

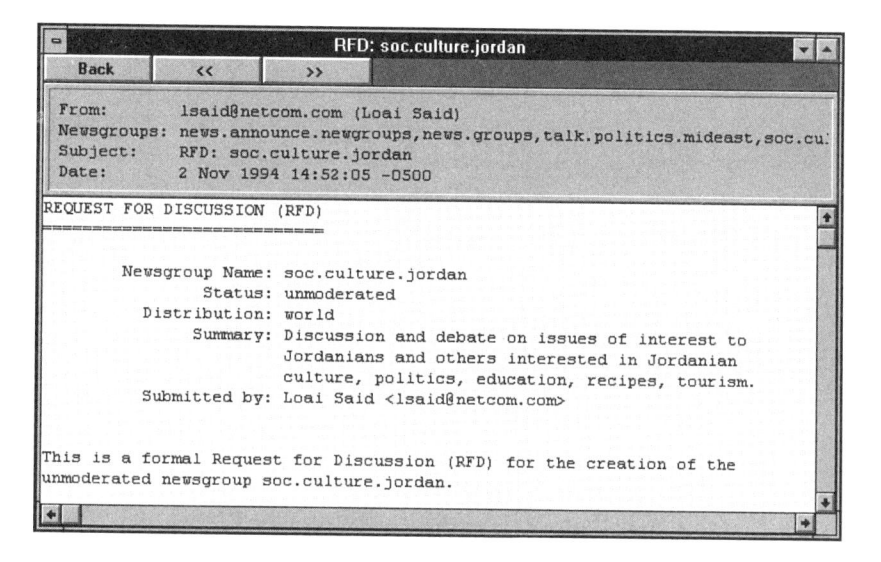

A good example of how to begin an RFD.

All newsgroups must have a charter. The next part of your RFD will be the group's proposed *charter*. The charter tells the reader what the group will be about, what kinds of topics are expected, and so on. The following figure shows the charter included in the RFD shown above.

Part 1 ➤ *The USENET Nitty-Gritty*

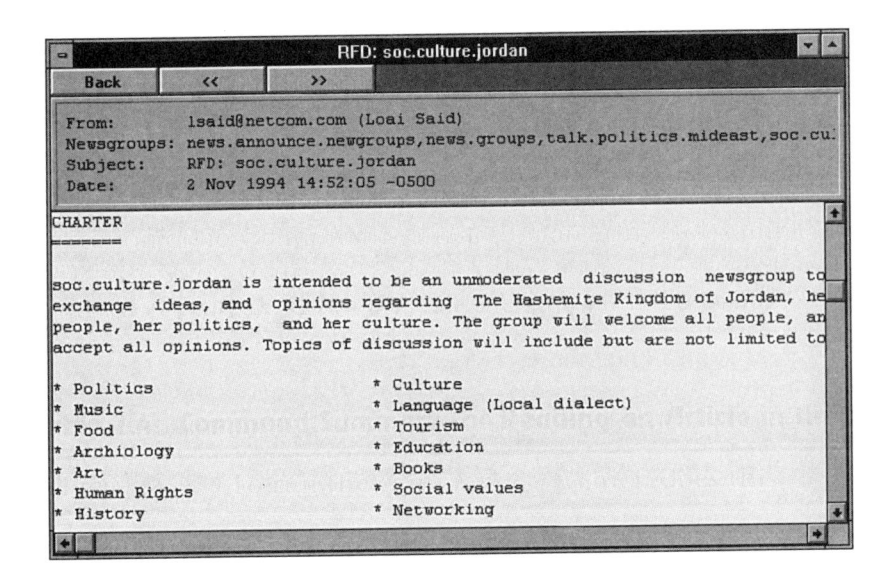

```
┌─────────────────── RFD: soc.culture.jordan ──────────────▼─┐
│ Back      <<       >>                                      │
│                                                            │
│ From:        lsaid@netcom.com (Loai Said)                  │
│ Newsgroups:  news.announce.newgroups,news.groups,talk.politics.mideast,soc.cu│
│ Subject:     RFD: soc.culture.jordan                       │
│ Date:        2 Nov 1994 14:52:05 -0500                     │
│                                                            │
│ CHARTER                                                    │
│ =======                                                    │
│                                                            │
│ soc.culture.jordan is intended to be an unmoderated  discussion  newsgroup to│
│ exchange  ideas, and  opinions regarding  The Hashemite Kingdom of Jordan, he│
│ people, her politics,  and her culture. The group will welcome all people, an│
│ accept all opinions. Topics of discussion will include but are not limited to│
│                                                            │
│ * Politics                    * Culture                    │
│ * Music                       * Language (Local dialect)   │
│ * Food                        * Tourism                    │
│ * Archiology                  * Education                  │
│ * Art                         * Books                      │
│ * Human Rights                * Social values              │
│ * History                     * Networking                 │
└────────────────────────────────────────────────────────────┘
```

An example of a group charter.

Include a rationale for your group. The most common question asked about a new group is "Why?" Why do we need it? Why aren't the existing groups good enough? Why that name and not this one? As far as possible, you should try to anticipate this kind of carping; put everything into a rationale in your RFD.

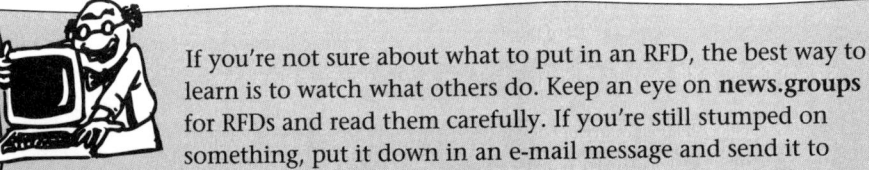

> If you're not sure about what to put in an RFD, the best way to learn is to watch what others do. Keep an eye on **news.groups** for RFDs and read them carefully. If you're still stumped on something, put it down in an e-mail message and send it to **group-advice@uunet.uu.net**. There are veteran newsmongers available at this address to answer your questions.

Step 3: Debating in news.groups

Once the RFD is posted to **news.groups**, the fun begins. For a period of 30 days or so, anyone and everyone is free to take their best shots at your proposal. You'll likely receive lots of suggestions about things like the group name, the group charter, and whether the group should be moderated. If, at the end of the discussion period, these and other issues haven't been fully resolved, it's normal to "take the discussion offline" and resume the debate via e-mail. In this case, once you've finalized everything, you post a second RFD showing the new info.

Step 4: The Official Call for Votes

Okay, your RFD has been put through the wringer and there is general agreement on the name, charter, and so on. The next step is to ask the USENET community to vote yea or nay on whether the group should be officially created. This requires another post: the Call for Votes (CFV). The CFV lists the name and charter of the would-be newsgroup, and then gives instructions for voting via e-mail. The voting period is usually 22 days.

By far the easiest way to set up a CFV is to take advantage of the hardy Usenet Volunteer Votetakers (UVV). They're a group of neutral, third-party votetakers who gather and count the votes for a newsgroup proposal. To arrange a CFV for your proposal, send a message to Ron Dippold at **rdippold@qualcomm.com**. (Try to do this as soon as possible after your RFD discussion period expires.)

Step 5: The Results

Once the voting period is finished, the votetaker will post the results of the vote to **news.announce.newgroups** and any other groups that saw the CFV (including **news.groups**). The Subject line of the post will look something like this:

```
RESULT: rec.crafts.bedazzler passes 205:30
```

The first number is a tally of the YES votes, and the second number is the tally of the NO votes. The body of the article contains, among other things, the names and e-mail addresses of each voter and what his or her vote was. The lack of secrecy is to ensure that the vote was legit. There's a five-day waiting period after the vote is posted, in which objections to the result can be posted. If no one cries "Foul!"—and if the YES forces get at least 100 votes more than the NO forces (and at least two-thirds of the legitimate votes cast)—the moderator of **news.announce.newgroups** creates the group.

Part 1 ➤ *The USENET Nitty-Gritty*

> Actually, the moderator of **news.announce.newgroups** doesn't create the newsgroup directly. Instead, he or she sends out a "control message" to each system administrator (the person who oversees the network at your service provider). The system administrator then decides whether to honor the new group request. This is almost always a mere formality for groups created in the **comp**, **misc**, **news**, **rec**, **sci**, **soc**, and **talk** hierarchies.

The Least You Need to Know

This chapter presented you with a virtual cornucopia of USENET bits and bites. Here's a recap to help things digest:

- ➤ If you don't have a newsreader, you can still keep abreast of the latest news by using a Gopher site such as **gopher.bham.ac.uk**.

- ➤ If you also need to post sans newsreader, use e-mail. Try *newsgroup*@cs.utexas.edu for regular posts, or **anon@anon.penet.fi** for anonymous stuff.

- ➤ To get only the news you need, try out the Stanford Netnews Filtering Service.

- ➤ Head for the **alt.binaries.pictures** groups to get pics of landscapes, celebrities, and things I can't mention here.

- ➤ If USENET doesn't cater to your favorite hobby, movie star, or fetish, you can try creating your own newsgroup.

Part 2
Start Spreading the News: A Guide to Popular Newsreaders

Chapter 5, "Useful USENET Tidbits," showed you ways to read and post articles without using newsreader software. But you wouldn't climb a mountain without the necessary ropes, pulleys, and funny shoes, so why tackle the mountain of USENET news without specialized equipment? Oh sure, you could still get the job done, but it'd be a lot harder, a lot slower, and a lot less convenient.

No, today's modern USENET surfer takes full advantage of the available newsreader technology. And with literally dozens of newsreaders kicking around—most of them costing exactly nothing—there's just no excuse for surfing naked. The nine chapters here in Part 2 show you the ins and outs of ten of the most popular newsreader programs around today. We'll cover software for UNIX, Windows, and the Mac, as well as three online services: CompuServe, America Online, and Delphi.

Chapter 6

Venerable UNIX Newsreaders: rn and trn

In This Chapter
- Subscribing and unsubscribing to newsgroups
- Reading articles
- Following up and posting
- Taking advantage of **trn**'s threads
- A no-muss, no-fuss primer that'll have you reading and posting in no time flat

Although Windows and Macintosh machines have made inroads in the last year or two, most of the Internet lives, eats, and breathes UNIX. Most of the networks are UNIX-based, most service providers are UNIX shops, and most of the sites you can surf to on the Net run UNIX. So it should come as no surprise that most newsreader software is available for UNIX platforms. There are dozens of UNIX newsreaders, but over the years two have emerged as the most popular: **rn** and its threaded cousin **trn**. This chapter takes a good look at these veterans of the USENET wars, and shows you how they can make your life online easier.

rn and trn: The Lowdown on the Hi-Fi

Both **rn** and **trn** are designed to let you read articles without having to perform all kinds of convoluted acrobatic maneuvers. In fact, if you're not too fussy about the news you read, you can get through an entire **rn** or **trn** session using only one or two keys.

The downside to this simplicity is the Spartan interface you get with both **rn** and **trn**. There are no pretty pictures to gawk at, no handy menus to help you out; it's just you and a few prompts. Fortunately, there are really only a few commands you'll use regularly, and a couple you'll use occasionally; the rest you can probably ignore. (Just in case, however, I've summarized most of the available **rn** and **trn** commands in tables throughout this chapter.)

So what's the difference between **rn** and **trn**? Well, they're identical except that **trn** is *threaded* (that's what the "t" in **trn** stands for). This means that **trn** can recognize threads in a newsgroup and organize your reading accordingly. Other than that, the two programs are identical.

> To keep up with the latest news about newsreaders, be sure to tune into the **news.software.readers** group. You'll find FAQs for popular newsreaders, announcements about new releases, and lots of technical help. If you're having a problem with your newsreader, you can post a question. Chances are that someone else has had the same problem and can recommend a solution.

Cranking Up rn and trn

To start **rn**, just type **rn** and then press **Enter**; for **trn**, type **trn** and press **Enter**. If you're starting the program for the first time, you'll see the following message:

```
Trying to set up a .newsrc file -- running newsetup...
```

The **.newsrc** file keeps track of, among other things, the newsgroups you've subscribed to; we'll talk more about this all-important file a little later on. You'll also see a long-winded preamble that gives you a few tips for using the program. Finally, first-timers will also see the following, potentially confusing, instruction:

Chapter 6 ➤ *Venerable UNIX Newsreaders: rn and trn*

```
[Type space to continue]
```

This doesn't mean you should type the word "space"—or, for that matter, the phrase "space to continue." It's just UNIX-ese for pressing the Spacebar.

That's the end of the first-time-user stuff. Now (and each subsequent time you start **rn** or **trn**), you'll see a list of the first five newsgroups from your **.newsrc** file. For example:

```
Unread news in rec.humor.funny  4 articles
Unread news in rec.juggling  40 articles
Unread news in rec.puzzles  43 articles
Unread news in alt.society.civil-liberties  3 articles
Unread news in news.group  298 articles
etc.
```

This gives you an indication of how much work lies ahead. "Now wait just a cotton-picking minute! How can I have newsgroups in this .newsrc thingamajig if I'm just starting out?" The answer depends on which version of **rn** or **trn** you're using:

➤ Some versions automatically stuff your **.newsrc** file with *every* newsgroup carried by your service provider. Yikes! In this case, you should read the section "How to Tame a Wild .newsrc File" later in this chapter to learn the easiest way to unstuff **.newsrc**.

➤ Later versions will automatically (and sensibly) subscribe you to just **news.announce.newusers**.

Now the program will look for any new groups that have been created since the last time you started **rn** or **trn**. If there are any, you'll see a prompt similar to the following:

```
Newsgroup alt.fan.tarantino not in .newsrc -- subscribe? [ynYN]
```

This is as good a time as any to talk about these prompts, since you'll be spending much of your **rn/trn** life responding to them. Each prompt contains two parts: a question, and a list of possible responses in square brackets (**[ynYN]**, in the above example). Here are some things to bear in mind when responding to a prompt:

> Each letter in the response list represents a specific choice you can make. In most cases, you just tap the letter you want on your keyboard, and **rn** or **trn** will respond accordingly.

> **rn** and **trn** differentiate between uppercase and lowercase letters. So, for example, pressing **y** will produce a different response than pressing **Y** (i.e., holding down the **Shift** key while tapping **y**).

> Responses fall into two categories: those that require only a single letter, and those that require multiple letters (such as the name of a newsgroup). For responses that require only a single letter, you need only press the letter on your keyboard; you don't have to press **Enter** to set things in motion. For responses that require multiple letters, you'll need to press **Enter** when you've finished typing the entire command.

> The most common responses are **y** (for **yes**), **n** (for **no** or, sometimes, **next**), and **q** (for quit).

> In a list of responses, the first letter is the default choice. If you like, you can select the default simply by pressing the **Spacebar**.

> You can get help at any prompt by pressing **h**. This throws up a list of all the possible responses you can make, and provides a brief explanation of each one.

*If you'd prefer that **rn** or **trn** not prompt you about new groups, start the program with the -q (for quiet) option (i.e., you'd type **rn -q** or **trn -q** and then press **Enter**).*

Okay, back to the action. If **rn** or **trn** prompts you about a new group, press **y** to subscribe to it, **n** to skip it, **Y** to subscribe to every new group (keep in mind, however, that there could be dozens of new groups), or **N** to bypass all the new stuff.

When that rigmarole is done, the program goes through your subscribed groups; for those who have unread articles, it asks whether or not you want to read them:

```
******   4 unread articles in rec.humor.funny -- read now? [ynq]
```

You can either press **y** to begin reading the articles, **n** to move on to the next group, or **q** to bail out of the program. (If you're using **trn**, you'll also see a plus (+) command. See "Selecting a Thread in trn," later in this chapter for details.) If you choose **y**, see the section titled

"Reading the News," later in this chapter. If you choose **n** for all the newsgroups, you'll eventually see the following prompt:

```
****** End of newsgroups -- what next? [npq]
```

From this prompt, you can either select a newsgroup to read, subscribe or unsubscribe to a group, quit the program, or perform some other command. (I'll discuss the various choices you have throughout the rest of this chapter.) As you work with both **rn** and **trn**, keep in mind that you'll always be doing one of three things:

➤ Selecting a newsgroup.

➤ Selecting an article.

➤ Reading an article.

Each of these topics has a unique set of commands and techniques; I'll cover each one (including working with threads in **trn**) in later sections of this chapter. For now, though, let's digress a little, and take a closer look at the **.newsrc** file.

How to Tame a Wild .newsrc File

As I mentioned earlier, some versions of **rn** and **trn** create a **.newsrc** file that subscribes you to every newsgroup. This is, of course, absurd—no sane individual would ever want to read thousands of groups. This means you'll need to modify **.newsrc** to cut the number of subscribed newsgroups down to a manageable size. As you'll see later in this chapter, both **rn** and **trn** have commands that can unsubscribe individual groups, but I assume you have better things to do over the next week or two. The better way is to use your favorite UNIX text editor to do the job.

For now, you should quit the program by pressing **q** until you're back at the UNIX prompt. Start your text editor and load the **.newsrc** file. If you're using the **vi** editor, for example, you'd start it with the command **vi .newsrc**. When the editor loads, you'll see a bunch of lines that look like the following:

```
rec.humor.funny: 1-740
rec.juggling: 1-9310,9312
alt.society.civil-liberties: 1-2848
```

Part 2 ➤ *Start Spreading the News: A Guide to Popular Newsreaders*

```
news.groups: 1-46517
news.announce.newusers! 1-463
alt.destroy.the.earth!
```

Here's what all this gobbledygook means for us mere mortals:

➤ The numbers tell you which articles have been read. (Each article posted to a newsgroup is given a number.) In **rec.humor.funny**, for example, I've read articles 1 through 740. In **rec.juggling**, I've read articles 1 through 9310 and article 9312. (Actually, "read" is a bit of a misnomer; an article will be marked as read not only if you actually do read the thing, but also if it expires before you get a chance to read it.)

➤ If you're subscribed to a newsgroup, you'll see a colon (:) following the group name.

➤ If you're unsubscribed to a group, you'll see an exclamation point (!) following the group name. (In the above example, I'm unsubscribed to **news.announce.newusers** and **alt.destroy.the.earth**.)

When you edit your **.newsrc** file, you can do two things: you can change the order of the groups, and you can change the newsgroup subscriptions. Why would you want to change the group order? Well, because this is the order in which **rn** or **trn** presents the groups for reading. So if you have a fave group you want to read first every day, you'd just move the group to the top of the **.newsrc** file.

If you make a mess of your **.newsrc** file and would like to start with a fresh one, type **newsetup** and press **Enter** at the UNIX prompt. This program creates a shiny new **.newsrc** file, and saves your old one under the name **.oldnewsrc**.

Changing the subscriptions is a simple matter of changing a group's colon to an exclamation point (to unsubscribe to the group), or vice versa. In most cases, you'll want to unsubscribe to every group, and then add by hand the groups you want to read within **rn** or **trn**. If you're using **vi** and you want to unsubscribe every group, type the following command:

```
:%s/:/!/
```

When you're done, press **Enter**. **vi** trudges through the entire file, replacing every colon in sight with an exclamation point. When the command has finished its dirty work, save your

70

changes and exit the editor. In **vi**, for example, type **ZZ** (yes, they have to be uppercase) to save your changes and quit.

Selecting a Newsgroup

Before you can read any articles, you need to tell **rn** or **trn** which group you want to work with. To help you do this, each program offers a number of commands for playing with newsgroups. How do you know when these commands are available? Easy—just look for prompts that take either of the following forms:

```
****** 4 unread articles in rec.humor.funny -- read now? [ynq]
****** End of newsgroups -- what next? [npq]
```

At any one of these prompts, you can either select a subscribed group from your **.newsrc** file, or you can subscribe to a new group.

Subscribing and Unsubscribing to a Newsgroup

If you're just starting out, you'll need to subscribe to the newsgroups you want to read. (I'm assuming, of course, that you've already cleaned out the subscribed groups in your **.newsrc** file, as described in the last section.) To subscribe to a group, you use the **g** command, like so:

```
g newsgroup
```

Here, *newsgroup* is the name of the newsgroup you want to subscribe to. For example, to subscribe to the group **rec.sport.hockey**, you'd enter the command **g rec.sport.hockey** and press **Enter**. One of two things will happen, depending on whether or not the group is already in your **.newsrc** file.

If the group is in **.newsrc**, you'll see a prompt similar to the following:

```
Newsgroup rec.sport.hockey is unsubscribed -- resubscribe? [yn]
```

In this case, press **y** to subscribe to the group.

If the group isn't in your **.newsrc** file, you'll see the following prompt:

```
Newsgroup rec.sport.hockey not in .newsrc -- subscribe? [ynYN]
```

In this case, press **y** to subscribe to the group. Now you'll get another prompt:

```
Put newsgroup where? [$^.Lq]
```

This prompt wants to know where to put the group in **.newsrc**. Your choices are listed in the following table.

Press	To
$	Put the group at the bottom of **.newsrc**.
^	Put the group at the top of **.newsrc**.
.	Put the group before the current newsgroup.
L	Display the **.newsrc** file.
q	Abort without subscribing.

In either case, yet another prompt will appear asking whether or not you want to read the unread articles in the new group.

When you want to unsubscribe to a newsgroup, first select the group you no longer want to bother with (as described in the next section), and then enter the **u** command.

Selecting Newsgroups from Your .newsrc File

Once you've subscribed to all the groups you want to read, you'll usually select your groups from the **.newsrc** file. To select a specific newsgroup, use the **g** *newsgroup* command. For example, if you're subscribed to **rec.humor.funny**, you can select that group by using the command **g rec.humor.funny**. To cycle through the subscribed groups in order, use either **n** (to go to the next group that has unread messages) or **p** (to go to the previous group that has unread messages).

For groups with long names (or if you can't remember the full name of the group), you can search for part of the name. To search forward, use the slash (/) command, like so:

/pattern

Here, *pattern* is some chunk of the newsgroup name (it could be a couple of words, a single word, or even part of a word). For example, the command /**news** finds the first newsgroup that includes the word **news** in its name. To continue the search, keep pressing /. If you'd prefer to search backward, use a question mark (?) instead of a slash.

Table 6.1 summarizes these commands and more.

Table 6.1 Command Summary for Selecting a Newsgroup in rn and trn

Use this command	To do this
g *newsgroup*	Go to (or subscribe to) *newsgroup*.
u	Unsubscribe to the current newsgroup.
n	Go to the next group with unread articles.
N	Go to the next group.
p	Go to the previous group with unread articles.
P	Go to the previous group.
^	Go to the first group with unread articles.
1	Go to the first group.
$	Go to the last group.
-	Go to the last group that was displayed.
/*pattern*	Search forward for the first group with a name that includes *pattern*.
/	Search forward again, using the previous pattern.
?*pattern*	Search backward for the first group with a name that includes *pattern*.
?	Search backward again, using the previous pattern.
l *pattern*	List all unsubscribed groups with a name that includes *pattern*.
L	List the contents of **.newsrc**.

Selecting an Article

Now that you've selected a group to work with, your next task is to select an article to read. In the simplest case, you'd just press **y** to start in with the first unread article. If you'd prefer to check out the article subjects first, press the equal sign (=) instead. In this case, you'll see a list of article numbers and their Subject lines:

```
741 Clinton's Popularity
742 To bake the chicken
743 Yes, I'm WAY behind!
744 Cooking lessons
```

To select one of these articles, just type its corresponding number and press **Enter**.

Once you're reading an article, there are several commands that take you to a different article. Use **n** to display the next unread article, **Ctrl+N** to display the next unread article with the same subject (i.e., the next unread article in the same thread), **p** to move backward to the next unread article, and **Ctrl+P** to move backward to the next article with the same subject within the same thread.

If you're looking for a particular subject, you can use our old friends **/** and **?**. Use **/***pattern* to find the next Subject line containing *pattern*. **?***pattern* is similar except that it searches backward.

Table 6.2 lists these and other useful commands for selecting an article.

Table 6.2 Command Summary for Selecting an Article

Use this command	To do this
y	Start reading articles in the selected newsgroup.
=	Display a list of Subject lines.
n	Go to the next unread article.
Ctrl+N	Go to the next unread article within the same thread.

Use this command	To do this
N	Go to the next article.
p	Go back to the previous unread article.
Ctrl+P	Go back to the previous unread article within the same thread.
P	Go back to the previous article.
^	Go to the first unread article.
$	Go to the last article.
j	Junk this article (mark it as read).
c	Catch up (mark all articles as read).
k	Kill the current subject (mark all articles with the same subject as read).
/*pattern*	Search forward for the first Subject line that includes *pattern*.
/	Search forward again, using the previous pattern.
?*pattern*	Search backward for the first Subject line that includes *pattern*.
?	Search backward again, using the previous pattern.
q	Quit the current newsgroup.

Selecting a Thread in trn

As I've said, **rn** and **trn** are almost identical programs. The only major difference is that **trn** organizes newsgroups into threads, which can make life a lot easier. To select a thread in **trn**, you press the plus sign (+) at one of the newsgroup selection prompts. When you do, you'll see a screen that looks something like this:

Part 2 ➤ *Start Spreading the News: A Guide to Popular Newsreaders*

```
  rec.puzzles           43 articles

a David Moews           6    What proportion of integers have initial
digit 1?
  Dave Ring
  Dave Ring
  David Meows
  Dik T. Winter
  Dik T. Winter
b Dave Dodson           2    Words starting with 'S', pronounced 'SH'
  Michael A. Phipps
c+Patrick Rockwell      3    Probability problem.
  Richard Weber
  Kevin Brown
```

The articles are displayed in thread order, and each thread is assigned a letter, or *thread ID*. In the example just given, there are three threads: **a**, **b**, and **c**. The first line of each thread shows the name of the original contributor (provided, that is, the original article hasn't yet expired), the number of articles in the thread (**6**, in the case of thread **a**), and the subject of the thread.

To select the threads you want to read, just press the thread's letter. You'll see a plus sign (+) appear beside the thread ID. If you make a mistake, just press the letter again to deselect the thread. If there are more threads to check out, press the greater-than key (>) or the **Spacebar**. When you're done, press **Z** or **Tab** to start reading the articles.

Reading the News

At long last, we get to the heart of the matter: reading news articles. This is, happily, a fairly straightforward affair. If the entire article fits on your screen, just go ahead and read it; then select the next article. If the article is too big to fit in one screen, you'll see the following at the bottom of the screen:

```
--MORE--(69%)
```

This tells you there are more lines to come, and gives you an indication of how far into the article you are. (In this example, the

69% means you've read 69% of the article.) Just press the **Spacebar** to continue reading. You can also use the keys outlined in Table 6.3 while reading an article.

Table 6.3 Command Summary for Reading an Article

Use this command	To do this
Spacebar	Display the next page.
d	Display the next half page.
b	Display the previous page.
q	Go to the end of the article.
Ctrl+R	Redisplay the article.
v	Redisplay the article, including the header.
Ctrl+X	Use rot13 to decode the article.
g *pattern*	Search for text that contains *pattern*.
G	Search again for text that contains the previous pattern.

Saving an Article

If an article contains some memorable text, you might want to save it in its own file for posterity. **rn** and **trn** give you two commands to accomplish this:

➤ The **s** *file* command saves the article to a file named *file*.

➤ The **w** *file* command is the same as **s**, except it doesn't include the article header in *file*.

For example, to save an article *sans* header to a file named **somenews**, you'd enter the command **w somenews** and press **Enter**. The program will then display the following prompt:

> When you're thinking up snappy names for your files, make sure you avoid spaces and backslashes (/). These are no-nos in UNIX file names.

```
use mailbox format? [ynq]
```

If you select **y**, the program saves the file in the same format used by e-mail messages. If you're not sure what to do, just press **n**.

Following Up an Article

If you get the urge to rebut an article's arguments or otherwise join in on a newsgroup discussion, **rn** and **trn** make it easy to post follow-ups. With the article you want to follow up displayed, press **F**. When the program asks if you're sure you want to follow up, press **y** (you may also have to press **Enter**). Now the following prompt appears:

```
Prepared file to include [none]:
```

If you've already created a text file to use in the follow-up, enter the file name and press **Enter**. Otherwise, just press **Enter**. The next prompt asks you to specify the text editor to use (the default is probably **vi**). Press **Enter** to accept the default, or type the name of your preferred editor and press **Enter**. When the editor loads, you'll see that the entire text from the original article has been inserted. At this point, you need to do two things:

➤ Edit the original text to include only those lines that are absolutely necessary for your reply.

➤ Add your own text.

When you're done, exit the editor (be sure to save your changes). You'll see a prompt similar to the following:

```
Send, Abort, Edit, or List?
```

Press **s** to send the message, **a** to abort the whole operation, **e** to edit the message, or **l** to display it (again, you may need to press **Enter**).

> If you'd prefer to reply to an article by sending the author an e-mail message, use either the **R** or **r** command. The **R** command inserts the original article text in the message, whereas the **r** command does not.

Posting an Original Article

rn and **trn** come with a program called **Pnews** that you can use to post your own original articles. To check it out, use either of the following methods:

➤ At the UNIX prompt, type **Pnews** and press **Enter**. The program will then prompt you to enter a newsgroup and a subject. In each case, type the appropriate data and press **Enter**. To avoid these prompts, you can specify a group and subject when you start **Pnews**. For example, to post an article to **rec.humor.funny** with the Subject line **Yet another blonde joke**, you'd start **Pnews** with the following command:

```
Pnews rec.humor.funny 'Yet another blonde joke'
```

➤ In **rn** or **trn**, select the group you want to use, select any article, and then type **f**. In this case, you'll see the following prompt:

```
Are you starting an unrelated topic? [ynq]
```

Since you're posting an original article, type **y**. You'll next be prompted for the subject of your article. Type the Subject line and press **Enter**.

In both cases, **Pnews** then prompts you to enter the distribution for your article. In most cases, you'll enter **world**, but you can easily restrict your post, if necessary. For example, enter **local** to restrict the post to the current site. Also, **usa** restricts the distribution to U.S. sites, **can** gives you Canada-only distribution, and so on.

Pnews then asks whether you're sure you want to go through with the post. There's no "Of course, silly" option, so just press **y** (and possibly **Enter**, as well). Now you'll get the following familiar prompt:

```
Prepared file to include [none]:
```

From here, you follow the same procedure I described in the last section for posting a follow-up.

The Least You Need to Know

This chapter showed you the basics of two time-tested UNIX newsreaders: **rn** and **trn**. Here's a nostalgic look back:

- **rn** and **trn** are loaded with options, but you can get away with using only a couple of keystrokes per session, if need be. The two programs are identical, except that **trn** organizes and displays articles in threads.

- To start **rn**, type **rn** and press **Enter**. To start **trn**, type **trn** and press **Enter**.

- The **.newsrc** file identifies which newsgroups you've subscribed and unsubscribed to, and tracks which articles you've read.

- You manage both programs by responding to a series of prompts. For each prompt, press the **Spacebar** to select the default option. Also, press **h** to display a list of the available commands for each prompt. For single-letter commands, just press the letter on your keyboard. For multiple-letter commands, type the letters and then press **Enter**.

Chapter 7

A UNIX Newcomer: tin

In This Chapter

- Subscribing and unsubscribing to newsgroups
- Reading articles
- Saving articles for posterity
- Following up and posting
- Putting **tin**'s pedal to its metal to get up to speed quickly

Most of the older UNIX newsreaders (such as **rn** and **trn**) were designed in an era when USENET was at least manageable. There were very few newsgroups 10 or 12 years ago, so these programs concentrated more on reading articles efficiently. But now, with thousands of groups flooding our machines every day, it's easy for these older programs to get swamped.

In response to the ever-growing deluge of groups, the **tin** newsreader was developed back in 1991. As you'll see in this chapter, **tin**'s strength is that it makes it easier to manage a large number of groups, while still maintaining a relatively simple interface. For these reasons and more, **tin** is rapidly becoming the newsreader of choice in the UNIX world.

> You'll be happy to know there's a **tin** FAQ list maintained by the guy who wrote the program (Iain Lea). It's posted regularly in the **news.software.readers** group under the name "FAQ: The TIN newsreader."

Breaking the tin Ice

To start **tin**, type **tin** and press **Enter**. If you're starting the program for the first time, you'll see an introductory message. Then **tin** connects to your news server and, if you've worked with **tin** before, the program checks to see if there are any new newsgroups that have materialized since your last session. If there are, you'll see a prompt that looks something like this:

```
Subscribe to new group alt.fan.tarantino (y/n/q) [n]:
```

In this case, **tin** has detected a new group called **alt.fan.tarantino**, and it's asking if you want to subscribe to it. Press **y** (for "yes") to subscribe to the group, **n** or **Enter** (for "no") to avoid the group like the plague, or **q** (for "quit") if you want to bail out of **tin** altogether.

tin then displays the following dispatches:

```
Reading news active file...
Reading attributes file...
Reading newsgroups file...
```

The first time you crank up **tin**, you'll also see a **Creating .newsrc** message. The **.newsrc** file holds all the vital statistics for your USENET universe: which groups you're subscribed to, which articles you've read, and which groups you're unsubscribed to. By default, **tin** crams every last one of your service provider's groups into your initial **.newsrc**. Since few people are foolish enough to try reading every newsgroup (there are, after all, thousands of them), you'll need to modify **.newsrc** so you're subscribed to only those groups you really want to read. There are **tin** commands you can use to unsubscribe to individual

Chapter 7 ➤ *A UNIX Newcomer: tin*

groups (or even multiple groups), but they take forever. By far the fastest way is to edit **.newsrc** directly. To find out how this is done, hike back to Chapter 6 and check out the section titled "How to Tame a Wild .newsrc File." (If you'd like to edit **.newsrc** before continuing with **tin**, press **Q** (uppercase) to quit the program and return to the UNIX prompt.)

When **tin** finishes its preliminaries, it displays the Group Selection screen (see the figure on the next page). The bottom of the screen presents you with a summary of some of the available **tin** commands. Since you'll be confronted with such a summary in all the **tin** screens, let's take a moment to try and knock some sense into it.

> If you're panicking because your **tin** screen doesn't have the handy summary of commands at the bottom, don't sweat it. All you have to do to set the world right is press **H** (uppercase). Once you've become a true **tin**-smith, you may not need to refer to the summary. In this case, you can press **H** again to remove the summary and give yourself a bit more room to maneuver.

In most cases, you run a **tin** command just by pressing a letter on your keyboard. The summary uses two methods to show you which keys to press. In the first method, the letter is part of the command name and **tin** marks the letter with a right parenthesis, like so:

```
h)elp
```

In this case, you'd simply press **h** to display a help screen (a list of the **tin** commands). In the second method, if the letter you press isn't part of the command name, the summary uses an equals sign (=), as shown here:

```
j=line down
```

This means you'd press **j** to move down one line in the list of newsgroups. (I'll talk more about these commands in the next section.) Notice, too, that **tin** differentiates between uppercase and lowercase letters. So, for example, pressing **s** runs one command (subscribe), while pressing **S** (**Shift+S**) runs a different command (subscribe pattern).

Part 2 ➤ *Start Spreading the News: A Guide to Popular Newsreaders*

Use the Group Selection screen to pick out the group you want to read.

Selecting a Newsgroup

Before you can read articles, you have to select the group you want to work with. Selecting a group is, not surprisingly, the province of the Group Selection screen. This screen displays the subscribed groups from your **.newsrc** using four columns of data:

➤ The first column shows an identification number that **tin** assigns to each displayed group.

➤ The second column shows the number of unread articles in the group.

➤ The third column shows the name of the group.

➤ The fourth column shows the group description. These descriptions are culled from a master list that gets sent around to each news site. If, for some reason, you'd prefer not to see these descriptions, you can toggle them off and on by pressing **d** (for description).

At this point, you have two choices: you can subscribe to a new group, or you can select a subscribed group from the list.

84

Working with Newsgroup Subscriptions

If you're just starting out, you'll need to subscribe to the newsgroups you want to read. (I'm assuming, of course, that you've already weeded out all the subscribed groups in your **.newsrc** file, as described earlier.) To subscribe to a group, press **g** to run the **goto** command. **tin** will display the following prompt at the bottom of the screen:

```
Goto newsgroup []>
```

Type the name of the group you want to subscribe to, and then press **Enter**. For example, to subscribe to the group **alt.backrubs**, you'd type **alt.backrubs** and press **Enter**. **tin** then asks where you want the group to appear in the list:

```
Position alt.backrubs in group list (1,2,..,$) [1]>
```

The number in the square brackets (e.g., **[1]**) is the default position, which you select by pressing **Enter**. Otherwise, type the position number (or **$** if you want the group to appear at the end of the list) and then press **Enter**. **tin** adds the group to the Group Selection list.

To unsubscribe to a newsgroup, highlight the group name in the Group Selection list (I'll show you how to do this in the next section), and then press **u** to run the **unsubscribe** command. The letter **u** appears to the left of the group's identification number. (The next time you start **tin**, the group won't appear in the Group Selection list.) If you change your mind and decide you want to subscribe to the group after all, select the group and press **s** (for **subscribe**).

Instead of unsubscribing or subscribing to one group at a time in the Group Selection list, you can work with multiple groups that have similar names. For example, you might want to unsubscribe to every group in the Group Selection list that contains the word **startrek**. To do this, press **U** to invoke the **unsubscribe pattern** command. You'll see the following prompt at the bottom of the screen:

```
Enter regex unsubscribe pattern>
```

> As I mentioned earlier, when you're just starting out with **tin**, the Group Selection list contains every single group. Instead of editing **.newsrc**, you might be tempted to run the U command and enter ***** as the pattern to unsubscribe to every group. This will work, but it will take, quite literally, hours to complete the task.

Here, "regex" means *regular expression*. What's a regular expression? Good question. In simplest terms, it's just a shorthand notation for describing a pattern of letters. Regular expressions can get pretty scary, but we can safely ignore most of the truly arcane symbols. For our purposes, we only need to know about one symbol: the asterisk (*). The asterisk is used to match zero or more characters in a group name. Here are some examples that illustrate how this works:

This expression	Matches all group names
news*	Beginning with *news* (i.e., every group in the **news** hierarchy).
*answers	Ending with *answers* (e.g., **alt.answers**, **comp.answers**).
startrek	Containing the text *startrek*.

To subscribe to a bunch of groups that match a pattern, press **S** to run the **subscribe pattern** command.

Selecting Newsgroups from the List

When you've subscribed to all the groups you want to read, you can then pick out a group to work with from the Group Selection list. The first thing you should notice is that **tin** always highlights the currently selected group. To move this highlight, **tin** gives you the following options:

➤ To move the highlight down one line, press **j** or the **down arrow** key (if your terminal has one).

➤ To move the highlight up one line, press **k** or the **up arrow** key (again, if the terminal you're using has such a key).

➤ If you have more than a screenful of groups, you can display the next screen by pressing the **Spacebar** (or **Page Down**), and you can display the previous screen by pressing **b** (or **Page Up**).

➤ To head directly to a group, press **g** to select the **goto** command. **tin** will prompt you to enter the group name, and it will display the name of the last group you used **goto** to jump to. If the displayed group is the one you want, just press **Enter** to select it. Otherwise, type the name of the group you want to select and press **Enter**.

When the group you want is highlighted, press **Enter** to display the group's threads.

tin also gives you a couple of commands that will select a group and display its threads in one fell swoop. If the group name is displayed in the Group Selection screen, type the group's identification number and press **Enter**. If you just want to go to the next group that contains unread articles, press **Tab**.

> To make the Group Selection list easier to navigate, press **r** to toggle the list between showing all the groups and just those with unread articles.

For groups with long names (or if you can't remember the full name of the group), you can search for part of the name. To search forward, type a slash (/) to select the **search pattern** command. **tin** displays the following prompt:

```
Search forwards []>
```

Type a piece of the newsgroup name you want to locate (it could be a couple of words, a single word, or even part of a word). For example, the command **/rec** finds the first newsgroup that includes the word **rec** in its name. To continue the search, press / and then press **Enter**. If you'd prefer to search backwards, type a question mark (?) and enter your search text in the **Search backwards** prompt.

Table 7.1 summarizes the commands that work in the Group Selection list and any other list that **tin** displays.

Table 7.1 Command Summary for All tin Lists

Press	To run the command	Which does this
j	line down	Moves the highlight down one line.
k	line up	Moves the highlight up one line.
Spacebar	page down	Displays the next page.
b	page up	Displays the previous page.

continues

Table 7.1 Continued

Press	To run the command	Which does this
$	last	Highlights the last item in the list.
<n>	set current to n	Reads the item with the id number n.
Tab	next	Reads the next unread item.
/	search forward	Searches forward for the first item with a name that includes a specified pattern.
?	search backward	Searches backward for the first item with a name that includes a specified pattern.
r	toggle all/unread	Toggles the list between all items and just those with unread articles.

Table 7.2 lists the main commands available for the Newsgroup Selection list.

Table 7.2 Command Summary for the Newsgroup Selection List in tin

Press	To run the command	Which does this
N	next (don't read)	Highlights the next group with unread articles.
g	goto	Highlights (or subscribes to) a specified group.
u	unsubscribe	Unsubscribes to the highlighted group.
s	subscribe	Subscribes to the highlighted group.

Press	To run the command	Which does this
U	unsubscribe pattern	Unsubscribes to all groups that match a specified pattern.
S	subscribe pattern	Subscribes to all groups that match a specified pattern.
Enter	read current group	Reads the highlighted group.
d	description	Toggles Group Selection list descriptions on and off.

Selecting an Article

When you open up a newsgroup to read it, **tin** displays the thread selection list, as shown in the figure on the next page. This list shows you the available threads in the newsgroup, and divides the info for each thread into five columns:

➤ The first column shows an identification number that **tin** assigns to each thread.

➤ The second column shows a plus sign (+) if the thread contains unread articles.

➤ The third column shows the number of unread articles in the thread. (If the thread has a plus sign in the second column but no number in the third column, it means there is only one unread article in the thread.)

➤ The fourth column shows the Subject line of the thread.

➤ The fifth column shows the name of the person who posted the original article.

In the figure that follows, for example, thread #2 is unread, it has 8 articles, the original Subject line is "Chronic Pain Relief & Releases of Endorphins," and the original poster was someone named "The Spy."

Part 2 ➤ *Start Spreading the News: A Guide to Popular Newsreaders*

```
┌─ tor.hookup.net ──────────────────────────────────┐
│                                                   │
│         alt.backrubs (11T 22A 0K 0H R)      h=hel │
│  1   +      alt.backrubs archive: policy clarification   J. Blustein
│  2   + 8    Chronic Pain Relief & Releases of Endorphins The Spy
│  3   +      Cool Backrub                                 WYATT M GREENE
│  4   +      BALANCE CHAIR for the Back                   J. Blustein
│  5   +      Massage swap wanted                          James Loper
│  6   + 2    backrubs                                     Steve Briggs
│  7   +      LOS ANGELES BACK RUB EXCHANGE                Ron MALE LA CA eme
│  8   + 3    Extracts and Oil                             Brian Higginbotham
│  9   + 2    How come this newsgroup is so dead?          Jody Andrew Garnet
│ 10   +      [alt.backrubs] FTP archive site              J. Blustein
│ 11   +      Springfield Area Backrubs                    Ackermann Timothy
│
│
│   <n>=set current to n, TAB=next unread, /=search pattern, (K)ill/select
│   a)uthor search, c)atchup, j=line down, k=line up, K=mark read, l)ist thread
│   |=pipe, m)ail, o=print, q)uit, r=toggle all unread, s)ave, t)ag, w=post
│                       *** End of Articles ***
└───────────────────────────────────────────────────┘
```

The thread selection list shows the available threads for the selected group.

> The top of the thread selection list shows the name of the newsgroup followed by a few incomprehensible numbers and letters. What does this gibberish mean? The first part (**11T**), tells you the number of threads in the list; the second part (**22A**) tells you the total number of articles in the threads; the third part (**0K**) tells you the number of killed articles; the fourth part (**0H**) tells you the number of hot articles; the final part (**R**) appears if the thread selector list is set up to display only threads with unread articles.

To read a thread, highlight it and press **Enter**. (Conveniently, **tin** lets you highlight a thread using the same commands you learned for highlighting a group in the Group Selection list.) **tin** displays the first article in the thread.

If you'd like to check out the authors and number of lines for each article in the thread, press **l** to select the **list thread** command. **tin** displays a new screen that shows you the following info for each article in the thread: whether the article has been read, the number of lines in the article, and the author of the article. To read an article, highlight it and press **Enter**. To return to the thread selection list instead, press **q**.

If you don't want to bother reading a particular thread, highlight it and press **K** to run the **mark read** command. **tin** will mark the thread as read. If none of the thread subjects turns your crank, you can mark everything as read by pressing **c** to select the **catchup** command.

Table 7.3 lists these and other useful commands for selecting a thread in **tin**.

Table 7.3 Command Summary for Selecting a Thread in tin

Press	To run the command	Which does this
Enter	read current thread	Displays the first article in the highlighted thread.
l	list thread	Displays the articles in the highlighted thread.
K	mark read	Marks the highlighted thread as read.
c	catchup	Marks all the threads as read.
C	catchup and read	Marks all the threads as read and reads the next group with unread articles.
N	next	Displays the next unread article.
P	previous	Displays the previous unread article.
q	quit	Returns to the Newsgroup Selection list.

Reading an Article

When you read a thread (or when you read a specific article from the thread), **tin** displays a new screen that shows the header at the top, followed by the article body. If the entire article fits on your screen, just go ahead and read it and then press the **Spacebar** to move on to the next article. If the article is too big to fit in one screen, you'll see the following at the bottom of the screen:

    --MORE--(69%)

This tells you there are more lines to come and gives you an indication of how far into the article you are. (In this example, the **69%** means you've read 69% of the article.) Just press the **Spacebar** to continue reading. You can also use the keys outlined in Table 7.4 while reading an article.

Table 7.4   Command Summary for Reading an Article in tin

Press	To run the command	Which does this
Spacebar	page down	Displays the next page.
b	page up	Displays the previous page.
$	last	Moves to the end of the article.
d	toggle rot13	Toggles the article between rot13 and regular text.
Ctrl+L	redisplay page	Redisplays the current page.
Ctrl+R	redisplay first	Redisplays the first page.
q	quit	Returns to the thread selector list.

Saving an Article

If you'd like to save a copy of an article to a file in your home directory, press **s** to run the **save** command. **tin** then displays the following prompt:

    Save a)rticle, t)hread, h)ot, p)attern, T)agged articles, q)uit:

To save the article, press **a**. In the **Save filename** prompt that appears, enter a name for the file and press **Enter**. Yet another prompt appears, asking you which "Process" to use. You can safely ignore this prompt, so just press **n** (for **none**).

Following Up an Article

If you get the urge to rebut an article's arguments or otherwise join in on a newsgroup discussion, **tin** makes it easy to post follow-ups. With the article you want to follow up displayed, press **f** to run the **followup** command. **tin** then loads the text editor and inserts the entire text from the original article. At this point, you need to do two things:

➤ Edit the original text to include only those lines that are absolutely necessary for your reply.

➤ Add your own text.

When you're done, exit the text editor (if you're using **vi**—which is usually the default editor for **tin**—you exit by pressing **ZZ**). You'll see a prompt similar to the following:

```
q)uit, e)dit, i)spell, p)ost:
```

Press **p** to send the message, **e** to edit the message, **i** to start the interactive spell check, or **q** to bail out of the operation.

> If you'd prefer to reply to an article by sending the author an e-mail message, press either **R** or **r**. The **r** command inserts the original article text in the message, whereas the **R** command does not.

Posting an Original Article

tin has a **write** command that lets you post original articles to the newsgroup of your choice. To try it out, use either of the following methods:

➤ At the UNIX prompt, type **tin -w** and press **Enter**. The program will then prompt you to enter a newsgroup and a subject. In each case, enter the appropriate data and press **Enter**.

➤ In **tin**, select the group you want to use and then type **w**. When the program prompts you for a **Post subject**, type your Subject line and press **Enter**.

From here, **tin** starts the text editor (the default editor is usually **vi**) so you can create your article. When you're done, press **ZZ** to exit **vi**; **tin** will then display the following prompt:

```
q)uit, e)dit, i)spell, p)ost:
```

Press **p** to post the article, **e** to edit it, **i** to start the interactive spell-check, or **q** to abort.

The Least You Need to Know

This chapter took you on a tour of the **tin** newsreader, one of the newcomers to the ranks of UNIX news software. Here are a few highlights:

➤ **tin** was designed to let you work with large numbers of newsgroups.

➤ To start **tin**, type **tin** and press **Enter**.

➤ The **.newsrc** file identifies which newsgroups you've subscribed and unsubscribed to, and tracks which articles you've read. When you run **tin** for the first time, your **.newsrc** file is set up to subscribe to every group available from your access provider.

➤ Use the Group Selection list to select which newsgroup you want to read. One way to read a group is to highlight it and press **Enter**.

➤ When you've selected a group, use the thread selection list to choose which thread you want to read. You can read a thread by highlighting it and pressing **Enter**.

➤ When you've finished reading an article or thread, press **q** to return to the thread selection list, and then press **q** again to return to the Group Selection screen.

Chapter 8

Blowing Your Own Horn with Trumpet

In This Chapter

- How to get a copy of Trumpet
- Subscribing and unsubscribing to newsgroups
- Reading articles
- Following up and posting
- Everything you need to know to ensure you and Trumpet make beautiful USENET music together

For most USENET newcomers, it doesn't matter all that much how they read the news; no, the sheer fact that USENET exists and works is amazing enough. "Some guy from Finland just called me a butt-head. Cool!" So, for years, USENETers happily suffered through ugly, unwieldy command-line newsreaders such as **rn**, **trn**, and **tin** (which were covered in the last two chapters). Then Windows came along, and a lightbulb clicked on over someone's head: "Hey, we can use this Windows thing to make reading the news a breeze!"

People all over the world slapped their heads in amazement. USENET? Easy? Imagine that! It's true, though, as you'll see in this

Part 2 ➤ *Start Spreading the News: A Guide to Popular Newsreaders*

chapter. We'll play around with one of the first—and, for now, one of the most popular—Windows newsreaders: Trumpet.

Getting Your Hands on Trumpet

If you don't have a copy of Trumpet, you'll need to use anonymous FTP to get the Trumpet file and install it on your system. Fortunately, this is a fairly straightforward affair, as the following steps show:

1. Load your FTP software and send it off to **ftp.utas.edu.au** (this is a site at the University of Tasmania).

2. When you're connected, change the directory to **/pc/trumpet/wintrump**, and then FTP the file **wtwsk*???*.zip**. (You'll need to substitute the *???* for whatever is the latest version number of Trumpet. As I write this, the current version is 1.0A, so the filename is **wtwsk10a.zip**.) This archive contains all the Trumpet files you need.

3. For Trumpet to work properly, you'll also need a copy of Winsock, the software that lets programs such as Trumpet talk to your service provider. Change to the directory **/pc/trumpet/winsock**, and FTP the file **twsk*???*.zip**. (Again, replace *???* with the latest version number of Winsock. The current version is 2.0B, so the filename is **twsk20b.zip**.)

4. Using File Manager, create a separate directory called **WTRUMPET**; copy the Trumpet ZIP file into this directory, and then decompress the file. (You use the program PKUNZIP to decompress a ZIP file. PKUNZIP is available in hundreds of Internet sites around the world. For example, anonymous FTP to **ftp.psi.com**, head for the **/src/dos** directory, and grab the file **PKUNZIP.EXE**.) If you need some help with this File Manager stuff, may I not-so-humbly suggest picking up a copy of *The Complete Idiot's Guide to Windows 3.1*, by (blush) Paul McFedries?

5. Copy the Winsock ZIP file to WTRUMPET, decompress it with PKUNZIP, and then copy the following files to your WINDOWS directory: **tcpman.exe** and **winsock.dll**.

6. In Program Manager, create an icon for Trumpet. (The file that starts Trumpet is in the WTRUMPET directory; its name is **wt_wsk.exe**.)

That's it, you're ready for action. In the next section, I'll show you how to start Trumpet and set it up for your system.

> Keep in mind that Trumpet and Winsock are *shareware* products. If you plan to use them regularly, be a good citizen and register them with the developer. You'll find the details in the documentation that comes with both products. Trumpet costs $40; Winsock is a mere $25 (those prices are, of course, subject to change at any time).

Before You Start Playing with Trumpet

Trumpet works, in most cases, by using your modem to exchange pleasantries with your access provider's USENET news computer. These exchanges use either SLIP (Serial Line Interface Protocol) or PPP (Point-to-Point Protocol) so the two machines can understand one another's lingo. So before you can start Trumpet, you need to dial up your access provider and establish either a SLIP or PPP connection. How you do this depends on how your Internet connection is set up:

➤ Many access providers supply their customers with a "dialer" program that will establish the connection automatically.

➤ If you have no dialer software, you need to use the TCPMAN.EXE program that came with the Winsock files. Setting up TCPMAN is not for the faint of heart, so you should commandeer the nearest Internet guru and get him to set things up for you. If you're really feeling your oats and want to try it for yourself, look for a file named INSTALL.TXT (there's also a Word for Windows file named INSTALL.DOC, if you prefer) in your Trumpet directory. The section titled "Installing the Winsock for use over Internal SLIP/PPP" tells you everything you need to know. Good luck!

Starting Trumpet with a Flourish

If you created a Program Manager icon for Trumpet, as described earlier, go ahead and double-click on it to get things started. (If you don't have a Trumpet icon, you can also start the program by pulling

Part 2 ➤ *Start Spreading the News: A Guide to Popular Newsreaders*

down the File menu in Program Manager or File Manager, selecting the **Run** command, entering **c:\wtrumpet\wt_wsk.exe**—assuming you unzipped Trumpet in the C:\WTRUMPET directory—and then selecting **OK**.) When you load Trumpet for the first time, you'll see the Trumpet Setup dialog box appear, as shown in the following figure.

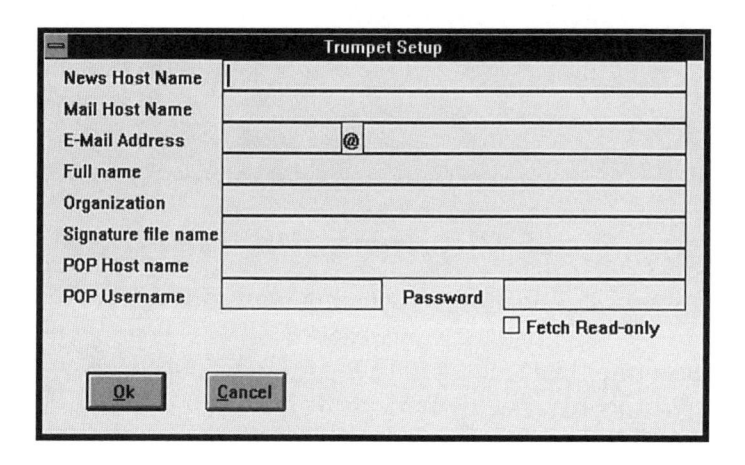

Use the Trumpet Setup dialog box to tell Trumpet a little about yourself.

You use this dialog box to give Trumpet the details it needs to connect to your news host (the computer at your access provider that handles USENET news), as well as a few other vital statistics about your system. Here's a quick rundown for each field (if you're not sure about any of this stuff, contact your system administrator or access provider):

> **News Host Name**—This is the Internet name of the computer that handles your USENET connection (this machine is also known as a *news server*). Enter a domain name (mine is **nnrp.tor.hookup.net**) or one of those dotted addresses (e.g., **123.456.78.90**).
>
> **Mail Host Name**—This is the Internet name of the computer that handles your e-mail. You only need to fill in this field if you think you'll be replying to some articles via e-mail.
>
> **E-Mail Address**—Use these two fields to enter your e-mail address. The first field is for your user name; the second field is for your domain name. For example, my e-mail address is **paulmcf@hookup.net**, so I'd enter **paulmcf** in the first field and **hookup.net** in the second field.

Chapter 8 ➤ *Blowing Your Own Horn with Trumpet*

Full name—This field will appear along with your e-mail address in the From line of your posts. You'll usually enter your name, but you're free to use any other alias that suits your fancy.

> When filling in the **Full name** field, don't use any of the following characters:
>
> ( ) " , < >

Organization—Use this optional field to enter a company name that will appear as part of the header in articles you post yourself.

Signature file name—Rather than typing a signature each time you post, you can use Notepad or some other text editor to create a text file containing your signature. You can then use this field to enter the drive, directory, and file name of the text file.

POP Host name—Although I won't go into it in this chapter, you can use Trumpet to get your e-mail messages. If you want to use this feature, enter the Internet name of the computer that stores your e-mail. (This will usually be the same as the name you entered in the **Mail host name** field.) Also, be sure to fill in the **POP Username** and **Password** fields.

When you're done, select **Ok**. Now you may also see the Network Configuration dialog box. When this dialog box appears, it collects the following info from you:

IP address—This is the IP (Internet Protocol) address of your computer. This will usually be a dotted address (e.g., 123.456.78.90, and your system administrator or access provider can let you know the correct value.

Time server—This is yet another address for a computer in your access provider's system. They can let you know the proper address.

Domain Suffix—This is the second half of your e-mail address (the part to the right of the "at" (@) sign).

When that rigmarole is all taken care of, select **Ok** to continue. Trumpet connects to your news host and then grabs the full list of available groups. After a few seconds, the Subscribe to News Groups dialog box appears. For now, just select **OK** to return to the main Trumpet window so we can take a look around. (By the way, if you ever need to make changes to the Setup info, pull down the File menu and select the Setup command to display the Trumpet Setup dialog box, or select the Network Setup command to display the Network Configuration dialog box.)

As you can see in the figure that follows, the Trumpet window is divided into two main sections. The top part of the screen (I'll call it the *group list*) displays the newsgroups you're subscribed to; the bottom part of the screen (I'll call it the *article list*) displays the unread articles in the selected group. Since you're just starting out with Trumpet, both windows will be empty. Your first order of business—which we'll get to in the next section—will be to subscribe to some newsgroups.

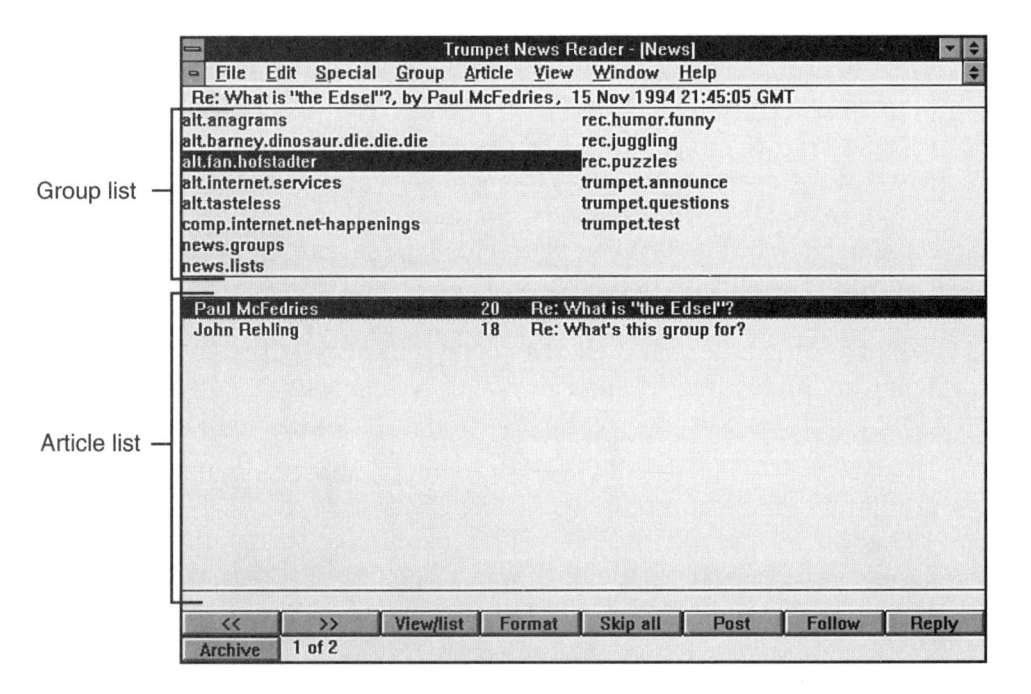

Where the action is: the Trumpet window.

If you become a dedicated Trumpet player, you'll be happy to know there are several newsgroups devoted exclusively to Trumpet. For example, **trumpet.questions** is the place to post if you have any queries about Trumpet. If you'd like to suggest

Chapter 8 ➤ *Blowing Your Own Horn with Trumpet*

> an enhancement to Trumpet, send your idea to **trumpet.feedback**. If you find a bug in Trumpet, you can let everyone know by posting to **trumpet.bugs**. If you'd like to try a test post or two, you can use the group **trumpet.test**. Finally, any new Trumpet versions or upgrades will be trumpeted (sorry about that) in the **trumpet.announce** group.

Subscribing and Unsubscribing in Trumpet

When you first load Trumpet, the group list is depressingly bare. To cheer things up a bit, you'll need to subscribe to a newsgroup or two so you can start reading articles. Begin by pulling down the Group menu and selecting the Subscribe command. Trumpet takes a few seconds to check for new groups and, if it finds any, it displays the Subscribe dialog box with the message **There are new news-groups**. In this case, just select **OK** to continue. You'll eventually see the Subscribe to News Groups dialog box, which will be similar to the one shown in the following figure.

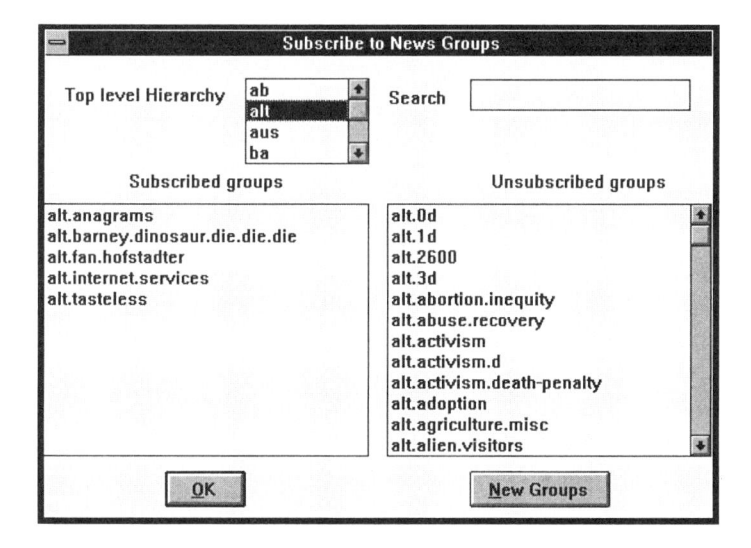

Use the Subscribe to News Groups dialog box to subscribe to your favorite newsgroups.

To subscribe to a newsgroup, you can use any of the following techniques:

101

> If Trumpet detected any new groups, they'll appear in the **Unsubscribed groups** list. If you'd like to subscribe to one of these groups, click on the group name. Trumpet will move the name to the **Subscribed groups** list.

> To pick out a group from a hierarchy, first use the **Top level Hierarchy** list to choose the hierarchy you want. Trumpet displays the hierarchy's unsubscribed groups in the **Unsubscribed groups** list, and the hierarchy's subscribed groups in the **Subscribed groups** list. Now just click on the group you want in the **Unsubscribed groups** list.

> If you know the name of the group, activate the **Search** text box and enter some or all of the group name. Trumpet will display all the group names that match your search text in the **Unsubscribed groups** list. Again, just click on the one you want to add it to the **Subscribed groups** list.

If you forget about Trumpet for a while (perhaps for about half an hour or so), your news host may automatically disconnect you. If you then try to do something, Trumpet will display a dialog box telling you the connection was closed. To get hooked up again, pull down the File menu and select the Reconnect command.

When you're done, click **OK** to return to the main Trumpet window. Trumpet will display your selected groups in the group list.

When a group wears out its welcome, you can unsubscribe to it by clicking on it in the group list, pulling down the Group menu, and selecting the Unsubscribe command. (If your group list is a real fiasco, you can get a clean slate by selecting the Special menu's Zap all subscribed groups command.)

Reading News with Trumpet

Okay, now that you've picked out some interesting groups, it's time to read what people have to say. The first thing you need to do is have Trumpet load the Subject lines for the group you want to read. To do this, just double-click on the group name. After a few seconds (or a few minutes, depending on how many articles there are), Trumpet fills the article list with info divided into three columns:

Chapter 8 ➤ *Blowing Your Own Horn with Trumpet*

- ➤ The first column tells you the name of the person who posted the article.

- ➤ The second column tells you the number of lines in the article.

- ➤ The third column tells you the Subject line of the article.

If you see a subject that looks like it might be worth a peek, double-click on it. (You can also click on it and then click on the **View/list** button at the bottom of the screen.) Trumpet temporarily hides the group and article lists, and uses the entire window to display the article, as shown in the figure that follows.

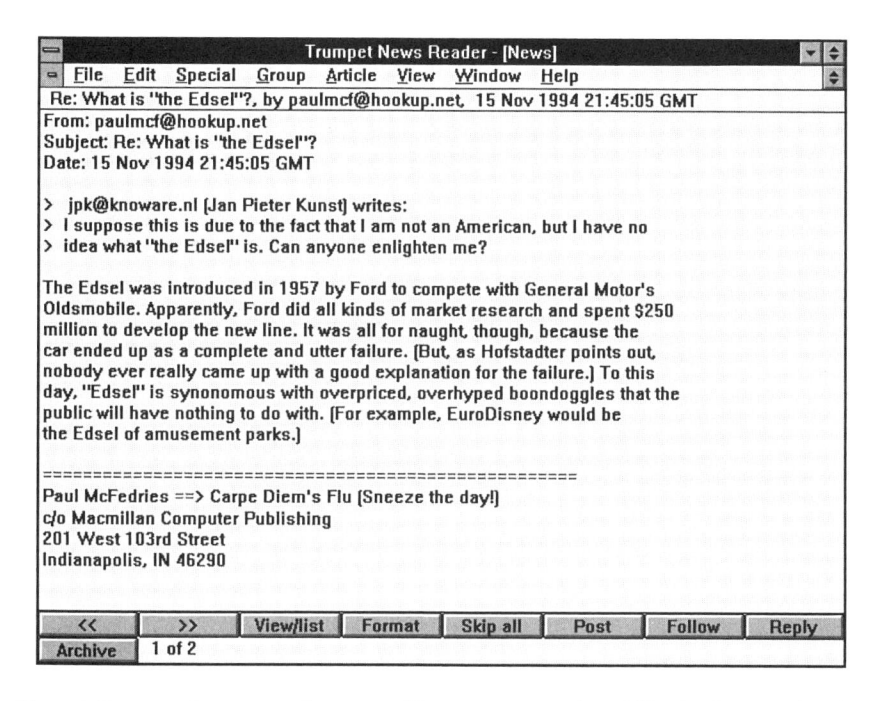

To get the maximum real estate, Trumpet uses the full window to display each article.

Once you've read the article, you can move on to the next article by clicking on the >> button at the bottom of the screen. To go back to the previous article, click on the << button. If you'd prefer to return to the article list, click on the **View/list** button.

Trumpet's Group menu also has a few commands that operate on multiple articles. Here's a rundown:

Read all—Marks all the articles in the current group as read, and clears out the article list. (If you want to mark all the articles as read *and* move on to the next group, click on the **Skip all** button instead.)

Unread all—Marks all the articles in the current group as unread. Why would anyone need to "unread" articles? Well, once you've read an article, Trumpet assumes you don't want to see it again. That way, if you go ahead and read an article, then display a different group, and then return to the previous group, the article you just read won't appear in the list. If you need to see the article again, you need to "unread" it.

Unread 20—Marks the last 20 articles you read in the current group as unread.

> The shortcut key for the Unread 20 command is **Ctrl+U**.

Unread 10—Marks the last 10 articles you read in the current group as unread.

Catch up—Marks all articles in the current group as read. This command is faster than Read all, because Trumpet doesn't bother to scan the group to see which articles are unread.

What if you just want to bypass a single article and mark it as read? No problemo. Just click on the article to highlight it, pull down the Article menu, and select the Skip command. (You can also just press **Ctrl+S**.)

The View menu also has a few commands worth checking out:

Full headers—This command toggles the article between displaying the full header (a dozen fields in all), and a more compact version (just the From, Subject, Summary, Keywords, and Date lines).

Word wrap—If the article has long lines that won't fit entirely on your screen, activate this command to wrap the text at the screen border so you can read everything.

Rot13—This command toggles the article between regular text and the rot13 encoding. (See Chapter 2, "So Just What the Heck Is USENET, Anyway?," to learn more about rot13.)

Archiving an Article

One of the unpleasant truths about USENET is that most of the verbiage you'll read will be only so much hot air, hokum, and out-and-out hogwash. Don't be discouraged, though; there are still plenty of gems out there to be mined. And occasionally—especially in the moderated groups—you'll come across an article worth saving for the ages. It could be a good joke, info you need for a project, or just a useful FAQ you'd like to keep handy. Trumpet, bless its digital heart, gives you not one, but *two* different ways to hang onto an article: you can save it to a "folder," and you can save it to its own text file.

Filing an Article in a Folder

In your USENET travels, you may see people talking about "offline" newsreaders. An offline newsreader is a program that lets you grab some interesting-looking articles and read them later on when you've severed your connection to the Internet. This is handy for people who pay through the nose for their connection time and want to minimize the time they spend online.

The good news is that Trumpet is an offline newsreader. Its approach is to copy articles to your computer and insert them in special *folders*. You can then open these folders at any time (such as when you're offline); your articles will be there, waiting patiently for you. You'll usually set up a folder for each newsgroup you read, but you're free to create your own folders.

To save an article to a folder, follow these simple steps:

1. Select the newsgroup containing the article you want to save, and then either highlight the article in the article list, or read the article.

2. Pull down the Article menu and select the Move Article to folder command. If this is the first time you're saving an article from this newsgroup, Trumpet will display a dialog box asking if you want to create a folder for the group (see the figure on the next page). Otherwise, Trumpet reads the article and saves it to the group's folder.

> You can also select the Move article to folder command by pressing **Ctrl+V** or by clicking on the **Archive** button.

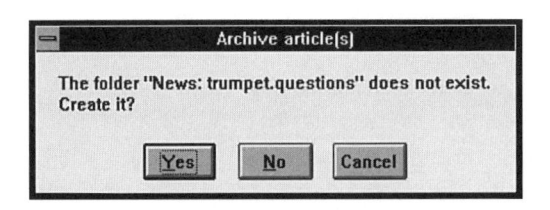

Part 2 ➤ *Start Spreading the News: A Guide to Popular Newsreaders*

[Dialog box: Archive article(s) — "The folder 'News: trumpet.questions' does not exist. Create it?" with Yes, No, Cancel buttons]

Trumpet politely asks if you want to create a folder for the current newsgroup.

3. If you want to create the folder, select **Yes**. Trumpet sets up the folder and saves the article.

   If you'd like to save the article to a different folder, select **No**, highlight the folder you want in the Select Mail Folder dialog box that appears, and then select **Ok**. (I'll show you how to create your own folders in a sec.) Trumpet then saves the article to the folder you selected.

To read one of your saved articles, pull down the **Window** menu and select the **Mail** window. The Mail window is similar to the News window you've been looking at until now. The top part of the window shows your folders; the bottom part of the window shows the articles in each folder. To read something you've saved, double-click on the folder containing the article, and then double-click on the article.

Once you've saved an article, you can treat it like any other: you can save it to a file (which I'll show you how to do in the next section), and you can send a follow-up (which we'll talk about later in the chapter). The Mail window also lets you do the following:

➤ To delete an article from a folder, highlight it, pull down the Article menu, and select the **Delete Article** command. (Alternatively, you can press **Ctrl+D**.)

➤ To move an article to a different folder, highlight it and select the Article menu's Move Article to folder command (or press **Ctrl+V**). Use the Select Mail Folder dialog box to pick out a group and then select Ok.

➤ To create your own folder, pull down the Special menu and select the Insert Folder command (or highlight an existing folder and press the **Insert** key). In the Insert folder dialog box that appears, enter the title of the folder, and then select **OK**.

➤ To delete an existing folder, highlight it and select the Special menu's **Delete** folder command (or press the **Delete** key). Trumpet displays the Delete Folder dialog box, asking you to confirm the deletion. Select **OK** to carry out the execution.

When you're done with the Mail window, pull down the **W**indow menu and select **News** to return to the News window.

Saving an Article to a File

If you'd prefer to save an article to a separate text file all its own, Trumpet is up to the task. Highlight the article (or read it), pull down the Article menu, and select the **S**ave to file command. In the File Save As dialog box that appears, use the Directories list to pick out a suitable location for the file, and enter the name of the file in the Fi**l**ename text box. When you're ready, select **OK**.

Following Up an Article

When reading a newsgroup, you may get the urge to answer someone's question, refute someone's argument, or just take the wind out of someone's sails. This means, of course, that you have to post a follow-up article. Here's how it's done in Trumpet:

1. Either highlight the article in the article list or read the article.

2. Pull down the Article menu and select the Follow command. (For faster service, try pressing **Ctrl+F** or clicking on the **Follow** button.) Trumpet displays the Post Article dialog box and loads the text from the original article (as shown in the figure on the next page).

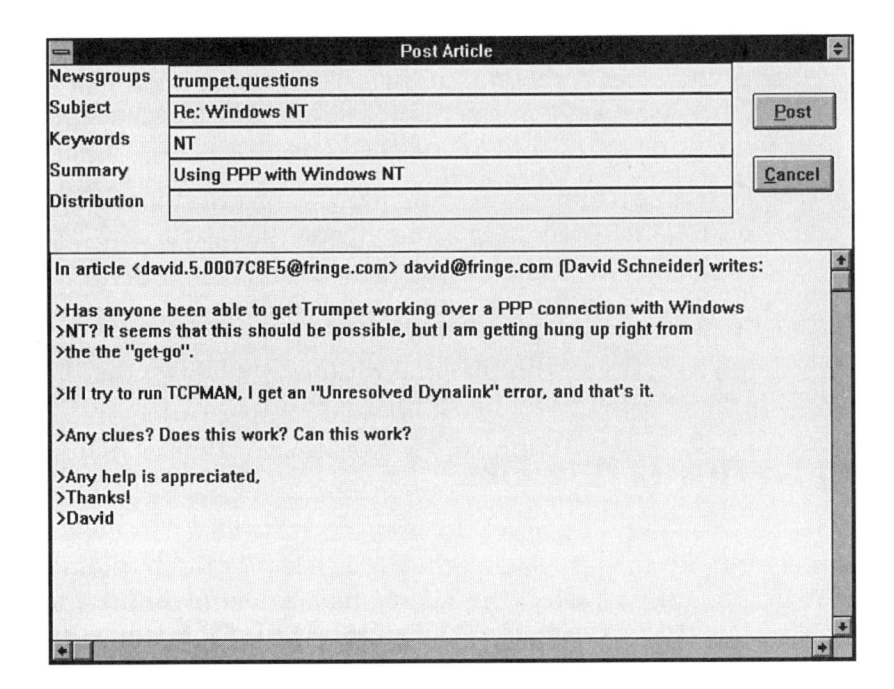

Part 2 ➤ *Start Spreading the News: A Guide to Popular Newsreaders*

```
┌─────────────────────── Post Article ───────────────────────┐
│ Newsgroups  │ trumpet.questions                    │        │
│ Subject     │ Re: Windows NT                       │  Post  │
│ Keywords    │ NT                                   │        │
│ Summary     │ Using PPP with Windows NT            │ Cancel │
│ Distribution│                                      │        │
├────────────────────────────────────────────────────────────┤
│ In article <david.5.0007C8E5@fringe.com> david@fringe.com  │
│ [David Schneider] writes:                                  │
│                                                            │
│ >Has anyone been able to get Trumpet working over a PPP    │
│ >connection with Windows                                   │
│ >NT? It seems that this should be possible, but I am       │
│ >getting hung up right from                                │
│ >the the "get-go".                                         │
│                                                            │
│ >If I try to run TCPMAN, I get an "Unresolved Dynalink"    │
│ >error, and that's it.                                     │
│                                                            │
│ >Any clues? Does this work? Can this work?                 │
│                                                            │
│ >Any help is appreciated,                                  │
│ >Thanks!                                                   │
│ >David                                                     │
└────────────────────────────────────────────────────────────┘
```

When you follow up an article, Trumpet copies the article text to the Post Article dialog box.

3. If necessary, edit the **Newsgroups**, **Subject**, **Keywords**, **Summary**, and **Distribution** text boxes. (In most cases, you can just leave these as they are. For more info, see "Posting an Original Article," later in this chapter.)

4. Cut out any unnecessary text from the original article. (In the figure above, I've already cut out the original header information.)

5. Enter your own text in the article body.

6. Select the **P**ost button. Trumpet sends the follow-up on its merry way.

> If you'd prefer to reply to an article by sending its author an e-mail message, select the **A**rticle menu's **R**eply command. (The shortcuts are **Ctrl+R** or the **R**eply button.) The Mail Article dialog box that appears is similar to the Post Article dialog box we looked at earlier. When you're ready to go, click on the **S**end button.

108

Posting an Original Article

When the impulse to post something original hits, Trumpet is ready, willing, and able. Here's what happens:

1. In the group list, highlight the newsgroup to which you want to post.

> You can post to more than one newsgroup, but you can only select one newsgroup at a time in the group list. To post to multiple groups, you add them to the Newsgroups field, as described in Step 3.

2. Select the Article menu's **Post** command. (Pressing **Ctrl+P** or clicking on the **Post** button will get you there faster.) Trumpet displays the Post Article dialog box.

3. This dialog box is identical to the one you worked with in the last section. In this case, however, you'll need to fill in some or all of the following text boxes to define your article header:

   Newsgroups—By default, this field shows the name of the current newsgroup. You can change this group, or add more groups if you need to cross-post the article.

   Subject—Enter the subject of the article.

   Keywords—You can use this field to enter one or more keywords that categorize your article. Some folks use the contents of the Keywords line (in combination with the Subject line) to decide whether or not an article is worth reading.

   Summary—This field lets you enter a summary of the article's contents. It's more useful in a follow-up article than in an original, because on a follow-up you can't use the Subject line to describe your article.

   > If you specified a signature file when you set up Trumpet, the program will add the signature text automatically when you post the article. *Don't* add a signature by hand, or you'll end up with a *double sig*: two signatures in one post. This will automatically brand you as a newbie.

Distribution—This field determines, on a general level, which Internet sites will receive the article. You'll usually enter **world** to get the maximum distribution, but you can also choose **local** (posted only to your site), **usa** (U.S. sites only), **can** (Canada), or **na** (North America). Ask your service provider to send you a complete list of Distribution options.

4. Enter your text in the article body.
5. Select the **P**ost button. Trumpet fires off the article.

The Least You Need to Know

This chapter showed you how easy USENET can be—if you have the right interface. Here's an encore presentation of some of this chapter's more memorable Trumpet solos:

➤ When you start Trumpet for the first time, the Trumpet Setup dialog box appears so you can enter the info the program needs to get your news.

➤ To subscribe to a newsgroup, select the Group menu's Subscribe command.

➤ To unsubscribe to a newsgroup, highlight the group in the group list, and then select the Group menu's Unsubscribe command.

➤ Reading an article is a snap: just double-click on the group and then double-click on the article.

➤ To save an article, pull down the Article menu and select either **M**ove Article to folder (to place the article in a folder for offline reading), or **S**ave to file (to copy the article to its own text file).

➤ If you want to write a follow-up to the article you're reading, select the Article menu's **F**ollow command (or choose **R**eply to send a rebuttal via e-mail).

➤ To post an article of your own, highlight the group you want to crash, and then select the Article menu's Post command.

Chapter 9

Pulling News Out of Thin Air: Working with AIR News

In This Chapter

➤ Newsgroup subscribing and unsubscribing

➤ How to set up personal groups

➤ Reading articles

➤ Following up articles and posting originals

➤ A treasure trove of news techniques and tactics that'll have you walking on AIR

Until recently, the Internet *zeitgeist* encouraged an altruistic, do-it-for-fun-and-not-for-profit attitude. One of the consequences of this disposition was a plethora of programs that were either free (like the **rn**, **trn**, and **tin** newsreaders covered in Chapters 6 and 7) or shareware (such as the Trumpet newsreader covered in Chapter 8). In recent years, however, the Internet has welcomed a flood of immigrants who are used to applications that have tech-support departments, manuals, and frequent upgrades, and who (most importantly) don't mind paying for these conveniences.

Part 2 ➤ *Start Spreading the News: A Guide to Popular Newsreaders*

So now all kinds of companies are popping up with commercial software packages that up the ante in terms of Internet access. One of the first, and one of the most popular, of these packages is the Internet In a Box suite of Windows applications from Spry, Inc. In this chapter, we'll look at the newsreader that comes with this collection: AIR News.

Walking on AIR News

At this point, I'm assuming you have Internet In a Box installed and properly set up, and that you've used the Dialer program to establish a connection with your service provider. To start AIR News, open the **Internet In A Box** program group and select the **AIR News** icon. You'll see the AIR News window appear, as shown in the following figure.

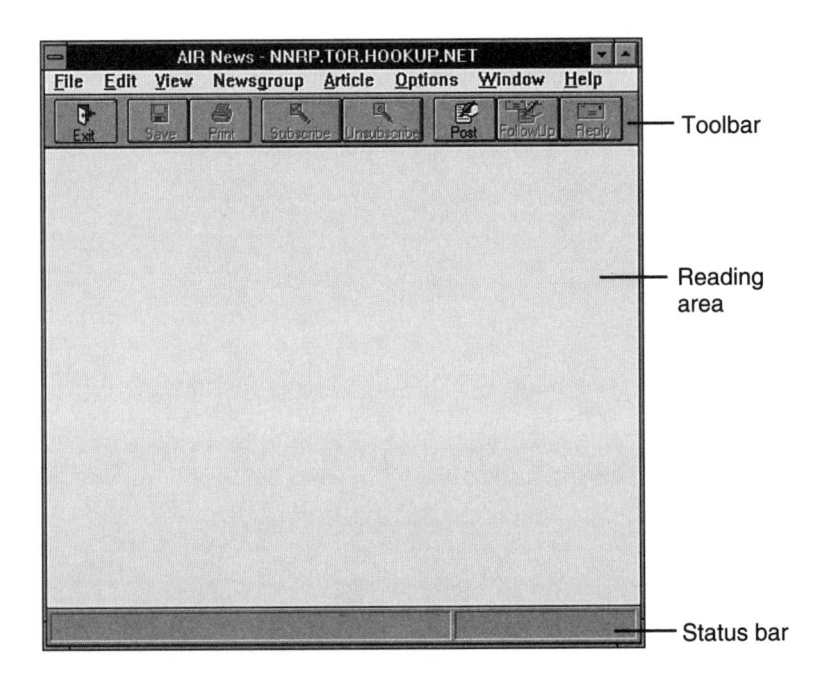

The AIR News window, ready and rarin' to go.

As you can see, the AIR News window is fairly straightforward. You have a toolbar that gives you single-click access to the AIR News

112

functions you'll use most often, a reading area where the windows containing your group and article lists (as well as the articles themselves) will appear, and a status bar that will report on the progress of your AIR News operations.

Filling the Newsgroup Browser Window

AIR News uses a window called the Newsgroup Browser to list all the groups available from your access provider. So your first order of business is to populate this window with the complete group list. To do this, pull down the **Window** menu and select **Newsgroup Browser**. AIR News contacts the news computer at your access provider, and then takes a minute or two (depending on how many groups there are) to grab all the data. When it's done, AIR News displays the Newsgroup Browser window.

> New groups are foisted upon us every day, so your Newsgroup Browser list will be out of date before long. To update it, pull down the Newsgroup menu and select the Refresh command.

You'll be using the Newsgroup Browser to select the groups you want to read or subscribe to. To make this chore a bit easier, you can view the Browser in either of two modes: list or tree. In the figure shown on the next page, the Newsgroup Browser on the left is in list mode. This means all the groups are visible, and they appear in alphabetical order. The Newsgroup Browser on the right is in tree mode. Here, the Browser only shows the group hierarchies. Displaying the groups in each hierarchy is similar to displaying subdirectories in File Manager: double-click on the hierarchy's folder icon to display the groups, and double-click on the icon again to hide them. To switch between these modes, pull down the **View** menu and activate either **Tree** or **List**.

Which mode should you use? Well, that depends on how you'll be using the Newsgroup Browser. If you'll be strolling through the groups looking for interesting targets, list mode is best. If you're looking for a specific hierarchy or group, you'll be better off in tree mode.

Part 2 ▶ *Start Spreading the News: A Guide to Popular Newsreaders*

List mode   Tree mode

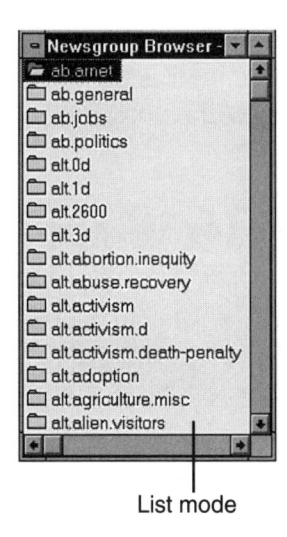

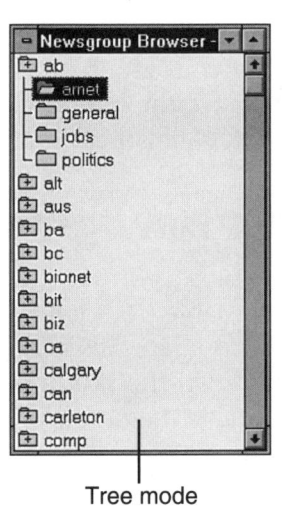

You can view the Newsgroup Browser either in list mode (left) or tree mode (right).

Finding a Newsgroup Needle in the Browser Haystack

The Newsgroup Browser's modes can certainly make the groups easier to manage, but you have thousands of groups to worry about. If you've got your heart set on reading or subscribing to a specific newsgroup, you still have to wade through lots of groups to locate the one you want (especially if the group resides in one of the more populous hierarchies such as **alt** or **comp**). Fortunately, AIR News has a Find feature that will take some of the drudgery out of your searches. To try it out, follow these steps:

1. Make sure the Newsgroup Browser is open, and then select the Edit menu's Find command. AIR News displays the Find dialog box.

2. Use the Find What text box to enter the name of the newsgroup you're looking for. If you're not sure of the name, just enter a

Chapter 9 ➤ *Pulling News Out of Thin Air: Working with AIR News*

piece of it; Find will match every newsgroup name that contains the text you enter. For example, to find the group **alt.sex.fetish.startrek** (I told you the Internet was a bizarre place!), you could just enter **startrek**.

3. Select the Find button. AIR News scours the newsgroup list and then displays all the matching group names in the **Results** list. (See the example in the following figure.)

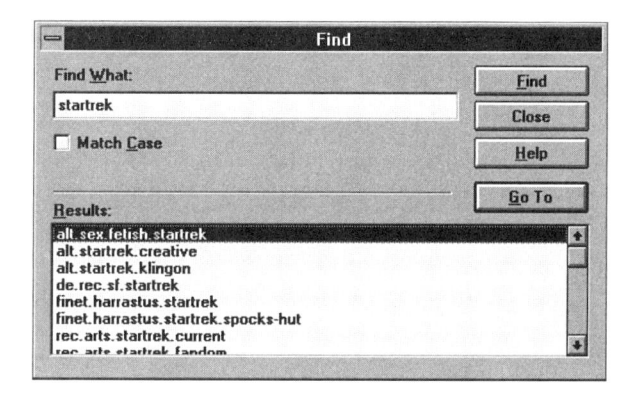

```
Find What:
startrek
☐ Match Case

Results:
alt.sex.fetish.startrek
alt.startrek.creative
alt.startrek.klingon
de.rec.sf.startrek
finet.harrastus.startrek
finet.harrastus.startrek.spocks-hut
rec.arts.startrek.current
rec.arts.startrek.fandom
```

When AIR News is finished searching, it displays the goodies it found in the Results list.

4. If the group you want is in the list, click on it to highlight it, and then select the Go To button. AIR News will highlight the group in the Newsgroup Browser.

5. Select **Close** to return to the Browser.

AIR Traffic Control: Subscribing and Unsubscribing

If you just want to take a quick look at a newsgroup, double-click on it in the Newsgroup Browser, or highlight the group and select the **News**group menu's **Read** command. AIR News will load the Subject lines and authors for the group's articles, and then display them in a separate window. You can then read the groups at your leisure (see the "Reading the News" section for details).

More than likely, however, you'll want to subscribe to some groups and read them regularly. AIR News handles subscriptions using *personal groups*. The idea is that you create a personal group for each type of newsgroup you subscribe to. For example, if you're a fan of *Dr. Who*, *Star Trek*, and the like, you'd set up a personal group called, say, "Science Fiction." When you subscribe to groups like **rec.arts.drwho** or **alt.startrek.klingon**, you can tell AIR News to store them in your Science Fiction personal group. Then, any time you're in a sci-fi mood, you can open up the Science Fiction personal group and access all the newsgroups therein.

AIR News comes with several predefined personal groups, such as Music, Sports, and Television. You can either use one these groups, or you can create your own. Here are the steps to plow through to create and open a personal group:

1. Pull down the **Window** menu and select **Personal Group**. AIR News displays the Open Personal Group dialog box, as shown in the following figure.

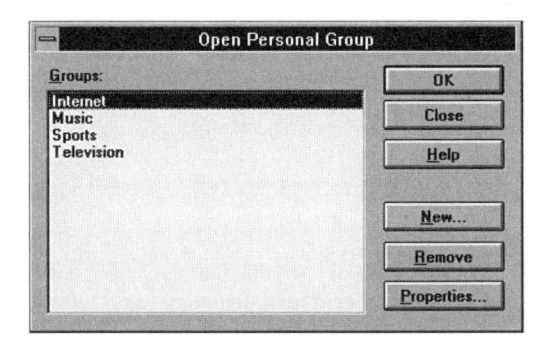

Use the Open Personal Group dialog box to open and create personal groups.

2. If you want to create a personal group, select the **New** button. The Newsgroup Properties dialog box appears. If you just want to open an existing personal group, skip to step 4.

3. Use the **Description** text box to enter a name for the personal group (up to 127 characters), and then select **OK**.

4. To open a personal group, highlight it in the **Groups** list and then select **OK**. AIR News opens a new window that lists the subscribed newsgroups for the personal group you selected.

Chapter 9 ➤ *Pulling News Out of Thin Air: Working with AIR News*

> Let's look at a few other tidbits that will round out your personal groups education. For starters, you'll notice that each personal group window shows not only the name of the subscribed newsgroups, but also the number of articles in the group. You may have panicked when you saw groups with hundreds or even thousands of articles. Don't sweat it; these numbers just represent, more or less, the total number of articles that have been posted to the group *in its lifetime.* The number of articles you have to read will always be much smaller.
>
> Secondly, what do you do if you don't like the name of a personal group? No problem: select the **Window** menu's **Personal Group** command, highlight the group in the Groups list, and then select Properties. In the Newsgroup Properties dialog box, modify the Description field and then select **OK**.
>
> Finally, what about deleting personal groups you no longer need? In this case, fire up the **Personal Group** command, highlight the group you want to nuke, and then select the **Remove** button.

Okay, let's get down to the subscribing brass tacks. AIR News gives you two different methods for subscribing to newsgroups:

➤ In the Newsgroup Browser, highlight the newsgroup you want to subscribe to. Pull down the News**g**roup menu and select **S**ubscribe, or click on the **Subscribe** button in the toolbar. The Open Personal Group dialog box appears. In the Groups list, highlight the personal group you want to use; then select **OK**. AIR News opens the personal group and adds in the newsgroup.

➤ Open the personal group you want to use, drag the newsgroup from the Newsgroup Browser, and drop it anywhere inside the personal group's window. (Forgotten how to drag-and-drop? Here's a quick refresher course: place the mouse pointer over the newsgroup name, and then press and hold down the left mouse button. Move the mouse pointer so it rests anywhere inside the personal group window, and then release the mouse button.)

If you get sick of a particular group (believe me, it happens), you should unsubscribe to it to get it out of your life. Open the appropriate personal group, highlight the newsgroup name, and then either select the Newsgroup menu's Unsubscribe command, or click on the toolbar's **Unsubscribe** button.

117

Part 2 ▶ Start Spreading the News: A Guide to Popular Newsreaders

Reading the News

With your newsgroups subscriptions in place, it's time to get the show on the road and start reading articles. Begin by opening the personal group that contains the newsgroup you want to read. Then either double-click on the newsgroup, or highlight it and select the Newsgroup menu's **Read** command. AIR News loads the header data for the group's articles and displays it in a separate window, as shown in the figure below.

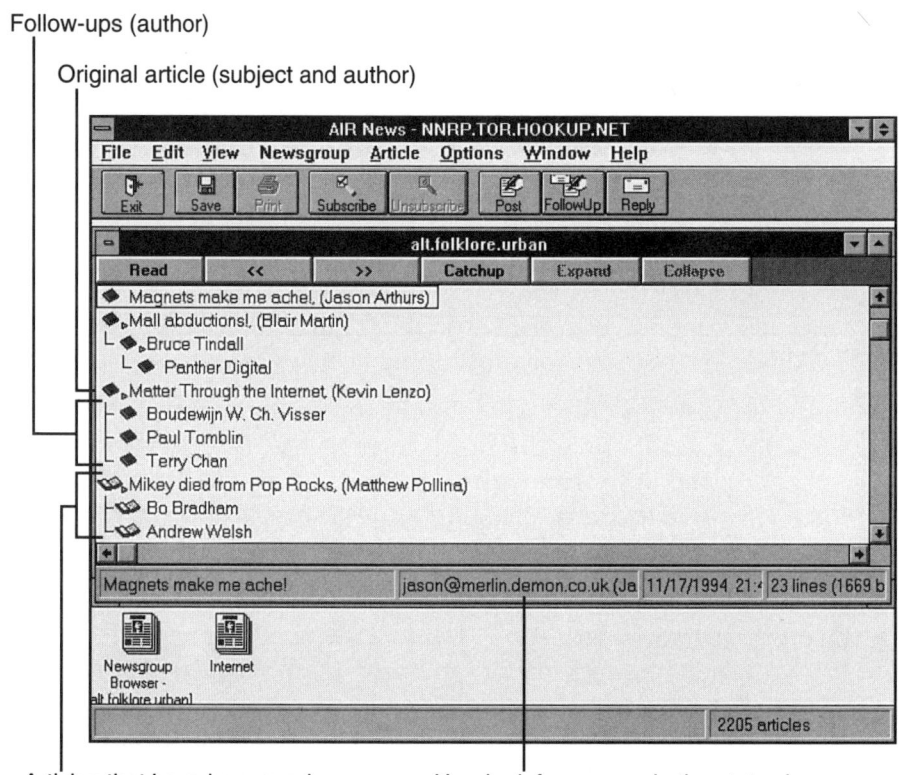

Follow-ups (author)
Original article (subject and author)
Articles that have been read
Header info appears in the status bar.

AIR News displays the articles' Subject lines and author names for the selected newsgroup.

The window shows the available articles, organized alphabetically by thread. For original articles, AIR News displays both the Subject line and the author. Follow-ups are shown branching off from the original, and only the author's name is displayed. (If you'd like more info about

118

each article, highlight it and check out the status bar: it shows the e-mail address of the author, the date and time the article was posted, and how many lines are in the article.) The book icons to the left of each post tell you whether or not you've read the article: if the book is closed, the article is unread; if the book is open, the article has been read.

You can also view the articles in different sort orders. Pull down the View menu and select from Sort by A**u**thor, Sort by D**a**te, Sort by Lines, or Sort by Su**b**ject. In each case, you can also choose either Sort **A**scending (to sort from 0 to 9 and A to Z) or Sort **D**escending (from Z to A and 9 to 0) in the View menu.

If a particular article catches your eye, you can read it by using any of the following techniques:

➤ Double-click on it.

➤ Click on it, pull down the Article menu, and select Read.

➤ Click on it and then click on the **Read** button.

AIR News opens a new window, grabs the article text, and displays it in the window. Once you've read the article, you can move on to the next article—either by clicking on the >> button, or by selecting the Article menu's Next command. To return to the previous article, click on the << button, or select Previous from the Article menu. If you'd prefer to go back to the article list, click on the **Back** button, or select the newsgroup's window from the Window menu.

Saving and Printing an Article

To save the current article to a file, pull down the File menu and select the Save As command, or click on the **Save** button in the toolbar. In the Save Articles dialog box that appears, use the Directories list to pick out a location for the file, enter a name in the File Name text box, and then select **OK**.

If you'd prefer a hard copy of the current article, first make sure you printer is fired up and ready to receive. Now pull down the File menu and select Print, or click on the toolbar's **Print** button. (The Print command and **Print** button are only available while you're reading the article.) AIR News prints the article.

Following Up an Article

USENET is at its best when it's interactive: questions are asked and answered; the swords of conflicting opinions are crossed; debaters cut and parry to score points on contentious issues. The engine behind all this verbal jousting is, of course, the follow-up article. To post a follow-up in AIR News, follow these steps:

1. Either highlight the article in the article list, or read the article.
2. Pull down the Article menu and select the Followup command, or click on the **Follow Up** button in the toolbar. AIR News opens a Followup window and fills it with the text from the original article.
3. Cut out any unnecessary text from the original article.
4. Enter your own text in the article body.
5. Select Article menu's **Send** command, or click on the **Send** button. AIR News posts the follow-up.

> Instead of posting a follow-up article, you can reply directly to its author via e-mail. To do this, select the Article menu's Reply command, or click on the **Reply** button. The Reply window that appears is similar to Followup window you just saw. When you're done, click on the **Send** button.

Airing Your Views: Posting an Original Article

Feeling the urge to delurk and post an original article of your own? Here's how it's done in AIR News:

1. Open the personal group containing the newsgroup you want to pester, and highlight the group name. (If you don't subscribe to the group, you can also highlight its name in the Newsgroup Browser.)
2. Pull down the Article menu and select the Post command, or click on the toolbar's **Post** button. AIR News opens the Posting window, which is identical to the one you used for follow-ups.
3. Select the **Header** button, fill in the appropriate fields in the Posting Headers dialog box that appears, and then select **OK**.

4. Enter your text in the article body.
5. Select the **Send** button. AIR News posts the article.

Some AIR News Options

To make sure AIR News works the way you want it to, the program comes with an Options menu that contains a fistful of customization options. I won't cover every command on this menu, just the most useful ones. Here's a summary:

Signature—This command is a bit misnamed; it doesn't have anything to do with your signature. Instead, it displays the Signature dialog box where you can specify default values for three header lines: From, Organization, and Distribution. The From text box defaults to your e-mail address, but most people also add their full name (or whatever other alias you feel like hiding behind) in brackets. For example, here's what my From line looks like:

> **paulmcf@hookup.net (Paul McFedries)**

For Organization, enter your company name (if applicable); for Distribution, enter **world**.

Fonts—Use this command to change the fonts AIR News uses in the Newsgroup Browser, newsgroup windows, and article windows. In the Fonts dialog box that appears, select the **Choose** button for either **Browser**, **Newsgroups**, or **Articles**, pick out your font options in the Font dialog box, and then select **OK**.

Article Headers—This command controls the data you see in the header area when you read an article. In the Article Headers dialog box, choose either the All, None, or Selection option. If you choose the latter, use the list to highlight the header lines you want to see.

Other—This command displays the Other dialog box, which contains a collection of miscellaneous options. You can leave most of these options as they are. You should make sure, however, that the Auto-Attach File check box is activated—and you should enter the name and location of your signature file (if you have one) in the text box provided.

Save Workspace on Exit—If you activate this command, AIR News will save your current workspace each time you exit the program. This means it will remember which windows you had open, what they contained, and where they were located. Then, the next time you fire up AIR News, the program will display the windows automatically.

The Least You Need to Know

This chapter showed you how to fly around USENET using AIR News. Here's a bird's-eye view of our flight path:

➤ When you first start AIR News, select the **Window** menu's **Newsgroup Browser** command to load the complete list of newsgroups from your access provider.

➤ Before you can subscribe to a group, you need to open (or create) a personal group to hold it. Use the **Window** menu's **Personal Group** command to do this.

➤ To subscribe to a highlighted newsgroup, select the **Newsgroup** menu's **Subscribe** command, or drag the newsgroup into an open personal group.

➤ To unsubscribe to a newsgroup, highlight the group in the personal group and then select the **Newsgroup** menu's **Unsubscribe** command.

➤ You read an article just by double-clicking on it.

➤ If you want to follow up the article you're reading, select the Article menu's Followup command (or choose **Reply** to send a rebuttal via e-mail).

➤ To post an article of your own, highlight the group and then select the Article menu's **Post** command.

Chapter 10

Surveying Netscape's USENET Landscape

> **In This Chapter**
> - How to subscribe and unsubscribe, Web-style
> - How to read USENET news
> - How to follow up and post articles
> - A wealth of info on the World Wide Web's most competent newsreader

One of the pet peeves of most Internet users is the number of tools we're forced to wield to get anything done. If we want a file, we use our FTP software; if we want to find a file, we use Archie; if we need a Gopher document, we use Gopher software; and, of course, if we want to read news and post articles, we use a newsreader. Wouldn't life be simpler if we could use a single software package to perform all our Net chores?

Well, we're not quite there yet, but progress is definitely being made. Suites such as Internet In a Box still offer multiple tools, but at least they have a reasonably consistent look and feel. The closest we've come to the Internet Swiss Army knife is the Netscape World Wide Web browser. Netscape surfs the Web, of course, but it can also grab

Part 2 ➤ *Start Spreading the News: A Guide to Popular Newsreaders*

files and Gopher documents, send e-mail, and (most importantly for us) read USENET news. This chapter takes you on a tour of Netscape's surprisingly full-featured newsreader.

> The proverbial space limitations mean I have to put my blinders on and ignore most of the other slick features found in Netscape. So this chapter assumes Netscape is installed and properly set up, and that you know the basics of Web travel. If you're wondering where to get Netscape, send your FTP program to **ftp.mcom.com** and head for the **/pub/netscape** directory. Select either the **mac**, **unix**, or **windows** subdirectory (depending on which version you need), and then grab the files you see there.

Surf's Up: Getting Started with Netscape's Newsreader

To check out the Netscape newsreader, first start the program as you normally do. Before you can access USENET through Netscape, you need to tell the program where you get your news. Here are the simple steps to follow:

1. Pull down the Options menu and select the Preferences command. Netscape displays the Preferences dialog box.

2. In the drop-down list at the top of the dialog box, select **Directories, Applications, and News**.

3. Using the **News (NNTP) Server** text box, enter the Internet address of your access provider's mail computer (this is known as the *mail server* or the *mail host*). For many sites, this is simply the site name and domain.

4. In the **News RC File** text box, enter the name and location of the file you want Netscape to use to keep track of your newsgroups. The News RC file monitors your newsgroup subscriptions, and keeps tabs on which articles you've read in the subscribed groups.

5. Select **OK**.

6. Pull down the Options menu and select the Save Options command.

124

Chapter 10 ➤ *Surveying Netscape's USENET Landscape*

You're now ready to crank up the newsreader. Netscape gives you three ways to get the job done:

➤ Pull down the **Directory** menu and select the **Go** to Newsgroups command.

➤ Click on the **Newsgroups** button.

➤ Click on the **Go to Newsgroups** link in the Welcome to Netscape! page (which should be the first page you see when you start Netscape).

Netscape connects to your mail server and loads the info from your News RC file. (If you're starting the newsreader for the first time, you won't have a News RC file, so Netscape displays a dialog box letting you know it will create one for you. Select **OK** to continue.) You'll eventually see the Subscribed Newsgroups page, as shown in the following figure. This page lists your currently subscribed groups and shows you the number of unread messages in each group.

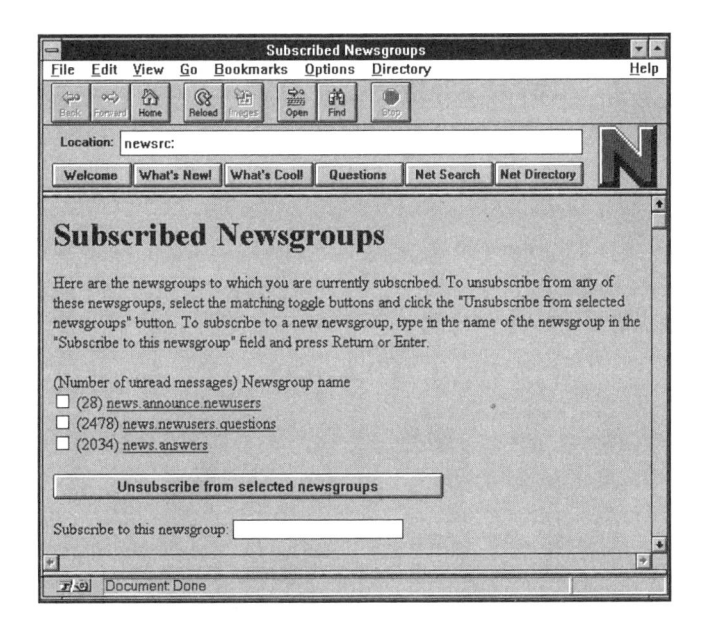

When you select Netscape's Go to Newsgroups command, the Subscribed Newsgroups page appears.

125

Handling Subscriptions in Netscape

Netscape courteously provides you with three pre-subscribed newsgroups: **news.announce.newusers**, **news.newusers.questions**, and **news.answers**. These are great for starters (especially if you're new to USENET), but you'll certainly want to add your favorite groups to the list.

If you know the name of the newsgroup you want, the easiest way to set up a subscription is to type the group's name in the **Subscribe to this newsgroup** field and press **Enter**. Netscape adds the newsgroup to the list.

What if you're not sure about a group's name, or you'd prefer to check out a group before committing to a subscription? In these cases, you can use Netscape's Newsgroups list page. To load this page, follow these steps:

1. Activate the **Location** bar (the one just below the toolbar). Alternatively, select the File menu's Open Location command (or press **Ctrl+L**) to display the Open Location dialog box.

2. If you're using the **Location** bar, delete any existing text.

3. Type **news:** followed by the subset of newsgroups you want to see. You specify the subset using the asterisk (*) operator to substitute for multiple characters. Here are some examples that show you how this works:

Enter this	To display this
news:news.*	All the groups in the **news** hierarchy.
news:rec.pets.*	All the **rec.pets** groups (e.g., **rec.pets.dogs**, **rec.pets.cats**). The following figure shows the results of this search.
news:*.answers	All the group names ending in **.answers** (e.g., **comp.answers**, **soc.answers**).
news:*fetish*	All the group names that include the word fetish.
news:*	All the newsgroups.

Chapter 10 ➤ *Surveying Netscape's USENET Landscape*

4. Press **Enter** or, if you're in the Open Location dialog box, select the **Open** button. Netscape rifles through all the newsgroups and selects the subset you specified.

> The problem with the Newsgroups list is that Netscape displays the groups in the order it receives them from the news server (which is to say, in no order at all). If you're dealing with a large subset (such as, say, **news:alt.***), you can track down the group you want by selecting the Edit menu's Find command (or by pressing **Ctrl+F**) to display the Find dialog box. Enter a piece of the group name in the Find What edit box, and then click on Find Next until you get to the group you want.

5. To see only a subset of the groups, activate the **Location** bar (the one just below the toolbar), or select the File menu's Open Location command to display the Open Location dialog box. Type **news:** followed by the group subset you want to see, and then press **Enter** (or, if you're in the Open Location dialog box, select the **Open** button). You specify the subset using the asterisk (*) operator to substitute for multiple characters. Here are some examples that show you how this works:

Enter this	*To display this*
news:news.*	All the groups in the **news** hierarchy.
news:rec.pets.*	All the **rec.pets** groups (e.g., **rec.pets.dogs**, **rec.pets.cats**). The following figure shows the results of this search.
news:*.answers	All the group names ending in **.answers** (e.g., **comp.answers**, **soc.answers**).
news:*fetish*	All the group names that include the word **fetish**.

Once you've got the group you want displayed on the Newsgroup list page, just click on it. When Netscape loads the group's articles, you can subscribe to the group by clicking on the **Subscribe** button.

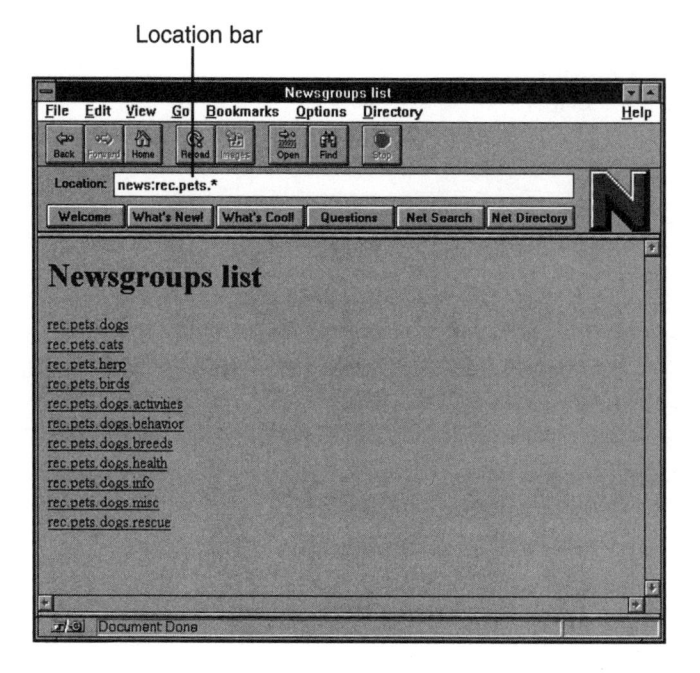

Part 2 ➤ *Start Spreading the News: A Guide to Popular Newsreaders*

Netscape's Newsgroups list.

When a subscribed group wears out its welcome, you should unsubscribe to it to keep your Subscribed Newsgroups page lean and mean. If you're viewing the group's articles, click on the **Unsubscribe** button at the top or bottom of the page. If you're in the Subscribed Newsgroups page, activate the check box beside the group name, and then click on the **Unsubscribe from selected newsgroups** button.

Reading Articles

Okay, now that you've got your fave groups subscribed, you can start reading articles. Your first chore is to display the list of unread articles for a group; you do that simply by clicking on the group name in the Subscribed Newsgroups page. Netscape loads the article data and displays it in a new page, as shown on the following page.

128

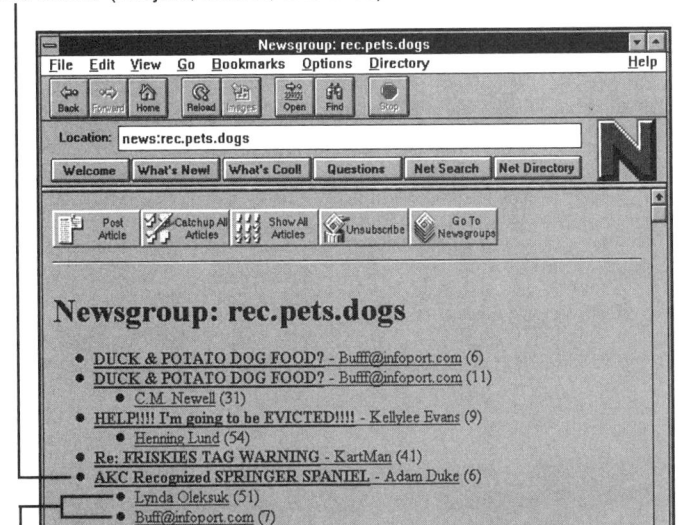

Chapter 10 ➤ *Surveying Netscape's USENET Landscape*

Original article (subject, author, and lines)

[Screenshot of Netscape newsgroup: rec.pets.dogs showing article list including "DUCK & POTATO DOG FOOD?", "HELP!!!! I'm going to be EVICTED!!!!", "Re: FRISKIES TAG WARNING", "AKC Recognized SPRINGER SPANIEL", and "GONNA KILL ALBANY DOG!!!!" threads]

Follow-ups (author and lines)

When you click on a group, Netscape displays the article Subject lines and author names.

The page shows the available articles, organized by thread and sorted by date, with the earliest articles at the top. For original articles, Netscape displays the Subject line, the author's name, and the number of lines in the article. (If the original article has expired, it's displayed in plain black text with no author. Articles that are still available are displayed in the underlined jump text.) Follow-ups are shown as bullets indented below the original, and only the author's name and the number of lines in the follow-up are displayed.

Reading an article is simplicity itself: just click on the subject. Netscape starts a new page and loads the article text, as shown in the following figure.

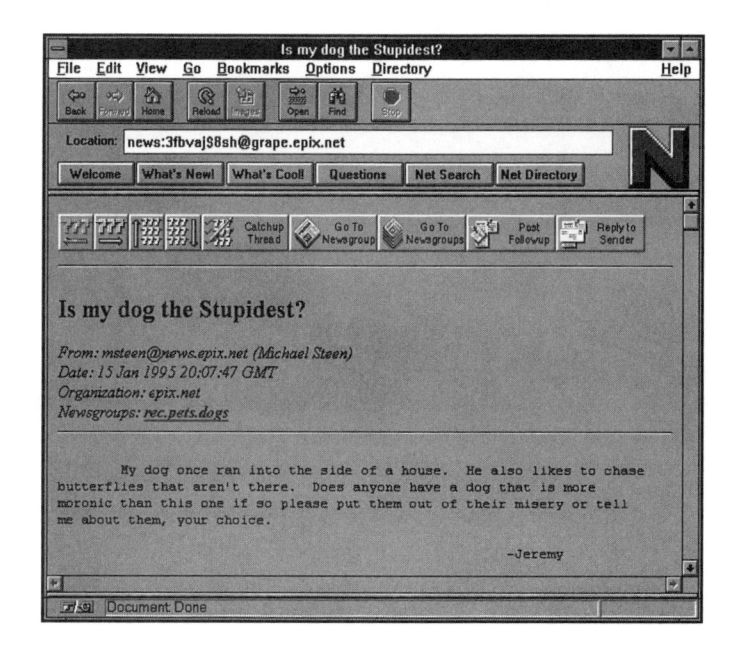

Part 2 ➤ *Start Spreading the News: A Guide to Popular Newsreaders*

When you select an article, Netscape displays it in a new page.

When you're done with the article, you can use the buttons shown in the following table to move on to bigger and better things.

Click on	To
	Display the previous article in the current thread.
	Display the next article in the current thread.
	Display the first article in the previous thread.
	Display the first article in the next thread.
	Mark all the articles in the current thread as read.
	Return to the newsgroup page.
	Return to the Subscribed Newsgroups page.

Saving an Article

If you find a particularly interesting or enlightening article (it happens from time to time), you should save it so you can refer to it at your leisure. In Netscape, you can save an article in one of two ways: you can save it to a file, or you can print it out.

To save the current article to a file, pull down the File menu and select the **Save As** command, or press **Ctrl+S**. In the Save As dialog box that appears, use the **Directories** list to pick out a location for the file, and enter a name in the File **Name** text box, and then select **OK**.

> The Save As dialog box displays a default extension of .HTM in the File Name text box. But the file you'll be creating will be a text file, so you'd be better off using an extension of .TXT.

If you'd prefer a hard copy of the current article, first make sure your printer is fired up and ready to go. Now pull down the File menu and select **Print**. Fill out the options in the Print dialog box that appears (such as the number of copies you want), and then select **OK**. Netscape prints the article.

Retorting: How to Follow Up an Article

Are you feeling like a Good Samaritan and want to respond to a question someone posted? Or perhaps you're feeling a bit ornery and want to give some netiquette-ignorant luser a piece of your mind. Hey, it's a free country, so why not write a follow-up article? Here's how you do it in Netscape:

1. Display the article you want to follow up.
2. Click on the **Post Followup** button at the top or bottom of the page. Netscape displays the USENET News Posting page, and inserts the original article's text in the **Message** field.

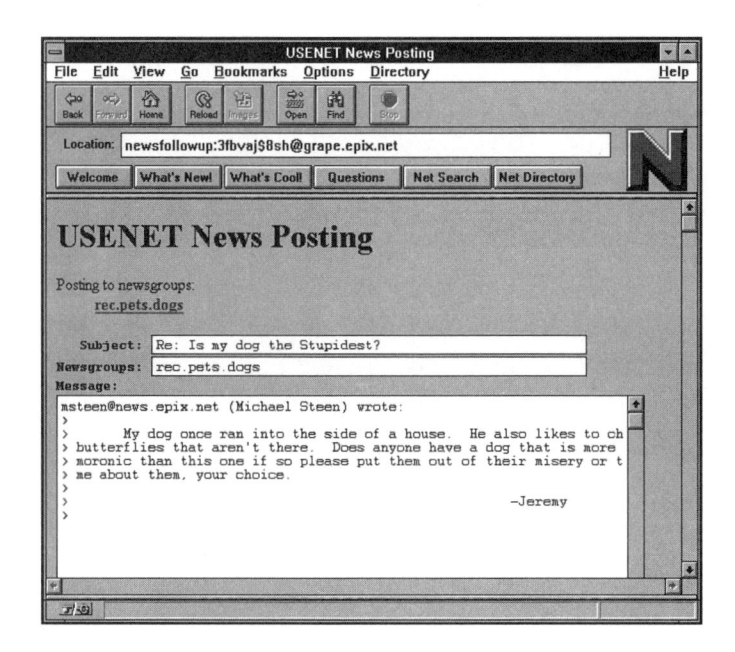

Part 2 ➤ *Start Spreading the News: A Guide to Popular Newsreaders*

When you follow up an article, Netscape displays the USENET News Posting page.

3. Cut out any unnecessary text from the original article.
4. Enter your own text in the article body.
5. Select the **Post Message** button at the bottom of the page. Netscape posts the follow-up.

Instead of posting a follow-up article, you can use e-mail to reply directly to the author. To try this out, follow these steps:

1. Select the **Reply to Sender** button at the top or bottom of the article page. Netscape displays the Mail Document dialog box.
2. Enter a subject in the **Subject** text box.
3. If you want to include the text from the original article, click on the **Include Document Text** button, and then edit the text as necessary.
4. Enter your own text.
5. Click on the **Send Mail** button. Netscape mails your reply.

Delurking: How to Post an Original Article

Got a question, an announcement, an essay, or just a basic tirade? Well, stop lurking and start posting! The following steps show you what to do to post an article using Netscape:

1. Display the page for the newsgroup you want to use.
2. Click on the **Post Article** button at the top or bottom of the page. Netscape displays the USENET News Posting page, which is identical to the one you used for follow-ups.
3. Use the **Subject** field to enter a Subject line for your article.
4. If you want to cross-post, enter the names of the other groups (separated by commas) in the **Newsgroups** field.
5. Enter your text in the **Message** field.
6. Select the **Post Message** button at the bottom of the page. Netscape posts the article.

The Least You Need to Know

This chapter gave you the 50¢ tour of Netscape's USENET landscape. Here's a recap of some sights we saw along the way:

➤ Before you use Netscape's newsreader for the first time, select the Options menu's Preferences command, and then enter the name of your news server in the dialog box.

➤ To start the newsreader, pull down the Directory menu and select Go to Newsgroups, or click on the toolbar's **Newsgroups** button.

➤ To subscribe to a newsgroup, enter its name in the **Subscribe to this newsgroup** field and then press **Enter**.

➤ To select a newsgroup from a list, use the Location bar to enter the subset of groups you want to see.

➤ To unsubscribe to a newsgroup, activate its check box in the Subscribed Newsgroups page and then click on the **Unsubscribe from selected newsgroups** button.

Part 2 ➤ *Start Spreading the News: A Guide to Popular Newsreaders*

- ➤ To read an article, display the newsgroup and click on the subject.

- ➤ If you want to follow up the article you're reading, click on the **Post Followup** button. Alternatively, click on the **Reply to Sender** button to send an e-mail response.

- ➤ To post an article of your own, open the newsgroup's page and click on the **Post Article** button.

Chapter 11

NewsWatcher: The Mac Newsreader of Choice

In This Chapter

- ➤ Where to find NewsWatcher
- ➤ Setting up NewsWatcher
- ➤ Working with newsgroups
- ➤ Reading articles
- ➤ Replying to articles and posting your own
- ➤ Using NewsWatcher to become one with your newsgroups

Mac users have quite a few options when it comes to newsreaders (including a version of the Netscape Web browser that we looked at in the last chapter). However, NewsWatcher has become the standard Mac news cruncher because it combines powerful features with a simple, easy-to-understand interface. This chapter tells you how to get your hands on a copy of NewsWatcher, how to set it up, and how to use it to read USENET and post your own articles.

Where to Get NewsWatcher

As with most other Mac Internet software, the most reliable and accessible FTP site is always **ftp.tidbits.com**. Look in the **/disk2/tidbits/select** directory for the file **newswatcher.sea**. It weighs in at about 500K (in *self-extracting archive* format), and expands to about 700K.

Getting NewsWatcher Ready for Action

The first time you use NewsWatcher, you may be asked whether you're using a Private, Shared, or Lab Mac. Even if you're not using a private Mac, select the **Private** button, and then click **OK** to move on.

Next, you'll see the Server Addresses dialog box appear, and you'll need to enter two vital crumbs of data:

News Server   This is the Internet name of the computer your access provider uses to dish out USENET news. Enter the machine's domain name (the one at my access provider is named **nnrp.tor.hookup.net**), or else use one of those hard-to-decipher dotted (or *IP*) addresses (e.g., **123.456.78.90**). If you're not sure about any of this, the system administrator or postmaster at your access provider will be able to help you out.

Mail Server   This is the Internet name of the computer that handles your e-mail. Filling in this field will enable you to respond to articles via e-mail. Again, enter either a domain name or an IP address.

> A **self-extracting archive**? Sounds kinda painful. Actually, it's a compression method that shrinks files so they take up less real estate in an FTP site, and so they take less time to travel to your computer. The beauty of a self-extracting archive (if beauty is the right term) is that you don't need any complicated "uncompress" programs to get at the file inside. You just double-click on the SEA file (such as NewsWatcher's **newswatcher.sea** file) and the full file unfolds itself lickety-split, no questions asked.

When you're done, click **OK**. Now NewsWatcher, ever curious, presents the Personal Information dialog box, which asks for three more tidbits of information:

Full name   This field will appear along with your e-mail address in the From line of your posts. You'll usually enter your name, but you're free to use any other alias that suits your fancy. (However, most USENETers find cute or silly aliases annoying or even rude. You're almost always better off just using your real name.)

Chapter 11 ➤ *NewsWatcher: The Mac Newsreader of Choice*

Organization Use this optional field to enter a company name that will appear as part of the header in articles you post yourself.

Email Address Use this field to enter your e-mail address.

> When filling in the **Full name** field, don't use any of the following characters:
>
> ( ) " , < >

When you've satisfied NewsWatcher's curiosity, click **OK** to continue. Now you'll wait (and wait, and wait...) while NewsWatcher transfers a full list of all the newsgroups from the news server. Since your access provider probably has access to thousands and thousands of newsgroups, you might want to go to lunch, take a nap, or watch that PBS Civil War documentary.

If your computer isn't outdated by the time the list is updated on your system, a few thousand newsgroups will appear in the Full Group List window. Congratulations! Now all you have to do is decide which of these thousands of newsgroups you want to subscribe to.

Before proceeding further, you need to create a new window to hold the newsgroups you'll be reading regularly. To do this, pull down the **File** menu and select **New Group Window**. NewsWatcher coughs up a new, empty window. Now select the **File** menu's **Save** command, enter a name for the window (such as **My Favorite Groups**), and then click **OK**.

Finding a Newsgroup Needle in the Full Group List Haystack

With all those thousands of newsgroups to choose from, there are bound to be groups to suit every taste, no matter how bad. If you play foosball competitively, there's a foosball group; if you read DC comics compulsively, there are groups for *Batman* and *Superman*; if you play Nintendo games until your fingers are blue, there's a Nintendo group; if you never leave your TV or computer unattended for more than about three hours, there are TV and computer groups to beat the band.

The problem is, how the heck do you find those foosball, comics, Nintendo, TV, or computer groups? I mean, that Full Group List has more groups than the national debt has dollars. Happily, NewsWatcher has a Find feature that makes it easy to pick out particular groups. To

137

try it out, first click inside the Full Group List window to make sure it's active. Then, pull down the **Edit** menu and select the **Find** command, or press **Command-F**. In the Find dialog box that appears, enter part of the group name you want to find (such as **foosball**), and then click **OK**.

Selecting Groups to Read

If you've got some time to kill, you should also take a leisurely browse through some of the hierarchies in the Full Group List. This way, you'll be sure not to miss any interesting groups that you might not have thought of otherwise.

Okay, once you've got a newsgroup highlighted in the Full Group List, just drag the item over to the new window you created earlier. (To drag a newsgroup, move the mouse pointer over the group name, hold down the mouse button, move the mouse pointer inside the other window, and then release the mouse button.) Continue to use Find to highlight group names, and then drag them to your group window. Rinse, repeat. The figure below shows the Full Group List and another window (My Favorite Groups) with a few selected groups.

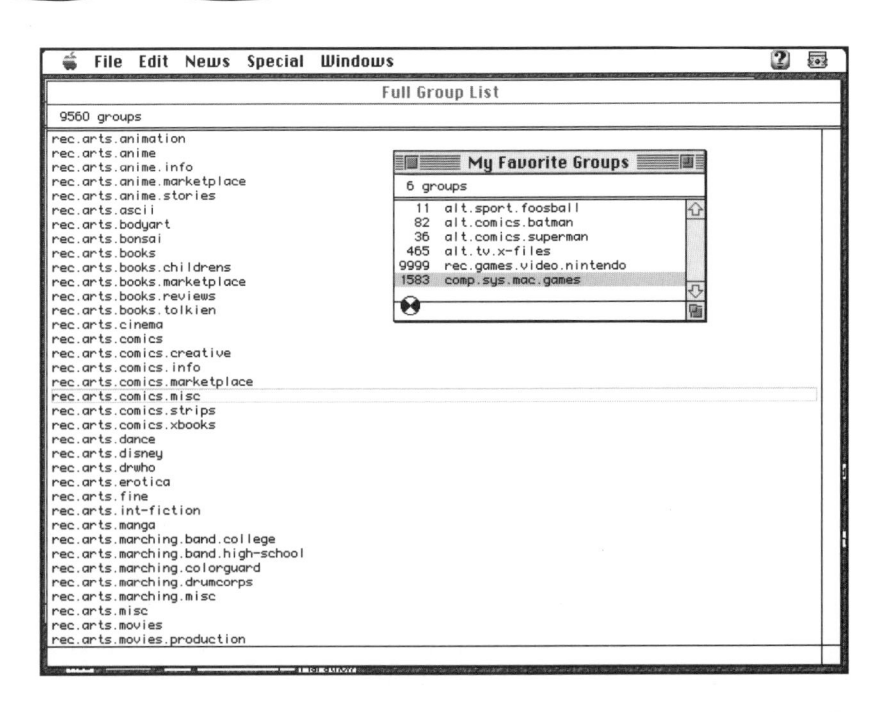

The Full Group List window and a custom window with a few selected groups.

138

Chapter 11 ▸ *NewsWatcher: The Mac Newsreader of Choice*

Reading Articles

Well, so far so good. You've figured out how to get around in the massive Full Group List, and you've even managed to add a group or two to your personal group window. Now we get down to brass tacks and actually start reading some articles.

For starters, you'll probably want to close that humongous Full Group List window. It's too bulky and cumbersome to be taking up your valuable screen real estate. (If you need to see it again later—say, to add more groups—just select the **Window** menu's **Show Full Group List** command.) Now, in your group window, find the group you want to read and double-click it. NewsWatcher opens a new window like the one shown here.

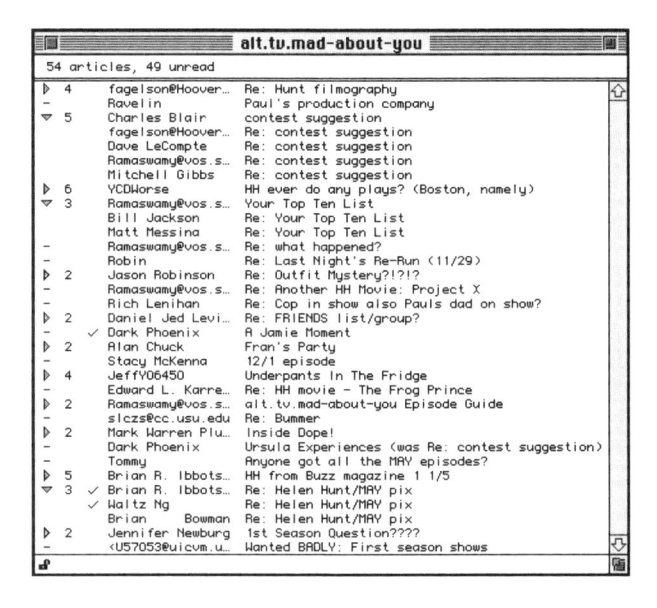

A typical newsgroup window.

The top of the window tells how many articles are in the newsgroup, and how many you haven't yet read. Each line with a little arrow represents a thread. Next to the arrow is a number indicating the number of follow-ups in the thread, the author, and the original subject. If you click a sideways-pointing arrow, it changes to a downward-pointing arrow; the list expands to include all the follow-ups in the thread and their authors. A hyphen next to an article indicates it is the only current article on that topic. A check mark to the left of the author's name indicates the article has been read.

If you see a subject that looks appealing, you can read it by double-clicking on it. Yet another window appears with the text of the article inside of it. To read the next article, press **Command-I**. To mark an article as read, even if you haven't read it, highlight it and press **Command-M**. (Why would you want to mark an article as read if you haven't even glanced at it? Well, the article might have an unappealing Subject line or an author who you know is a real bozo. By marking it as read, it won't appear the next time you read the group and you won't have to bother with it again.) To mark it as unread, press **Command-U**. To mark everything as read, press **Command-;**. If you want a little variety in your hand exercises, you can select self-explanatory options from the **News** menu (such as the **Next Article** command that lets you read the next article).

Saving and Printing an Article

If you come across some particularly breathtaking prose, a useful FAQ, or a knee-slappingly funny joke, you'll probably want to save it for future reference. NewsWatcher lets you save articles either by copying them to a file or by printing them.

To save an article, select the thread or message and press **Command-S**; the familiar Save As dialog box will appear. Enter the name and location for the file, and then click on the **Save** button.

To print an article, press **Command-P** to display the Print dialog box. Enter your print options and click on the **Print** button.

Following Up an Article

To follow up an article, press **Command-R**, or select **Reply** from the **News** menu. The contents of the current article will appear with > symbols in front of the text; these identify quotes and enclose quotations from the original message, which gives readers of the posting a context for the response. Cut out any text you don't need to get your point across, and then add additional comments based on your wisdom, experience, and invaluable insights. When you're ready to go, select the **Send** button.

If you have a comment regarding the post that you would rather not share with the entire readership of the newsgroup, you might wish to send e-mail instead of posting a follow-up within the newsgroup. Press **Command-E**, or select the **News** menu's **Send Message** command; the text of the message will appear in a mail window, allowing you to send e-mail to the original poster (or someone else) which contains all or part of the original message.

> Whether you run the **Reply** or **Send Message** command, you can choose where to send the response from the reply window itself. To send the reply to the newsgroup, activate the News icon at the top of the window; to send the reply to the author's e-mail address, activate the Envelope icon; to send a copy of the reply to yourself, activate the Head icon.

Posting an Original Article

If you have an original thought that isn't being covered in the current messages, you might want to post your own message. For instance, if you would like to complain about the absence of comic Steven Wright from *Mad About You* for the past 18 months, you might want to post an article stating this.

To post an original article, select the newsgroup you want to use and then press **Command-N**, and a new message window will appear. Be sure to fill in the Subject line in as much detail as possible within about 40 characters. Then enter your kernels of wisdom in the message area. When you've got everything off your chest, select **Send**.

Setting NewsWatcher Preferences

The people who design and write Macintosh Internet software always seem to make sure there are tons of different preference options available. NewsWatcher is no exception. You can specify the font and size of the text in the windows, change the news and mail servers, change your personal information, add a signature for placing at the bottom of each message you post, and a host of other options. To access the wide variety of preferences in NewsWatcher, select the **File** menu's **Preferences** command.

The Least You Need to Know

This chapter got you up to speed with the Macintosh newsreader, NewsWatcher. Here's a summary of what you learned:

➤ You can pick up the latest version of NewsWatcher at **ftp.tidbits.com**.

➤ Have your access provider give you your news and mail server name (or IP address) before you start mucking about with NewsWatcher.

➤ Create your own list of newsgroups by first selecting the **File** menu's **New Group Window** command to create a window, and then dragging the groups you want from the Full Group List to the new window.

➤ To read an article, double-click on the appropriate newsgroup and then double-click on the article.

➤ To follow up the current article, press **Command-R**.

➤ To post an original article to the current newsgroup, press **Command-N**.

Chapter 12

Checking Out the CompuServe Connection

In This Chapter

➤ Finding CompuServe's USENET section
➤ Subscribing and unsubscribing
➤ How to read USENET news
➤ How to follow up and post articles
➤ A compendium of CompuServe's Netnews components

Of all the people new to USENET, CompuServe users are likely to be the ones who are the least nonplussed by the whole thing. Why? Because CompuServe subscribers have had a USENET-like service for years: the *forums*. The forums are closely related to newsgroups; forum messages are basically the same as group articles, and even much of the slang and acronyms are the same. So if you've ever participated in a forum, USENET territory will feel very familiar.

Best of all, CompuServistas don't have to bother with all the usual rigmarole those other poor saps on the Internet have to put up with: locating an access provider, configuring protocols, finding software. As you'll see, reading the news on CompuServe is a simple matter of dialing in, jumping to the USENET section, and getting down to business. This chapter shows you how it's done.

Part 2 ➤ *Start Spreading the News: A Guide to Popular Newsreaders*

> To keep with the latest CompuServe gossip and happenings, there are (at this writing) three CompuServe newsgroups you should check. **compuserve.announce** keeps you informed of the latest CompuServe news; **compuserve.general** contains discussions about CompuServe; and you can use **compuserve.test** to post test articles.

A Word About Internet Prejudice

In your Internet e-mail address, the part to the right of the @ sign is called the *domain name*. For example, my e-mail address is **paulmcf@hookup.net**, so **hookup.net** is the domain name. (Or, to be technically correct, it's the domain name of my access provider.) Similarly, if your e-mail address is **12345.6789@compuserve.com**, your domain name is **compuserve.com**.

I'm letting you in on this chunk of network trivia so you'll understand a form of bias not uncommon among Net veterans: *domainism*. The idea is that certain Internet e-mail addresses are "cool" and others are "uncool." For example, addresses within educational domain names (the ones ending in **edu**, such as **mit.edu**) are definitely cool, while those from the big-time online services (such as CompuServe and America Online) are considered uncool.

I tell you this not to discourage you from getting on the Internet, but to prepare you, as a CompuServe user, for what may come your way. Keep in mind that the people who make these distinctions are a bunch of lamebrains. (If you saw them in person, I'm sure you'd recognize them from their sloping foreheads, protruding brow ridges, and hairy knuckles.) It's clear they put no more thought into their "beliefs" than do any other bigots, so the most sensible course of action, certainly, is just to ignore them altogether.

Finding the USENET Newsgroups on CompuServe

Once you've logged onto CompuServe, you can head directly to the USENET Newsgroups section by pulling down WinCIM's **Services** menu and selecting **Go** (or by pressing **Ctrl+G**). In the Go... dialog box, type **usenet** and then select **OK**.

Chapter 12 ➤ *Checking Out the CompuServe Connection*

CompuServe takes you to the USENET Newsgroups section and displays the main menu, as shown in the following figure. (As you can see, the figure shows the WinCIM version of the main menu. Unfortunately, I just don't have enough room to cover both the WinCIM and command-line versions of CompuServe's USENET section. The two are close enough, however, that you should still be able to figure things out if you're using the command-line. If you'd like to download WinCIM to your computer, type **GO WINCIM** and press **Enter** at any CompuServe prompt to get all the info you need.)

CompuServe's USENET Newsgroups main menu.

The first few menu items are documents designed for USENET newcomers. Here's a summary:

About USENET Newsgroups This is a general introduction to USENET. (You can also check out Chapter 2, "So Just What the Heck Is USENET, Anyway?," for more introductory stuff.)

Newsgroups Disclaimer This document warns innocent CompuServe types that USENET contains material that is "uncensored" and may be "offensive." It's just the usual "our lawyers told us to put this in so our behinds are covered in case you grow hair on your palms from reading alt.sex.spanking" type of disclaimer.

Newsgroup Etiquette This is a collection of netiquette do's and don'ts. (See also Chapter 3, "Learning Netiquette: Minding Your USENET Ps and Qs," for more on Netnews decency and decorum.)

Frequently Asked Questions   This is a list of questions specific to CompuServe's USENET section. It includes a helpful comparison between CompuServe forums and USENET newsgroups.

USENET Feedback   This item brings up another menu from which you can send suggestions, criticisms, or comments about CompuServe's Internet services.

With those preliminaries out of the way, it's now time to fire up CompuServe's newsreader by selecting the **USENET Newsreader (CIM)** menu item. CompuServe displays the USENET Newsgroups menu, as shown in the following figure. CompuServe also notifies you in the bottom left corner of the screen that you have left basic services, which means you will be charged accordingly.

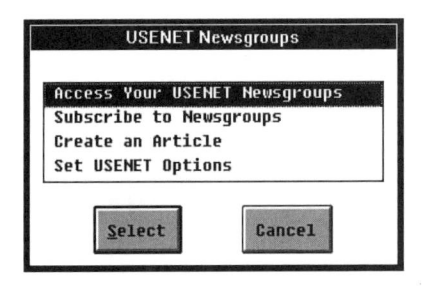

The main USENET Newsgroups menu.

In order to save some verbiage in the following sections, I'm going to assume you're adept at getting around in WinCIM and CompuServe itself. Just to make sure we're working from the same script, however, let me clarify what I mean when I tell you to "select" a menu item. In WinCIM, selecting a menu item means highlighting the item and choosing the Select button. (You can also double-click on the item.)

Setting CompuServe's USENET Options

Before getting down to the nitty-gritty of subscribing and reading, let's take a look at some USENET options you can set up within CompuServe. Here are the steps to follow:

1. Select the **Set USENET Options** menu item. CompuServe displays the Options dialog box.

2. Fill in the following fields:

   ➤ **Name**   This field appears in the From line of your posts, along with your e-mail address. You'll usually enter your full name, but you can remain semi-anonymous by entering any alias that suits your style. Why semi-anonymous? Well, suppose I entered **Writer Who Needs to Get Out More** in the **Name** field. Then, since my CompuServe address is 70033,541, the From line of my posts would look like this:

   ```
   Writer Who Needs to Get Out More <70033.541@compuserve.com>
   ```

   This is "anonymous" in the sense that no one knows who I am, but they can still send me messages (or, more likely, flames berating me for using a silly alias).

   ➤ **Organization**   This field appears in the Organization line of articles you post. Enter your company name, if applicable.

   ➤ **Default articles for newly subscribed groups**   This field limits the number of articles you see when you first subscribe to a group. By keeping the number relatively small (20 is the default), you can check out a group without incurring prohibitive connection charges. (Remember: CompuServe charges the same rate for its USENET access as it does for its forums.)

   ➤ **Display newsgroups with no articles**   Activate this check box to have CompuServe display a newsgroup even if it doesn't contain any articles to read.

   ➤ **Signature**   Use this box to enter a signature that will appear at the end of your articles.

3. Select **OK**. CompuServe saves your info and returns you to the USENET Newsgroups menu.

Subscribing and Unsubscribing in CompuServe

If you're new to CompuServe's USENET service, you'll need to subscribe to a newsgroup or two so you can start reading articles and posting your own epistles. To that end, let's plow through the various methods CompuServe gives you to subscribe to a newsgroup.

For openers, select the **Subscribe to Newsgroups** item from the USENET Newsgroups menu. The Subscribe to Newsgroups dialog box appears, as shown in the following figure.

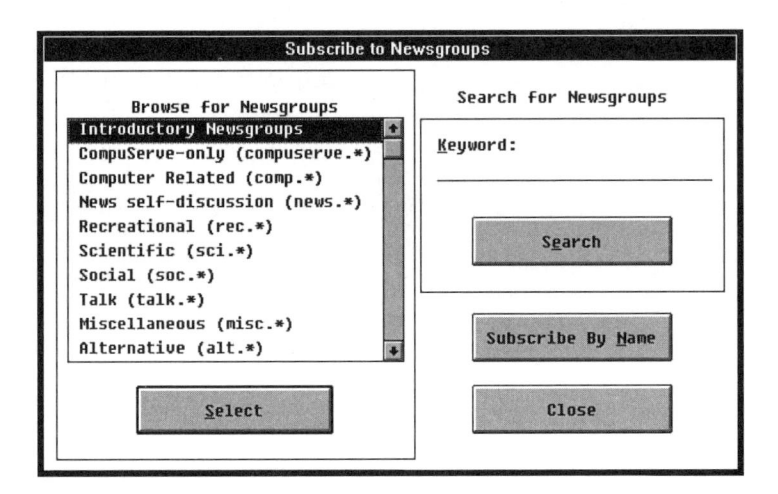

```
┌─ Subscribe to Newsgroups ─────────────────────┐
│  Browse for Newsgroups    Search for Newsgroups│
│  ┌──────────────────────┐                      │
│  │ Introductory Newsgroups│  Keyword:           │
│  │ CompuServe-only (compuserve.*)│ _____  │
│  │ Computer Related (comp.*)│                   │
│  │ News self-discussion (news.*)│               │
│  │ Recreational (rec.*) │    ┌─────────┐        │
│  │ Scientific (sci.*)   │    │ Search  │        │
│  │ Social (soc.*)       │    └─────────┘        │
│  │ Talk (talk.*)        │                       │
│  │ Miscellaneous (misc.*)│   ┌──────────────┐   │
│  │ Alternative (alt.*)  │    │Subscribe By Name│ │
│  └──────────────────────┘    └──────────────┘   │
│       ┌─────────┐            ┌─────────┐        │
│       │ Select  │            │  Close  │        │
│       └─────────┘            └─────────┘        │
└───────────────────────────────────────────────┘
```

Use the Subscribe to Newsgroups dialog box to set up your group subscriptions.

This dialog box gives you no less than four different ways to subscribe to a group. Three of these methods allow you to pick out newsgroups from a list; the fourth method lets you subscribe to a specific newsgroup. The next two sections give you the lowdown on each method. (By the way, when you've completed your subscription chores, select the **Close** button to return to the USENET Newsgroups menu.)

Subscribing to a Newsgroup from a List

If you're not sure which groups to subscribe to, CompuServe can display a list of newsgroups that includes a brief description of each one. There are three ways to display these lists:

➤ The "introductory" newsgroups include the CompuServe groups I mentioned earlier, as well as **news.announce.important**, **news.announce.newusers**, **news.answers**, and **news.newusers.questions**. To get a list of these groups, select **Introductory Newsgroups** from the **Browse for Newsgroups** list.

Chapter 12 ➤ *Checking Out the CompuServe Connection*

➤ The rest of the **Browse for Newsgroups** list contains the seven mainstream hierarchies (**comp**, **news**, **rec**, **sci**, **soc**, **talk**, and **misc**) as well as some alternative hierarchies such as **alt** and **bionet**. Selecting one of these items displays a list of the available groups in each hierarchy.

➤ You can also search for a newsgroup. This is handy if you're not sure about a group name, or if you'd like to subscribe to several groups with names that share a common word (e.g., **startrek**). Select the **Keyword** field, enter the search text (it could be a word in a group name or even part of a word), and then select Search. CompuServe displays a list of newsgroups with names or descriptions that match your search text.

With the list displayed, activate the check box beside each group you want to subscribe to, and then select Subscribe. When CompuServe has set up the subscriptions, a dialog box appears to let you know. Select **OK**, and then select **Cancel** to return to the Subscribe to Newsgroups dialog box.

Subscribing to a Newsgroup by Name

If you already know the name of the group you want to subscribe to, go ahead and select the Subscribe By Name button in the Subscribe to Newsgroups dialog box. In the dialog box that appears, enter the name of the group in the Newsgroup field, and then select **OK**. CompuServe displays a dialog box letting you know you're now subscribed to the group. Select **OK** to return to the Subscribe to Newsgroups dialog box.

> As part of CompuServe's ongoing plan to protect us from ourselves, the newsgroup lists don't include some of the racier groups (such as alt.sex and the like). They are available, but the only way to get to them is to use the Subscribe By Name feature.

Unsubscribing to a Newsgroup

If you get sick and tired of people ranting, raving, or just plain geeking out in a particular group, you should unsubscribe to the group right away before brain rot sets in. Here are the steps to trudge through to unsubscribe to a group in CompuServe:

Part 2 ➤ *Start Spreading the News: A Guide to Popular Newsreaders*

1. Display the USENET Newsgroups menu. (If you're still in the Subscribe to Newsgroups dialog box, select **Close**.)
2. Select the **Access Your USENET Newsgroups** item. The Access Newsgroups list appears, as shown in the following figure.

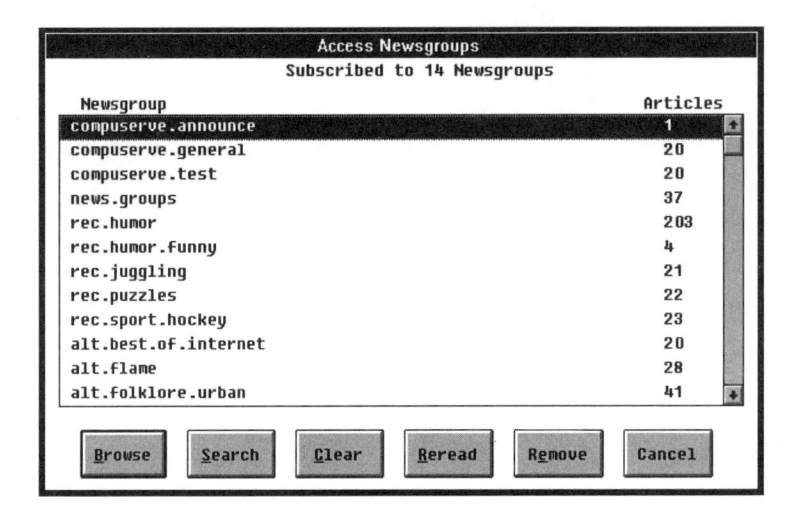

```
                    Access Newsgroups
                 Subscribed to 14 Newsgroups
   Newsgroup                                    Articles
   compuserve.announce                             1
   compuserve.general                              20
   compuserve.test                                 20
   news.groups                                     37
   rec.humor                                       203
   rec.humor.funny                                 4
   rec.juggling                                    21
   rec.puzzles                                     22
   rec.sport.hockey                                23
   alt.best.of.internet                            20
   alt.flame                                       28
   alt.folklore.urban                              41

   [Browse] [Search] [Clear] [Reread] [Remove] [Cancel]
```

Use the Access Newsgroups list to, among other things, unsubscribe to a group.

3. Highlight the newsgroup you want to blow away.
4. Select the Remove button. CompuServe asks whether you're sure you want to remove the group.
5. Select Yes. CompuServe sends the group back from whence it came.

Reading the News

Now we get to the good part: we read articles that have been posted to your subscribed groups. First, display the Access Newsgroups dialog box by selecting **Access Your USENET Newsgroups** from the USENET Newsgroups menu. This dialog box (see the figure shown above) lists each subscribed group and shows the total number of articles waiting to be read.

Chapter 12 ➤ *Checking Out the CompuServe Connection*

Next, select a group to read by highlighting the group name in the list and selecting the **B**rowse button. CompuServe displays the Browse dialog box that shows the Subject lines for the available articles and how many articles are in each thread.

To read a thread, highlight it and then select the **G**et button. CompuServe opens a new window and displays the text of the first article in the thread (see the figure below).

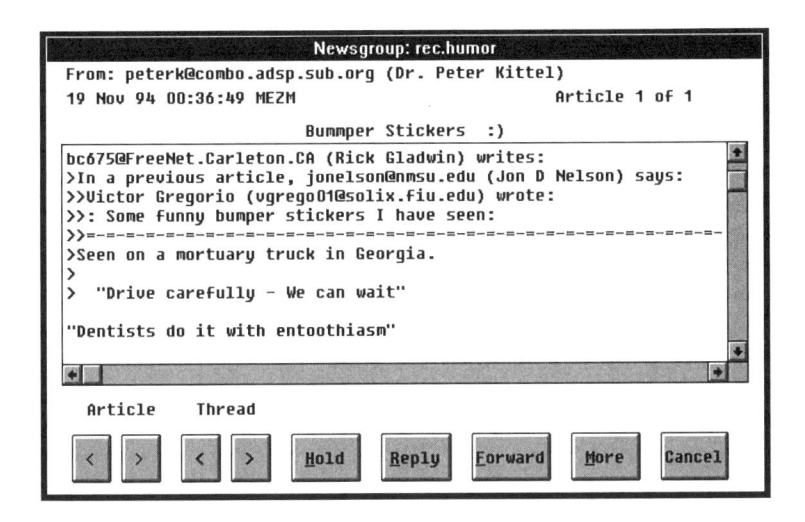

CompuServe displays the article text in a separate window.

To move through the article text, you can use the following buttons:

Article >   Moves to the next article in the current thread.

Article <   Moves to the previous article in the current thread.

Thread >   Moves to the first article in the next thread.

Thread <   Moves to the first article in the previous thread.

When you're done, select **Cancel** to return to the Access Newsgroups list.

Part 2 ▶ *Start Spreading the News: A Guide to Popular Newsreaders*

Saving an Article

With over seven million users writing tens of thousands of articles every day, there's bound to be some interesting material out there somewhere. If you happen to uncover a real gem (such as a useful FAQ, or "The Canonical List of Blonde Jokes"), CompuServe lets you save the article to a file on your computer. Here's what you do:

1. Highlight the article you want to save (as described in the last section).

2. Select the **More** button. CompuServe displays a dialog box showing more info for the article.

3. Select either **As is**—to save the article verbatim—or **Quoted**—to save the article without its header and with extra quote symbols (> characters) in case you want to use the material in a follow-up.

4. Select **Retrieve**. CompuServe displays the Save As dialog box.

5. Enter a name and location for the file, and then select **OK**. CompuServe downloads the article to your computer.

> If you want to save an entire thread, there is an easier way to go about it. In the Browse dialog box, highlight the thread and select Retrieve. When CompuServe asks if you want to retrieve the thread to a single file, select Yes or No, as appropriate. If you select Yes, CompuServe will display the Save As dialog box once for each article in the thread.

Writing a Rejoinder: How to Follow Up an Article

Whether it's responding to a query or just getting your two cents in during a debate, following up is an easy way to get quick posting experience. The following steps show you how to reply to an article either directly in the newsgroup or through e-mail:

1. In the Browse dialog box, read the article you want to follow up.

2. Highlight the text you want to include in your follow-up and select the Edit menu's Copy command.

3. Click on the **Reply** button. CompuServe displays the Reply to USENET Message dialog box.

4. If you want the follow-up to appear in the newsgroup, activate the Post to Newsgroup(s) check box. If you prefer to send the response through the e-mail system, activate the Send via E-mail check box.

5. Activate the **Message Contents** box, and then select the Edit menu's Paste command to paste the original article text.

6. Add a greater-than sign (>) to the beginning of each line from the original article.

7. Enter your own text.

8. Select the Send button. CompuServe posts the article and displays a dialog box to let you know.

9. Select **OK** to return to the article.

Posting an Original Article

As I've said before, original articles are the lifeblood of USENET because they get the discussions off the ground, and they give the rest of us something to read (as well as laugh at, sneer at, and hurl verbal abuse at). So if you're feeling creative, here's how to post an original article from CompuServe:

1. Get started by using either of the following techniques:

   ➤ If you're in the USENET Newsgroups menu, select the **Create an Article** item.

   ➤ If you're in the Access Newsgroups list, highlight the group you want to use, select **Browse**, and then select Create.

2. In the Create USENET Message dialog box that appears, use the Subject field to enter the subject of your article.

3. In the **Newsgroups** list, activate the check box for each group you want to use for the post. (If you're posting from the Access Newsgroups list, the check box for the current group will already be activated.)

4. Enter your article text in the **Message Contents** box.

5. Select the Send button. CompuServe posts the article, and then displays a dialog box to let you know everything went well.

6. Select **OK** to return to the article.

The Least You Need to Know

This chapter showed you how to surf USENET using CompuServe. Here are a few pointers to take with you on your travels:

- To display CompuServe's main USENET menu, pull down WinCIM's Services menu, select Go, enter **USENET**, and select **OK**.

- To start the newsreader, select **USENET Newsreader (CIM)** from the menu.

- Select the **Set USENET Options** menu item to set options such as your name, organization, and signature.

- To subscribe to a newsgroup, select the **Subscribe to Newsgroups** item, and then use the Subscribe to Newsgroups dialog box to pick out the group.

- To unsubscribe to a newsgroup, select the **Access Your USENET Newsgroups** item, highlight the group in the list that appears, and then select the Remove button.

- To display a group's articles, select the **Access Your USENET Newsgroups** item, highlight the group in the list that appears, and then select the Browse button.

- To read an article, highlight it and select the Get button.

- If you want to follow up the article you're reading, select the Reply button.

- To post an article of your own, either select **Create an Article** from the USENET Newsgroups menu, or display the group's articles and select the Create button.

Chapter 13

Chatting in Friendly Confines of America Online

In This Chapter

- ➤ Finding the Newsgroups area
- ➤ Subscribing and unsubscribing
- ➤ Reading the news with America Online
- ➤ Following up and posting articles
- ➤ Everything you need to know, from go to whoa

If you're already a member of America Online, you can read USENET news (and access a few other Internet services, to boot) without having to bother with the hassle of tracking down an access provider, endlessly configuring your computer to understand Netspeak, and scouring cyberspace for newsreader software. Granted, America Online's newsreader doesn't have all the highfalutin' features you'll find in the dedicated software packages—and it can even be downright infuriating at times—but it'll get the job done. And if you've been using America Online's message boards, you'll feel right at home with USENET. This chapter covers all the basic features of America Online's USENET connection.

A Word About Internet Prejudice

In your Internet e-mail address, the part to the right of the @ sign is called the *domain name*. For example, my e-mail address is **paulmcf@hookup.net**, so **hookup.net** is the domain name. (Or, to be technically correct, it's the domain name of my access provider.) Similarly, if your e-mail address is **dear_reader@aol.com**, your domain name is **aol.com**.

I'm letting you in on this chunk of network trivia so you'll understand a form of bias not uncommon among Net veterans: *domainism*. The idea is that certain Internet e-mail addresses are "cool" and others are "uncool." For example, addresses within educational domain names (the ones ending in **edu**, such as **mit.edu**) are definitely cool, while those from the big-time online services (such as America Online and CompuServe) are considered uncool.

I tell you this not to discourage you from getting on the Internet, but to prepare you, as an AOL user, for what may come your way. Keep in mind that the people who make these distinctions are a bunch of lamebrains. (If you saw them in person, I'm sure you'd recognize them from their sloping foreheads, protruding brow ridges, and hairy knuckles.) It's clear they put no more thought into their "beliefs" than do any other bigots, so the most sensible course of action, certainly, is just to ignore them altogether.

Finding America Online's Newsgroups Area

After you've signed in to America Online, you can head for the Newsgroups area using either of the following methods:

➤ Pull down the Go To menu and select the **Keyword** command (or press **Ctrl+K**). In the Go To Keyword dialog box, type **INTERNET** and select **OK**. Once inside the Internet Center, click on the **Newsgroups** button.

➤ If you'd prefer to bypass the Internet Center, select the Go To menu's **Keyword** command, type **NEWSGROUPS**, and select **OK**.

In either case, you'll eventually see the Newsgroups window, as shown in the following figure. The box on the left contains a list of documents that tell you about USENET and explain how to use the various buttons on the right side of the Newsgroups window.

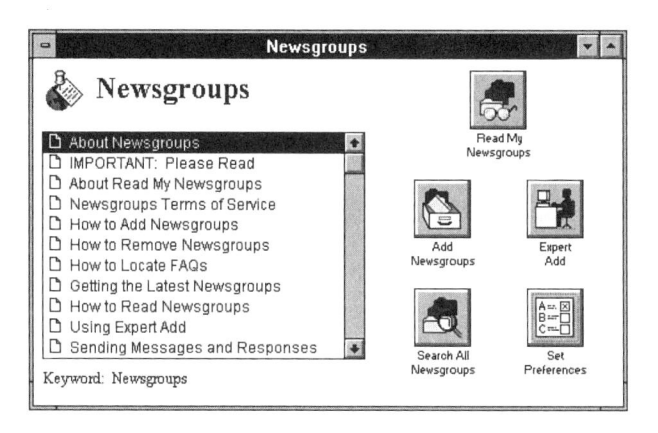

Chapter 13 ➤ *Chatting in Friendly Confines of America Online*

America Online's Newsgroups window.

Subscribing and Unsubscribing in America Online

America Online gets your USENET career off to a flying start by automatically subscribing you to no less than ten newsgroups. You get five groups from the **news** hierarchy: **news.announce.newusers**, **news.answers**, **news.groups.questions**, **news.groups.reviews**, and **news.newusers.questions**. The other five groups are all related to America Online itself:

> **** Important America Online Messages **** This group displays announcements about significant America Online happenings and new features. The Internet name for this group is **aol.motd**. (I'll explain why this group and the other AOL groups have two names in a second.)
>
> **Report America Online Newsgroup Bugs Here** If you discover a problem with America Online's Newsgroups area, use this group to let them know about it. Reading this group will also give you fair warning about bugs that others have discovered. The Internet name for this group is **aol.newsgroups.bugs**.
>
> **Help with Newsgroups** Use this group to post questions about America Online's Newsgroups area. The Internet name for this group is **aol.newsgroups.help**.

AOL Newsgroups Suggestion If you'd like to see some changes and enhancements to the Newsgroups area, post them to this group. The Internet name for this group is **aol.newsgroups.suggestions**.

Test Messages Go Here If you're just getting your feet wet with posting and following up, use this group for your tests and experiments. The Internet name for this group is **aol.newsgroups.test**.

As you can see, the names of the America Online-related groups don't look like normal USENET newsgroup names. The reason is that, to make USENET a bit more palatable for beginners, AOL has converted many group names into their English descriptions. So, for example, the group **aol.newsgroups.help** becomes **Help with Newsgroups**; similarly, **rec.motorcycles.harley** becomes **All aspects of Harley-Davidson motorcycles**. When you're subscribing, you can pick out your groups using either these descriptive names or the traditional USENET names.

To get the subscription show on the road, here are the steps to follow to subscribe to a group in America Online:

1. In the Newsgroups window, click on the **Add Newsgroups** button. America Online displays the Add Newsgroups-Categories window. This windows lists the seven mainstream hierarchies (**comp**, **news**, **rec**, **sci**, **soc**, **talk**, and **misc**), as well as **alt** and a host of lesser hierarchies (such as **aol** and **biz**).

2. Highlight the hierarchy you want to use, and then select the **List Topics** button. A new Topics window appears, showing the main topics in the hierarchy and the number of newsgroups in each topic. The figure that follows shows the window that appears for the **alt** hierarchy.

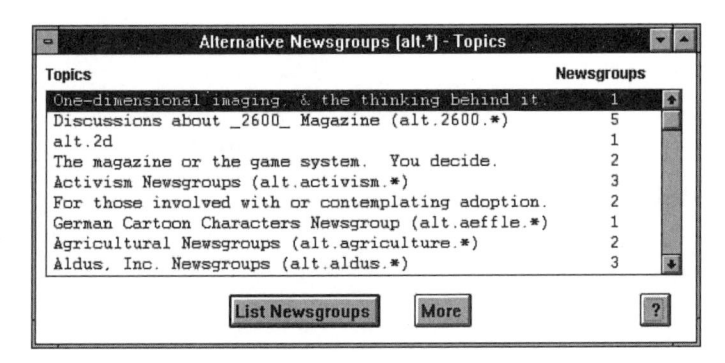

*The Topics window for the **alt** hierarchy.*

3. Highlight the topic you want and then select the **List Newsgroups** button. The Newsgroups window that appears lists the available newsgroups and the number of "subjects" (i.e., articles) that have appeared in the group over the past couple of weeks.

4. To see a list containing both the descriptive name and the Internet name for each group, select the **Internet Names** button. When you've finished with the list that appears, select **OK**.

5. Highlight the group you want to subscribe to and select the **Add** button. America Online displays a dialog box that tells you you've been subscribed to the group.

> Don't forget that for America Online lists that contain more than 20 items, you can select the **More** button to see more items in the list. Also, most America Online windows don't have any kind of "Close" button. Instead, you shut down a window by double-clicking on the **Control-menu box** in the upper-left corner of each window, or by pressing Ctrl+F4.

6. Select **OK**. America Online returns you to the Newsgroups window.

7. If you want to subscribe to more groups, repeat steps 5 and 6.

8. Close all the windows you just opened until you return to the Newsgroups window.

Other (Better) Ways to Subscribe

Whew! What a load to go through just to subscribe to a li'l ol' newsgroup. There *has* to be an easier way. Thankfully, there is, provided you know the name (that is, the Internet name) of the group you're looking for. In fact, this method is so easy I can describe it in a single (long) sentence: In the Newsgroups window, select the **Expert Add** button, type the name of the group in the Expert Add window that appears, select the **Add** button, select **OK** to say "Thanks!", and then close the Expert Add window.

America Online, ever eager to please, also gives you two other methods for scoping out and subscribing to newsgroups:

Part 2 ➤ *Start Spreading the News: A Guide to Popular Newsreaders*

> ➤ If you're not sure about a group's name, you can do a search for a word, or even part of a word, in the name. For example, fans of the rock group Rush could search for **rush** to find the group **alt.music.rush**. (Of course, you'll also find stuff like **alt.fan.rush-limbaugh**, but such are the hazards of inexact searches.) To try this out, select the **Search All Newsgroups** button in the Newsgroups window. In the Search Newsgroups window that appears, enter your search text and then select **Search**. America Online displays a Search Results window that lists the group names matching your search text. If you see the group you want, highlight it and select **Add**. As usual, select **OK** when America Online lets you know that you're subscribed to the group, and return to the Newsgroups window.

> ➤ The America Online powers-that-be also keep an eye out for new groups that have been added to USENET between your sessions. To see a list of these groups, select the **Expert Add** button in the Newsgroups window, and then select the **Latest Newsgroups** button in the Expert Add window. Again, if you see a group you'd like to subscribe to, highlight it, select **Add**, and so on.

> The prudes at America Online don't include some of the more risqué newsgroups (such as the **alt.sex** stuff) in their lists. You can get them, if you like, but the only way to do it is through the **Expert Add** button.

Unsubscribing to a Newsgroup

There are almost as many reasons to unsubscribe to a newsgroup as there are groups themselves. Whatever the reason, if a newsgroup just doesn't cut it for you any longer, here's how to bail out:

1. In the Newsgroups window, select the **Read My Newsgroups** button. The Read My Newsgroups window appears.

2. Highlight the newsgroup you want to nuke.

3. Select the **Remove** button. America Online lets you know the group has been unsubscribed.

4. Select **OK** to get back to the Read My Newsgroups window. (You may as well stick around this window, because we'll be using it in the next section.)

Reading Articles

For starters, you need to display the Read My Newsgroups window I talked about in the last section (if you're not there already). You do this by selecting the Newsgroup window's **Read My Newsgroups** button. This window lists each subscribed group and shows the number of unread articles and the total number of articles that have been posted to the group. (Confusingly, AOL uses a mixture of descriptive names and Internet names in this window. If you need clarification about a group name, select the **Internet Names** button to display a list that shows both names for each newsgroup.)

Once you have the Read My Newsgroups window on-screen, highlight the group with the articles you want to read and then select the **List Unread** button. (If you want to go back and check out an article you read previously—provided it hasn't yet expired—select the **List All** button, instead.) The window that appears (see the following figure) lists the subjects of all the group's unread threads, as well as the number of articles in each thread.

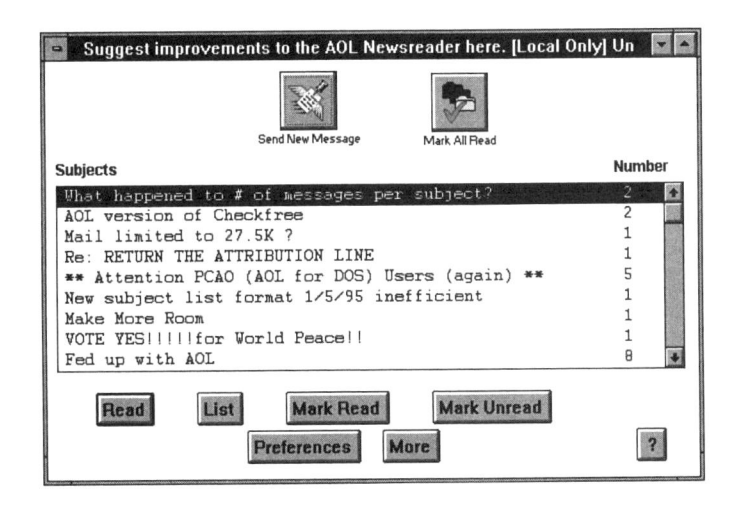

This window shows the Subject lines and number of articles in each thread.

Now highlight the thread you want to read and then select the **Read** button. America Online opens the article in its own window. The top of the window shows the Subject, From, Date, and Message-ID header lines, followed by the article text, followed by more header info.

> If you want to see more detail about a thread's messages before reading them, highlight the thread and select the **List** button. The window that appears shows the author's e-mail address and name, the number of lines in the article, and the date and time it was posted. To read an article from here, highlight it and select **Read**.

To move on to the next article, select the **Next->** button. To head back to the previous article, select the **<-Previous** button.

Saving and Printing an Article

To save the current article to a file on your computer, pull down the File menu and select the **Save** command (or press **Ctrl+S**). In the Save Text As dialog box that appears, use the Directories list to pick out a location, use the File Name text box to enter a name, and then select **OK**.

If you'd prefer a hard copy, make sure your printer is powered up and ready to go, and then select the File menu's **Print** command (or press **Ctrl+P**). In the Print Text dialog box, make your selections (such as the number of copies you want), and then select **OK**.

Talking Back: Following Up an Article

Here's how you post a follow-up article in America Online:

1. Read the article you want to follow up.

2. Highlight the text you want to include in your follow-up, and then select the Edit menu's Copy command.

3. If you want to send the response to the newsgroup, select the **Reply** button. America Online displays the Reply window. If you prefer to respond directly to the author via e-mail, select the **Reply to Author** button to display the Reply to Author window.

4. In the **Reply** box (it's called the **Response** box in the Reply to Author window), place the cursor where you want the original text to appear, and then select the Edit menu's **Paste** command to paste the original article text.

5. To make sure everyone knows you're quoting from the original article, place a greater-than sign (>) and a space at the beginning of each line in the original text.

6. Enter your own text.

7. If you're responding to the newsgroup and you want the author of the original article to get an e-mailed copy of your response, activate the **Copy author of original message via Email** check box.

8. If you want to include your signature in your response, activate the **Use signature (set in global preferences)** check box.

> How do you create a signature? Easy. Just return to the main Newsgroups window and select the **Set Preferences** button. In the Preferences dialog box that appears, use the **Signature** box to enter your signature, and then select OK.

9. Select the **Send** button. America Online posts the article and displays a dialog box to let you know.

10. Select **OK** to return to the article.

Posting an Original Article

Here are the steps to go through to post an article from America Online:

1. In the Read My Newsgroups window, highlight the group you want to use and select **List Unread Subjects**.

2. Select the **Send New Message** button. (This button also appears in the window you use to read an article.) America Online displays the Post New Message window.

3. Use the **Subject** field to enter the subject of your article.

163

Part 2 ➤ Start Spreading the News: A Guide to Popular Newsreaders

4. Use the **Message** box to enter your article text.
5. If you want to include your signature in the post (as described earlier), activate the **Use signature (set in global preferences)** check box.
6. Select the **Send** button. America Online posts the article and displays a dialog box to let you know everything went well.
7. Select **OK**.

The Least You Need to Know

This chapter took you through the ups and downs of reading USENET news through America Online. Here's the highlight film:

➤ To display America Online's Newsgroups area, pull down the Go To menu, select **Keyword**, enter **NEWSGROUPS**, and select **OK**.

➤ To subscribe to a newsgroup, select the **Expert Add** button, enter the name of the group in the Expert Add dialog box, and select **Add**.

➤ To unsubscribe to a newsgroup, select the **Read My Newsgroups** button, highlight the group in the list that appears, and then select the **Remove** button.

➤ To display a group's articles by thread, select the **Read My Newsgroups** button, highlight the group in the list that appears, and then select the **List Unread Subjects** button.

➤ To read an article, highlight it and select the **Read Messages** button.

➤ If you want to follow up the article you're reading, select the **Reply** button.

➤ To post an article of your own, highlight the group you want to use, select **List Unread**, and then select **Send New Message**.

Chapter 14

Doing the USENET Thing on Delphi

In This Chapter

➤ Starting up Delphi's newsreader
➤ Saving groups in your Personal Favorites list
➤ Reading and saving articles
➤ Following up and posting original articles
➤ An oracular look at Delphi's USENET newsreader

Of all the big-time online services, Delphi's name carries the most cachet in Internet circles. Part of the reason is that Delphi's Internet Special Interest Group (SIG) offers a more complete menu of Internet functions than do the other services. You can have all kinds of Net fun, including FTPing files, burrowing through cyberspace with Gopher, telneting to remote sites, and, of course, reading the news. And Delphi has offered this smorgasbord of services for a few years, so having "delphi.com" in your e-mail address is no mark of shame (as it sometimes is with CompuServe and America Online users; I talked about this domain prejudice—it's called *domainism*—in Chapters 12 and 13). This chapter shows you how to wield Delphi's newsreader to take you into the brave new world of USENET news.

Part 2 ➤ *Start Spreading the News: A Guide to Popular Newsreaders*

Before you rush headlong into cyberspace, please note that, due to *book* space limitations, I have to assume you've registered with Delphi, know how to log on, and are at least relatively familiar with the Delphi way of doing things. However, since I'll be telling you to select menu options all day long, let's at least make sure we're agreed on the procedure. To select a menu item in Delphi, you'll usually type the first few characters of the menu item's text, and then press **Enter**. To select the **Terms of Use** item, for example, you could type **TER** and press **Enter**. (Actually, since there are no other menu items that start with "T," you could get away with typing **T** and pressing **Enter**.) In some cases, the menu items will be numbered, so you select an item by typing its number and pressing **Enter**. If you use InterNav, you can also select a menu item by double-clicking on the first word in the item text.

Registering for Delphi's Internet Services

Before you can use Delphi's USENET section, you have to register for the Internet SIG so Delphi can charge you more money (an extra $3 a month as I write this). If you haven't registered already, here are the steps to follow:

1. Log onto Delphi and type **GO INT REG** at the Main Menu prompt. The Internet Registration Menu appears.

2. If you want to see what you're getting yourself into, select **Terms of Use** from the menu. The text that appears tells you a bit about Delphi's Internet SIG, gives you pricing info, and more. Press **Enter** after each screen until you're back at the Internet Registration Menu.

3. Select the **Register** menu item. Delphi asks if you've read and agree to the Terms of Use.

4. Type **YES** and press **Enter**. Delphi registers you for the Internet SIG.

5. Select the **Exit** item from the menu.

Getting Delphi's Newsreader Off to a Flying Start

Okay, now that you're a legitimate member of the Internet SIG, it's time to see what all the fuss is about. Type **GO INT** at any Delphi

Chapter 14 ➤ *Doing the USENET Thing on Delphi*

prompt and press **Enter**. A second or two later, Delphi displays the initial screen for the Internet SIG. Now press **Enter** to bring up the **Internet SIG Menu**:

```
About the Internet          Gopher

Conference                  IRC-Internet Relay Chat

Databases (Files)           Telnet

EMail                       Utilities (finger, traceroute, ping)

Forum (Messages)            USENET Newsgroups

Guides (Books)

Register/Cancel             Help

Who's Here                  Exit

Workspace                   Privacy Discussion (PGP)

FTP-File Transfer Protocol
```

Select the **USENET Newsgroups** item. Delphi now displays the **USENET Menu**:

```
About USENET Discussion Groups
USENET (Delphi Newsreader)
NN Newsreader (USENET)
Instructions for the NN Newsreader
Exit
```

The **About USENET Discussion Groups** item displays an introduction to USENET that you can read if you like. (See also Chapter 2, "So Just What the Heck Is USENET, Anyway?," for more introductory info.) To get Delphi's newsreader up to speed, select the **USENET (Delphi Newsreader)** option. Delphi displays the first page of the **USENET Discussion Groups** menu, as shown in the following figure. (Just so you know, the "NN Newsreader" menu options allow you to use a different newsreader—called **nn**—to work with USENET. **nn** is similar to **rn**, **trn**, and **tin** newsreaders I covered back in Chapters 6 and 7. In most cases, you'll find the Delphi newsreader easier to use.)

> If you'd prefer to bypass this menu and start the Delphi newsreader automatically, type **USE USE** at the **Internet SIG>** prompt and press **Enter**.

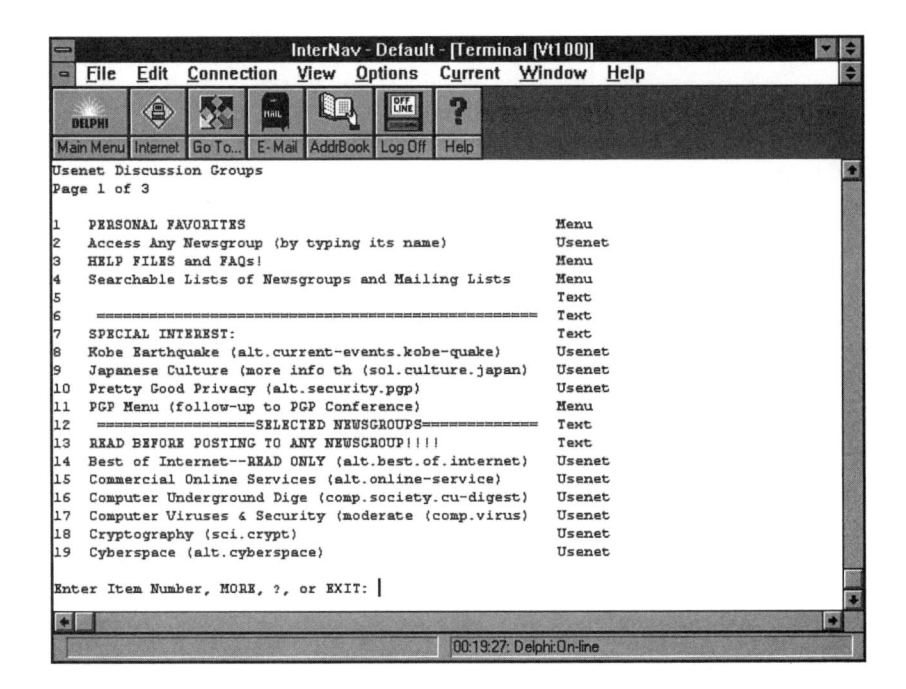

Part 2 ➤ Start Spreading the News: A Guide to Popular Newsreaders

*The first page of the **USENET Discussion Groups** menu.*

This menu (which changes all the time, and so may appear different on your screen) lists all of Delphi's newsreader options. Here's a quick summary:

PERSONAL FAVORITES—This item displays a menu of newsgroups that you've designated as your personal fave raves. (This is Delphi's way of saying you're subscribed to the groups.) This menu is empty when you first start the Delphi newsreader.

Access Any Newsgroup—This item lets you open up any newsgroup just by typing its name. If you know the name of the group you want, this is the fastest way to get to it.

HELP FILES and FAQs!—This item displays a menu that contains Help documents, FAQ lists, and menus containing other helpful documents.

Searchable Lists of Newsgroups and Mailing Lists—You can use this item to search for a particular newsgroup by entering part of the group's name.

168

SPECIAL INTEREST—This section presents newsgroups and other items that are particularly relevant to what's happening in the world.

SELECTED NEWSGROUPS—The rest of the menu (including the second page) lists over 30 newsgroups that the Delphi powers-that-be think you might be interested in. There's also a READ BEFORE POSTING TO ANY NEWSGROUP!!!! item that gives you some quick pointers on posting netiquette (most of which we discussed back in Chapter 3).

Adding Newsgroups to Your Personal Favorites List

Although the **USENET Discussion Groups** menu lists over 30 newsgroups in the **SELECTED NEWSGROUPS** section, the specific groups you see will change from time to time. So, if you have groups you want to read regularly, you'll need to add them to your Personal Favorites list. To do this, use either of the following methods:

➤ To choose one of the **SELECTED NEWSGROUPS**, type **SAVE** *n* and press **Enter**, where *n* is the group's number on the **USENET Discussion Groups** menu. For example, if **alt.cyberspace** is item 19, you'd type **SAVE 19** and press **Enter**. When Delphi asks you to confirm that you want the group saved to your Personal Favorites area, type **Y** and press **Enter**.

➤ For any other group, select the **Access Any Newsgroup** menu item, type in the name of the group, and then press **Enter** *twice*. After Delphi displays the list of threads for the group, type **SAVE** and press **Enter**. When Delphi asks for confirmation, type **Y** and press **Enter**. To return to the **USENET Discussion Groups** menu, type **BACK** and press **Enter**.

If you're not sure about the name of a newsgroup, you can perform a search using only part of its name. Select **Searchable Lists of Newsgroups and Mailing Lists**, then select **Newsgroup Lists**

169

from the menu that appears. Now choose either **Delphi Newsgroups (alt. thru cle.)** or **Delphi Newsgroups (comp. thru za.)**. If you'd prefer to see a list of new and deleted groups from the past week, select **List of new and deleted newsgroups this week**. You'll see the following prompt:

```
Press ENTER to display, D to Download, C to Cancel:
```

Press **Enter** to display the list. When the first page appears, type **FIND** *text*, where *text* is a word (or part of a word) from the group you want; you can enter up to 11 characters. Repeat the FIND command until Delphi displays the group you want. Once you've got the proper group name, type **TOP** and press **Enter** to return to the **Usenet Discussion Groups** menu. You can then use the **Access Any Newsgroup** item (as described earlier) to add the group to your PERSONAL FAVORITES list.

Reading Articles in Delphi

With all that out of the way, it's now time to get down to some serious time-wasting. I'm speaking, of course, of reading newsgroup articles. Your first big decision involves choosing a newsgroup to work with. Delphi gives you two options:

- ➤ To use a group from your Personal Favorites area, select the **PERSONAL FAVORITES** item in the **USENET Discussion Groups** menu. Delphi displays the PERSONAL FAVORITES menu. Now just type the number of the group you want and press **Enter**.

- ➤ If you want to use one of the **SELECTED NEWSGROUPS** in the **USENET Discussion Groups** menu, just type its number and press **Enter**.

In either case, you'll see a prompt similar to the following:

```
370 messages have been posted in the last 14 days. You've read
approximately 257.

Select which messages: Unread, All, Date or ?> [unread]
```

To see only those articles you haven't yet read, press **Enter** to accept the default value (**Unread**); to see every article, type **ALL** and press **Enter**; to see only those articles posted within a certain time

Chapter 14 ➤ *Doing the USENET Thing on Delphi*

frame, type **DATE** and press **Enter**. In this case, Delphi displays another prompt:

```
Show messages posted in last ____ days: [5]
```

Press **Enter** to see only the articles posted in the last five days; otherwise, type the number of days worth of articles you want to eyeball (enter a number between 1 and 14) and press **Enter**.

Delphi gathers the articles for the newsgroups and then displays a new menu (see the following figure). This menu tells you the Subject line for each thread in the group, as well as the number of articles in each thread.

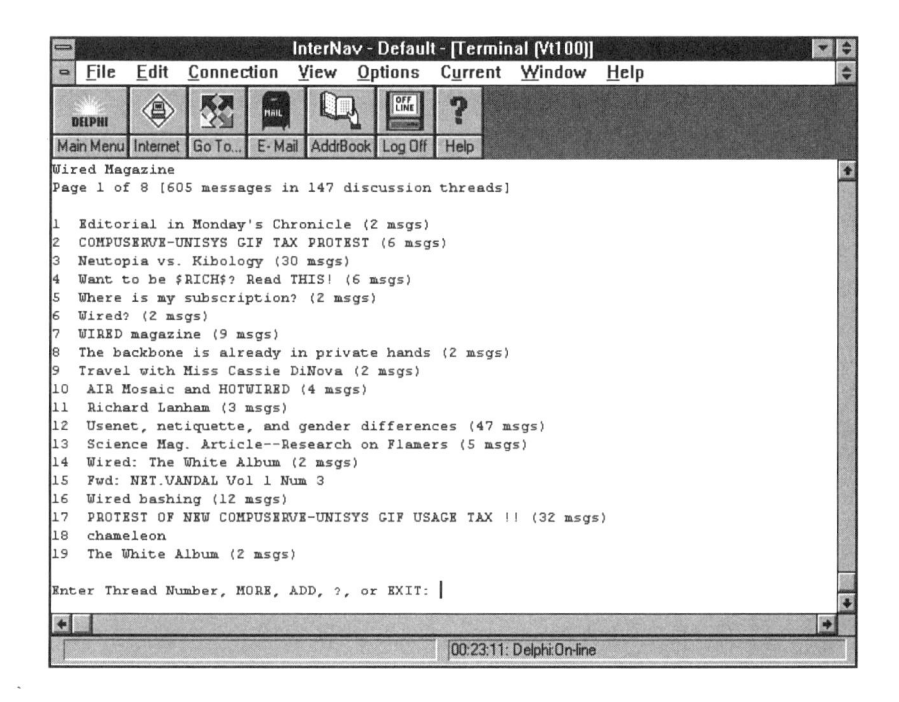

This menu shows the thread Subject lines and number of articles in each thread.

To read a thread, type its number and press **Enter**. Delphi cues up the first article in the thread and displays it on-screen. While reading a message, you can enter the following commands to move around:

READ NEXT   Displays the next article in the current thread.

171

LAST   Displays the previous article in the current thread.

NEXT THREAD   Displays the first article of the next thread.

PRIOR   Displays the first article in the previous thread.

CURRENT   Re-displays the current article.

HEADER   Displays the full header for the current article.

ROT   Decodes the current article using rot13.

GROUP   Takes you to the next newsgroup in the list.

Saving an Article to Your Personal Workspace

The *personal workspace* is your own, private chunk of Delphi real estate that you're free to do with what you will. Delphi stores some files in there (for example, your Personal Favorites group list is stored in a file named FAVORITES.SAV), you can create files in the workspace, and you can even use the workspace to edit files. One of the most common uses for the workspace is to save articles that have somehow struck your fancy (funnybone, whatever). To do this, display the article you want to save, type **FILE**, and press **Enter**. Delphi displays the following prompt:

    Filename:

Enter a name for the file—you can use up to 255 characters, and any combination of letters, number, periods (.), and underscores(_)—and press **Enter**. Delphi then copies the article to your workspace.

> When reading articles in Delphi, you can take advantage of the **Enter** key to make life easier. For example, if an article has multiple pages, pressing **Enter** displays the next page. If you're at the end of an article, pressing **Enter** displays the next article in the thread. If you're reading the last article in a thread, pressing **Enter** displays the first article of the next thread.

How to Create a Signature File in Delphi

Before I tell you how to post follow-ups and new articles, let's see how you go about creating a signature file. A signature, you'll recall, appears at the bottom of your articles, and they're a handy way to tell your readers a little more about yourself. A *signature file* is a text file that contains your signature. Here are the hoops you have to jump through to create a signature file in Delphi:

1. At any Delphi prompt, type **GO WORK** and press **Enter** to head for your personal workspace (the Delphi area that contains your personal files).

2. Type **CREATE SIG.TXT** and press **Enter**. This creates a new text file named SIG.TXT.

3. In the first line, type **.SIGNATURE**, followed by a space, followed by the first line of your signature.

4. Type in the rest of your signature (4 or 5 lines max).

5. Press **Ctrl+Z** to save the file.

6. At the **WS>** prompt, type **EDIT FAVORITES.SAV** and press **Enter**.

7. At the * prompt, type **INCLUDE SIG.TXT** and press **Enter**. This tells Delphi to use the file SIG.TXT as your signature.

8. Type **EXIT** and press **Enter**. Delphi saves the file.

Following Up an Article

Did you think of a snappy comeback while reading an article? Or perhaps the posters in a thread are indulging in some witty repartee and you'd like to join in the fun. Whatever the reason, if you have a riposte, rejoinder, or retort you'd like to get on record, the follow-up article is the way to go. Here's how it's done in Delphi:

1. Read the article you want to follow up.

2. To post the follow-up in the newsgroup, type **REPLY** and press **Enter**. If you'd prefer to respond via Delphi's e-mail system, type **MAIL REPLY** and press **Enter**. Delphi asks whether you want to quote sections of the original article in your reply.

3. If you don't want to quote the original article, just press **Enter** and then type in your article text. If you're using InterNav, Delphi will load its editor for you to type in your message. When you're done, select the **S**end button. Otherwise, press **Ctrl+Z** when you've finished. Skip ahead to step 7.

If you do want to quote the original article, type **Y** and press **Enter**.

4. If you chose **Yes** in step 3, Delphi displays the original article text and numbers each line. Type the range of lines you want to quote. For example, if you want to quote the first 5 lines, you type **1-5**. When you're ready, press **Enter**.

5. Enter your response to the quoted material; press **Ctrl+Z** when you're done. Delphi asks if you want to quote more material.

6. Repeat steps 3–5 until you've finished quoting what you need from the original article. If you created a signature file, Delphi displays the following prompt:

   ```
   Append signature from FAVORITES.SAV to message (y or n)?
   ```

7. Type **Y** and press **Enter** to include the signature. Now Delphi displays another prompt:

   ```
   Post, List, or Cancel?
   ```

8. To post the follow-up, type **POST** and press **Enter**. You can also enter the **LIST** command to take a peek at the article, or the **CANCEL** command to bail out of the operation.

Posting an Original Article

USENET has no shortage of people who enjoy proselytizing, evangelizing, sermonizing, and propagandizing in one form or another. If you'd like to take part, you need to post original articles of your own by following these steps:

1. Select the group you want to use for your post.

2. Type **ADD** and press **Enter**. Delphi prompts you for a subject.

3. Type the subject of your article and press **Enter**. Delphi prompts you to enter your article text. If you're using InterNav, Delphi will load its editor for you to type in your article. In this case, select the Send button when you're done. Otherwise, type in your article at the bottom of the screen; press **Ctrl+Z** when you're finished. If you created a signature file, Delphi asks if you want to include it in the article.

4. Type **Y** and press **Enter** to include the signature.

5. To post the article, type **POST** and press **Enter**. You can also enter the **LIST** command to view the article, or the **CANCEL** command to forget the whole thing ever happened.

Removing Newsgroups from Your Personal Favorites List

As you saw earlier in this chapter, Delphi has a SAVE command that you use to save a newsgroup to your Personal Favorites list. So it would be logical to assume there is some kind of "UNSAVE" command that would remove a newsgroup from the Personal Favorites list. Ah, if only life at Delphi were that simple. No, unfortunately, there is no "UNSAVE" command, or anything remotely close to it. Instead, the only way to blow away an unwelcome group is to edit a file called FAVORITES.SAV.

FAVORITES.SAV is stored in your Personal Workspace, and it contains (among other things) a list of the groups in your Personal Favorites list. Each group appears on a separate line that looks something like this:

```
.TOPIC Urban Folklore     alt.folklore.urban
```

Deleting a newsgroup from your Personal Favorites list is a matter of deleting the appropriate line in FAVORITES.SAV. Here are the specific steps to follow:

1. At any Delphi prompt, type **GO WORK** to enter your Personal Workspace. You'll know you're there when you see the **WS>** prompt.

2. Type **EDIT FAVORITES.SAV**. Delphi displays the first line of the file and the ***** prompt. (If you don't see this prompt, pressing **Ctrl+Z** should do it.)

3. If this line contains the name of a newsgroup you want to delete, type **DEL** and press **Enter**. Otherwise, press **Enter** to move on to the next line.

4. Repeat step 3 until you've deleted all the newsgroups you no longer need.

5. Type **EXIT** and press **Enter**. Delphi saves your changes and returns you to the **WS>** prompt.

The Least You Need to Know

This chapter took a prophetic look at Delphi's newsreader. Here's a summary of some things to remember in the future:

➤ Before starting up the Delphi newsreader, register for the Internet SIG by typing **GO INT REG** and pressing **Enter**.

➤ To start the newsreader, type **GO INT** and press **Enter**, select **USENET Newsgroups**, and then select **USENET (Delphi Newsreader)**.

➤ To add a group to your Personal Favorites list, select the group, type **SAVE**, and press **Enter**. To add a group from the **SELECTED NEWSGROUPS** list, type **SAVE** *n* and press **Enter**, where *n* is the number of the group.

➤ To display a group's articles by thread, display the Personal Favorites list and then enter the group's number. (You can also open a group from the **SELECTED NEWSGROUPS** list.)

➤ To read a thread, type its number and press **Enter**.

➤ If you want to follow up the article you're reading, type **REPLY** (to post the follow-up in the group) or **MAIL REPLY** (to send the follow-up via e-mail), and press **Enter**.

➤ To post an article of your own, open the newsgroup, type **Add**, and press **Enter**.

➤ If you want to remove a group from your Personal Favorites list, you need to delete the appropriate line from the FAVORITES.SAV file in your personal workspace.

Part 3
All the News That's Fit to Surf

Okay, you learned the ABCs of USENET back in Part 1, and you learned how to wield your favorite newsreader in Part 2. Now what? Well, now it's time to start having some fun as you subscribe to, read, and post to your favorite newsgroups. That's all well and good, I hear you say, but I don't have any favorite newsgroups yet. Hey, no problem; that's what the chapters here in Part 3 are for. I'll take you on newsgroup tours that'll cover entertainment, business, hobbies, politics, sports, you name it. In all, we'll look at hundreds of USENET's most popular groups, and I'll even tell you about any FAQs that are available, so you won't feel like a newbie when you wade into a new group.

Before you get started, though, a brief disclaimer is in order. One of the first things you'll notice about USENET is that things change—fast. There are always new groups coming online, old groups dividing into multiple subgroups, and dead groups falling by the wayside. Keeping up with all this is like herding cats, so you're bound to find a few discrepancies and omissions. If so, I apologize in advance. Happy surfing!

Chapter 15

Getting Star-Struck in the Entertainment Newsgroups

In This Chapter

➤ Selected television newsgroups

➤ Some movie newsgroups

➤ Newsgroups devoted to books, magazines, and comics

➤ Groups for music groupies

➤ An entertaining look at USENET's entertainment discussions

This chapter kicks off our newsgroup chapters with a tour of USENET's most popular entertainment groups. We'll cover TV, movies, books, magazines, music, and a whole lot more. So make up a batch of popcorn, get your autograph book ready, and let's get to it...

Browsing the Boob-Tube Groups

Television's pervasive influence in our culture is directly reflected in the wealth and diversity of the USENET groups related to the ol' idiot box. There are dozens of groups, with topics ranging from Barney the Dinosaur to *The X-Files*, so there's bound to be something to keep most couch-potatoes happy.

Part 3 ➤ *All the News That's Fit to Surf*

If you're looking for discussions related to TV as a whole, check out **rec.arts.tv**, one of the most heavily-traveled groups in USENET. Before diving in, be sure to read the FAQ with this title:
*** REC.ARTS.TV POSTING GUIDELINES ***

The next few sections take you through a selection of TV-related newsgroups from the **alt** hierarchy. If you want more information about TV, the Net has all kinds of TV resources, but one of the best is the Yahoo World Wide Web site. Point your favorite browser to the following URL:

```
http://akebono.stanford.edu/yahoo/bin/menu
```

In the list that appears, select the **Entertainment** link, and then select the **Television** link. The page that appears gives you links to Neilsen ratings, schedules, episode guides, and lots more.

Barney-Bashing to Melrose Mania

The following list describes some of the more popular TV-related newsgroups:

- ➤ If you love to complain about commercials (and, hey, who doesn't?), check out **alt.tv.commercials** to meet some kindred spirits.

- ➤ What is it about poor Barney the Dinosaur that throws people in paroxysms of rage at the mere mention of his name? Find out in the newsgroup devoted to full-time Barney-slamming: **alt.barney.dinosaur.die.die.die**.

- ➤ Beavis and Butt-head burnouts will love **alt.tv.beavis-n-butthead**. Here, you'll find people arguing over things like which episode was the best ever (and all without even a trace of irony).

- ➤ Tune in to **alt.tv.bh90210** to explore some of life's great mysteries with fans of Dylan, Clair, and that wacky Walsh family. (Example mystery: How come everyone hated Brenda when she was on the show, and they miss her now that she's off the show?)

- ➤ From New York—the city that doesn't sleep, but probably should—it's **alt.fan.letterman**. Read this group for just a few minutes, and you'll realize why Letterman is kicking Jay Leno's patootie (ratings-wise, that is). I mean, these people are *fanatics*!

Chapter 15 ➤ *Getting Star-Struck in the Entertainment Newsgroups*

Why they've even created a separate group just to hold Top Ten lists from the current week's shows: **alt.fan.letterman.top-ten**.

    FAQ Info:
        Articles:
            alt.fan.letterman Frequently Asked Questions (read
                before posting)
            alt.fan.letterman The Official David Letterman
                Song Book
        RTFM.MIT.EDU Directory:
            /pub/usenet-by-group/alt.fan.letterman

> Fans of other talk show hosts won't be disappointed. There's **alt.fan.jay-leno** for *Tonight Show* viewers, **alt.fan.conan-obrien** for *Late Night* night-owls, and **alt.fan.greg-kinnear** for *TalkSoup* watchers.

➤ Devotees of the prime-time soap *Melrose Place* meet in **alt.tv.melrose-place** to discuss the weekly plot twists and turns of fate of this popular *90210* offspring. Recent thread subjects included "Is Kimberly a man?" and "Susan Neck Theory" (don't ask me).

➤ Most women I know absolutely hate it when the men around them suddenly break into a Monty Python sketch that usually ends up with the guys yelling "Nee! Nee!" at the top of their lungs. Hey, it sounds like fun to me! If it does to you too, then you'll probably enjoy **alt.fan.monty-python**.

➤ Will Ed become a shaman? Will Cicely miss the doctor? Will Maggie's boyfriends ever stop dying on her? For the answers to these questions and many more *Northern Exposure* conundrums, dial up the popular newsgroup **alt.tv.northern-exp**.

    FAQ Info:
        Article:
            alt.tv.northern-exp Frequently Asked Questions
        RTFM.MIT.EDU Directory:
            /pub/usenet-by-group/alt.tv.northern-exp

- ► Admired by both viewers and critics alike, the gritty, steamy cop show *NYPD Blue* is also a hit on USENET. Head for **alt.tv.nypd-blue** to see what all the fuss is about.

- ► For a show that's supposed to be about "nothing," *Seinfeld* sure generates a lot of conversation. In particular, you'll find all kinds of Seinfeldian discussions in the very popular newsgroup **alt.tv.seinfeld**.

    ```
    FAQ Info:
        Article:
            alt.tv.seinfield FAQ List and Info File (part 01/03)
            alt.tv.seinfield FAQ List and Info File (part 02/03)
            alt.tv.seinfield FAQ List and Info File (part 03/03)
        RTFM.MIT.EDU Directory:
            /pub/usenet-by-group/alt.tv.seinfeld
    ```

- ► It may not be as good since Conan O'Brien left to pursue more lucrative pastures (doh!), but *The Simpsons* is still a popular show and **alt.tv.simpsons** remains one of the most highly-trafficked groups in USENET. Drop in to get the latest on the adventures of Homer, Marge, Bart, Lisa, Maggie, and the rest of the Springfield denizens.

    ```
    FAQ Info:
        Article:
            alt.tv.simpsons Frequently Asked Questions
        RTFM.MIT.EDU Directory:
            /pub/usenet-by-group/alt.tv.simpsons
    ```

- ► *The X-Files* is probably the most paranoid TV show ever made. Despite this (or, more likely, because if it), the newsgroup **alt.tv.x-files** generates hundreds of articles a day. Most of the X-philes who post to the group either discuss the plausibility of the show's latest alien-abduction-conspiracy theory, or express the writer's unrequited lust for either David Duchovny or Gillian Anderson (the show's co-stars). By the way, rumor has it that the *X-Files* braintrust (including executive producer Chris Carter) are regular lurkers.

Chapter 15 ➤ *Getting Star-Struck in the Entertainment Newsgroups*

```
FAQ Info:
    Article:
      DOWN & DIRTY DAILY X-FAQ
    RTFM.MIT.EDU Directory:
      /pub/usenet-by-group/alt.tv.x-files
```

The Best of the Rest

Unfortunately, I just don't have the space to cover absolutely every TV-related newsgroup. So, just to make things semi-complete, here's a short list of some popular TV groups not covered in the previous section:

alt.tv.brady-bunch	They're all drug addicts now :-), but they sure were cuddly back then.
alt.tv.mad-about-you	The cutest couple on television.
alt.tv.picket-fences	Tackling life's most serious issues in one hour.
alt.tv.ren-n-stimpy	Some change from Lassie, eh?
alt.tv.roseanne	Find out her marital status for this week.
alt.tv.sctv	SCTV (Second City TV) & alumni discussions.
alt.tv.snl	*Saturday Night Live*, older but not better.
alt.tv.talkshows.late	Late-night wars on the major networks.

Movie Newsgroups for Cinemaniacs

One of the busiest groups in all of USENET is **rec.arts.movies**. To give you an idea of how popular it is, a survey done in the summer of 1994 showed that this group generated an average of nearly 8,000 articles a month! Most of the chat revolves around the latest releases, but film buffs, it seems, are happy to talk about *any* movie, *any* time. A great place to find cinematic trivia.

If you're more interested in the technical side of moviemaking, get your clapper loader and head for **rec.arts.movies.production**. This group has fascinating discussions of special effects and equipment, a few want ads, and lots of advice on how to get your start in the behind-the-scenes aspect of show biz.

Part 3 ➤ *All the News That's Fit to Surf*

```
FAQ Info:
    Articles:
        rec.arts.movies Frequently Asked Questions
        LIST: Crazy Movie Credits
        LIST: MOVIE TRIVIA: in-jokes, cameos, signatures
        LIST: Movie BIOGRAPHIES list
        LIST: Movie Quotes (Part 1/2)
        LIST: Movie Quotes (Part 2/2)
        LIST: Movie Soundtracks
    RTFM.MIT.EDU Directory:
        /pub/usenet-by-group/rec.arts.movies
```

If you need quick access to movie tidbits (such as the names of a film's director or co-stars), point your World Wide Web browser software to the following site:

http://www.cm.cf.ac.uk/Movies/moviequery.html

This site gives you access to the Internet Movie Database, which is filled to the rafters with movie info and trivia.

To some extent, all moviegoers are film critics, but this criticism spans a wide range, from the simple grunt of approval to the polished prose of a Jay Scott or Pauline Kael. Between these extremes lie the dedicated posters who send in well-crafted, thoughtful, "man-in-the-street" reviews to the moderated newsgroup **rec.arts.movies.reviews**. The articles, as you might expect, are longish (about 100 lines, on average), but the presence of a moderator means you never have to wade through too many posts in one sitting.

Filmdom, of course, isn't just about the latest blockbuster or the acknowledged classics. There's a whole genre of cult movies that attracts some of the most rabid film freaks. If you count yourself part of this crowd, be sure to cultivate a relationship with the **alt.cult-movies** newsgroup. There's lots of trivia, news about upcoming cult filmfests, and descriptions of not-to-be-missed gems such as *Dr. Goldfoot and the Bikini Machine*.

If, in your lost youth, you spent many a midnight hour at the local theater throwing toast and doing the Timewarp with other *Rocky Horror Picture Show* aficionados, you'll definitely want to jump to the left and spend time in **alt.cult-movies.rocky-horror**.

Chapter 15 ➤ *Getting Star-Struck in the Entertainment Newsgroups*

```
FAQ Info:
    Article:
        Rocky Horror Theater List
    RTFM.MIT.EDU Directory:
        /pub/usenet-by-group/alt.cult-movies
```

If your taste runs toward monster movies, **alt.movies.monster** is the place you oughta be. You'll find discussions of current monster flicks, video releases, filmfests, and more.

Reading About Reading: Books, 'Zines, and Comics

Newsgroups devoted to reading books, magazines, and comics are some of the most well-thumbed spots on the Net. This section browses through a few of these groups for your reading pleasure.

Groups for Book Buffs

People have been predicting the demise of books ever since the first computers reared their vacuum-tubed heads in the 1940s. But, if the immense volume of traffic in USENET's book-related groups is any indication, books of all kinds still have a lot of life left in them. Of these groups, **rec.arts.books** is the most popular. This group features book reviews, lists of bookstores and books clubs, and lots of talk about just how wonderful books are.

The group **rec.arts.books.childrens** is devoted exclusively to KidLit. For new book announcements, book catalogues, and articles looking to buy or sell books, turn to **rec.arts.books.marketplace**. For reviews of computer and engineering books, try the groups **alt.books.technical** and **misc.books.technical**.

```
FAQ Info:
    Article:
        rec.arts.books Frequently Asked Questions (FAQ)
        Book Catalogues and Book Clubs List (rec.arts.books)
    RTFM.MIT.EDU Directory:
        /pub/usenet-by-group/rec.arts.books
```

Writer Fan Clubs

The whole point of USENET, of course, is to allow like-minded individuals to converse on topics of mutual interest. So it's only natural that many different fan clubs would spring up, and there are quite a few for writers. Here's a summary:

alt.books.anne-rice	Anne Rice aficionados.
alt.fan.dave-barry	Dave Barry buffs.
alt.fan.hofstadter	Douglas Hofstadter devotees.
alt.fan.holmes	Sir Arthur Conan Doyle detectives.
alt.books.stephen-king	Stephen King connoisseurs.
alt.books.toffler	Alvin Toffler addicts.
alt.fan.tolkien	J.R.R. Tolkien junkies.
rec.arts.books.tolkien	Ditto.
alt.fan.wodehouse	P.G. Wodehouse wonks.

Magazine Newsgroup Subscriptions

No true Net surfer would be caught dead without a copy of this month's *Wired* magazine. This publication is fairly broad-based, but many of its features and articles deal with the Internet and related issues. Once you've read the magazine, you can get truly wired by flipping to the **alt.wired** newsgroup. Other magazine groups to watch out for are **alt.mag.playboy**, **alt.motherjones**, and **alt.zines** (which covers all those underground 'zines that have sprung up over the past couple of years).

Conversing with Comics Connoisseurs

Comic books are a big business now, and long gone are the days when comics appealed only to kids. This is reflected in the diversity of newsgroups related to comic books and graphic novels (as many of them are called nowadays). For general discussions, try **rec.arts.comics.misc**; newspaper comic strips and editorial cartoons are covered in **rec.arts.comics.strips**; buying and selling comic collectibles is the charter of the **rec.arts.comics.marketplace** newsgroup;

if your taste runs more towards obscure, alternative comics, try **alt.comics.alternative**; finally, the moderated newsgroup **rec.arts.comics.info** has good reviews, FAQs, and more.

There are also several groups devoted exclusively to particular comics: X-Men fans can be found in **rec.arts.comics.xbooks**; Batman buffs hang out in the Batgroup **alt.comics.batman**; and Superman fans are up, up, and away in **alt.comics.superman**.

```
FAQ Info:
    Articles:
        Welcome to rec.arts.comics: Introduction
        Welcome to rec.arts.comics: Netiquette
        Welcome to rec.arts.comics: FAQ
        Welcome to rec.arts.comics: Glossary
        Welcome to rec.arts.comics: FTP Resources
        Welcome to rec.arts.comics: Mailing Lists
        Welcome to rec.arts.comics: Email and Other Net Resources
    RTFM.MIT.EDU Directory:
        /pub/usenet-by-group/rec.arts.comics.info
```

Hanging Out with Groupies, Roadies, and Other Music Fans

If you like music, USENET is the place to be—with well over a hundred groups that cover everything from alternative music to *a cappella*. Although most of the music groups cater to specific musical genres or to specific bands, there are a few whose charters are more general. For example, **rec.music.info** contains tons of information files that include FAQ lists, music charts from around the world (just in case you need to know this week's top 20 Austrian singles), and lists of Internet music resources (such as FTP sites and mailing lists).

Other groups to bear in mind include **rec.music.reviews**, where amateur music critics dump on the latest releases, **rec.music.videos**, where MTV and MuchMusic junkies discuss current music videos, and **rec.music.marketplace**, which brings together buyers and sellers of CDs, albums, and music collectibles.

Part 3 ➤ *All the News That's Fit to Surf*

> **FAQ Info:**
> Article:
> REC.MUSIC.INFO: Welcome to rec.music.info!
> RTFM.MIT.EDU Directory:
> /pub/usenet-by-group/rec.music.info

The rest of this section gets you into the groove by digging on some of the more popular of USENET's music newsgroups.

Rock 'n' Roll

What do you once you've read **alt.sex** and **alt.drugs**? Why, you read **alt.rock-n-roll**, of course. This group has lots of rock talk, reviews of albums, band info, and lots more. "Rock" is a pretty broad term, of course, so this group has spawned quite a few subgroups. Bobby-soxers and those still stuck in the '60s should try **alt.rock-n-roll.classic** and **alt.rock-n-roll.oldies**. If you think ballads are for wimps, you'll probably feel right at home in **alt.rock-n-roll.hard**. And if head-banging is your favorite participation sport, you can join your fellow metalheads in **alt.rock-n-roll.metal**, **alt.rock-n-roll.metal.death**, **alt.rock-n-roll.metal.heavy**, and **alt.rock-n-roll.metal.progressive**.

> There are a fistful of cool Net sites for music info. For example, the Yahoo Web page I mentioned earlier in this chapter has a huge list of music sites. If you're into rock and alternative, the new RockWWWeb page has lots of promise. Browse to **http://www.rock.net** to check it out.

Alternative

For general discussions of alternative music, subscribe to the group **alt.music.alternative**. One of the hallmarks of the alternative scene is the large number of female artists and all-grrrl bands. The group **alt.music.alternative.female** celebrates this welcome gender equality. Techno-lovers can rave on in **alt.music.techno**; the industrial scene is honored in **rec.music.industrial**; and the resurgent punk movement finds a home in **alt.punk** and **alt.punk.straight-edge**.

```
FAQ Info:
    Articles:
        FAQ: rec.music.industrial Part 1/2--Questions and
            History
        FAQ: rec.music.industrial Part 2/2--Mailorder Sources
            and Zines
    RTFM.MIT.EDU Directory:
        /pub/usenet-by-group/rec.music.industrial
```

Classical and Opera

If your musical tastes run more toward "the three Bs"—Bach, Beethoven, and Brahms—you'll find lots of kindred spirits in the highly popular newsgroup **rec.music.classical**. Discussions include the latest recordings, reviews of performances, and lots more.

Fans of classical guitar music (no, we're not talking "Classical Gas") will enjoy **rec.music.classical.guitar**. If the "pre-Baroque" era (i.e., before about 1685) turns your crank, you'll love **rec.music.early**. Finally, classical music performers can turn to **rec.music.classical.performing** for discussions of vocal and instrumental technique.

```
FAQ Info:
    Articles:
        FAQ: rec.music.classical
        Which Classical Music Newsgroup? (FAQ)
    RTFM.MIT.EDU Directory:
        /pub/usenet-by-group/rec.music.classical
```

Jazz, Folk, Country, and More

For jazz, try **alt.music.progressive** and **rec.music.bluenote** (which discusses the Blue Note jazz recording label). Honky-tonk men and women can line dance until their feet are sore in **rec.music.country.western**. If you're more of a folkie, you can find music conversations with a revolutionary air in **rec.music.folk**. If you can tell the difference between the Salsa you can dance to and the salsa you can eat, then you'll feel right at home in **rec.music.afro-latin**. Need to get the funk out your face? Then pay a visit to **rec.music.funky**. Finally, if modern reggae is your style, be sure to visit the island of **rec.music.reggae**.

Part 3 ➤ *All the News That's Fit to Surf*

Recording Artist Fan Clubs

Most of the USENET music groups deal with individual artists and bands, so these groups become basically informal fan clubs. Most of the chatter is a bit breathless and bit fawning, but, hey, that's what fan clubs do. Here's a list of some of the newsgroups that deal with individual artists and bands:

alt.fan.courtney-love	Hole lead singer and notorious Net gadabout.
alt.fan.jello-biafra	The Dead Kennedys' lead singer and punk icon.
alt.fan.jimi-hendrix	'Scuse me, while I kiss this guy!
alt.fan.laurie.anderson	Ms. Multimedia herself.
alt.fan.madonna	Play "Truth or Dare" online.
alt.fan.sting	The world's favorite pop-environmentalist.
alt.fan.u2	I'll be U2 and UB40.
alt.music.genesis	Genesis, in all their incarnations.
alt.music.nin	Digging Nine Inch Nails.
alt.music.nirvana	Mostly Kurt Cobain eulogies.
alt.music.paul-simon	Just who was that roly-poly little bat-faced girl?
alt.music.pearl-jam	The newly-crowned grunge kings.
alt.music.peter-gabriel	Digging in the dirt.
alt.music.rush	Is Neil Peart the best lyricist ever?
alt.music.smash-pumpkins	If hearing their songs 57 times a day isn't enough.
alt.music.smiths	You can talk about Morrissey's solo stuff, too.

Boldly Going: The Science Fiction Newsgroups

Scratch a technogeek, and you'll find a science fiction (SF) aficionado. So it's no surprise that USENET has a thriving collection of science fiction groups, as you'll see in this section.

Some places to start are in the following list:

▶ Science fiction conventions are a ritual that any true SF buff must join. To keep you posted on local and national "cons," keep an eye on the groups **rec.arts.sf.announce** and **alt.fandom.cons**.

```
FAQ Info:
    Article:
        Rec.arts.sf.groups, an introduction
    RTFM.MIT.EDU Directory:
        /pub/usenet-by-group/rec.arts.sf.announce
```

▶ Science fiction toys, collectibles, and memorabilia are always hot items. For proof, just check out the furious action in **rec.arts.sf.marketplace**, the place to be for buying and selling sci-fi merchandise.

▶ For many fans, the *science* of science fiction is its most attractive feature. If you have your own theories about faster-than-light travel and matter transport, you should definitely hang out in **rec.arts.sf.science**. Beware, though: the discussions can get real technical, real fast.

▶ There's no shortage of sci-fi stuff on both the big screen and the boob tube, and there's no shortage of USENET talk about both media. For movies, join the discussions **rec.arts.sf.movies** and **rec.arts.sf.starwars**. Sci-fi couch potatoes can get their fill in **rec.arts.sf.tv**, **rec.arts.drwho**, **rec.arts.tv.sf.babylon5**, and **rec.arts.tv.sf.quantum-leap**.

Sci-Fi Books

Most sci-fi nuts are created by reading, no *devouring*, books at an early age. (For me, it was the late Isaac Asimov's *Foundation* series and innumerable books with names like *Mutant 59: The Plastic Eaters*.) Here's a list of some of the newsgroups that discuss sci-fi books:

rec.arts.sf.written	General talk about current sci-fi books and authors.
rec.arts.sf.written.robert-jordan	The Robert Jordan fan club.
alt.books.isaac-asimov	The *I, Robot* guy.
alt.fan.douglas-adams	The hitchhiker's guide to Ford Prefect, et. al.
alt.fan.dune	For fans of Frank Herbert's interminable Dune series.
alt.fan.eddings	David Eddings: the one-man Book of the Month Club.

Trekker City: The Star Trek Groups

In the nearly 30 years since the original show aired, *Star Trek* has garnered an unbelievable number of devotees. These enthusiasts run the gamut from rabid, Klingon-faced, get-a-life Trekkers, to casual watch-whatever-current-series-are-on fans. USENET's *Star Trek* groups reflect this diversity, too, with a group for every taste and level of dedication. Check out the **rec.arts.startrek** and **alt.startrek** newsgroups for *Star Trek* discussions.

> There are, quite literally, dozens of FAQ lists for the *Star Trek* groups. Instead of listing them all here, do the anonymous FTP thing to the **rtfm.mit.edu** site, and check out the following directories:
>
> /pub/usenet-by-group/rec.arts.startrek.current
> /pub/usenet-by-group/rec.arts.startrek.misc
> /pub/usenet-by-group/rec.arts.startrek.tech
> /pub/usenet-by-group/alt.startrek.creative

Chapter 16

Getting Advice in the Business and Consumer Newsgroups

In This Chapter

➤ Newsgroups for business buffs
➤ Groups that tackle consumer issues
➤ Advice for investing your spare cash
➤ Newsgroups for buying and selling
➤ Want ads for the unemployed and disgruntled

In your USENET travels, you'll find many things in abundance: opinions, bombast, bluster, and lots of good old-fashioned hot air. But you also find advice—lots of advice. Whether you're starting up a business, buying a house, or looking for work, plenty of USENET citizens are only too happy to help.

This chapter takes you on a tour of a few newsgroups devoted to business and consumer topics. We'll also invest some time investigating the various investment groups, as well as the newsgroups that handle classified ads and want ads.

General Business Biz

Looking for new business opportunities? Need some business advice? USENET has several groups that cater to general business concerns, from startups to marketing, as listed below:

➤ The newsgroup **alt.business.misc** is the place to hang out if you're looking for a new business opportunity, if you want to connect with someone in the same business as you, or if you want some advice about a startup idea you have. It's like a cocktail party without the booze and small talk.

➤ If you've always dreamed of being your own boss, spend some time in the newsgroup **misc.entrepreneurs**. You'll find lots of advice about how to get a going concern going, from small business owners, venture capitalists, and the like.

➤ The concept of multi-level marketing (or MLM as those in the know like to call it) is simple: if you tell two friends about a product, and they each tell two friends, and each of them tells two friends, and so on, then theoretically you end up with a product that's widely known by word-of-mouth (either that, or you end up with no friends). Many people swear by it, and are ready to evangelize on the subject in the group **alt.business.multi-level**.

```
FAQ Info:
    Article:
        alt.business.multi-level FAQ (Frequently Asked
          Questions)
    RTFM.MIT.EDU Directory:
        /pub/usenet-by-group/alt.business.multi-level
```

➤ Tired of smuggling cigarettes and rum from tropical Caribbean locales? If you're looking for bigger (and more legal) fish to fry, the import-export business could be right up your alley. To find out, sneak into the newsgroup **alt.business.import-export** and see what you can bring back.

Conversing on Consumer Concerns

Thanks to the efforts of people like Ralph Nader, Phil Edmonston, and the staff of *Consumer Reports*, we consumers have more power than ever over where we choose to spend our hard-earned dollars.

Chapter 16 ➤ *Getting Advice in the Business and Consumer Newsgroups*

Thinking of forking out the bucks for a set of Ginsu knives or a Popiel Pocket Fisherman? Before you do, you might want to ask the folks who inhabit **misc.consumers** what they think. This group is designed to exchange info on any kind of consumer product: which brands are best buys; who gives good service; which products are unreliable, unsafe, or under investigation.

They don't call a house a "money pit" for nothing. If the mortgage payments don't get you, the repairs/upgrades/add-ons certainly will. If you're looking to at least reduce the size of the pit you're pouring your money into, I'd definitely recommend the newsgroup **misc.consumers.house**. This highly useful (and busy) group is loaded with tips for reducing household expenses, getting the best deals on repairs, advice for do-it-yourselfers, and lots more. And if you're just starting out, you'll find good info on financing, working with real estate agents, and choosing a home.

```
FAQ Info:
    Article:
        misc.consumers.house FAQ (frequently asked questions)
    RTFM.MIT.EDU Directory:
        /pub/usenet-by-group/misc.consumers.house
```

Not Just IRAs: Investment Advice

The most widely-read of the investment newsgroups is **misc.invest**. This group takes a general approach to personal investing, including interest vehicles, stocks, mutual funds, and more. If you're just getting started, this is the place to lurk or ask questions.

```
FAQ Info:
    Articles:
        misc.invest FAQ on general investment topics (part 1 of 6)
        misc.invest FAQ on general investment topics (part 2 of 6)
        misc.invest FAQ on general investment topics (part 3 of 6)
        misc.invest FAQ on general investment topics (part 4 of 6)
        misc.invest FAQ on general investment topics (part 5 of 6)
        misc.invest FAQ on general investment topics (part 6 of 6)
    RTFM.MIT.EDU Directory:
        /pub/usenet-by-group/misc.invest
```

Part 3 ➤ *All the News That's Fit to Surf*

If the stock market is your favorite way to lose money, check out **misc.invest.stocks**. Experienced bulls and bears give out stock tips, trade rumors about companies, and discuss their pet investment strategies.

By the way, if you're looking for cheap stock quotes, you can get free Dow Jones closing quotes (along with some pithy commentary) by gophering to **lobo.rmhs.colorado.edu**. Select **Other Information Services** from the top menu, then **Stock Market Closing Quotes**. You can also get free quotes on the World Wide Web from MIT's Experimental Stock Market Data site (shown in the following figure). Browse to **http://www.ai.mit.edu/stocks.html**. If you need prices for both stocks and futures, and don't mind paying for them, try QuoteCom on the WWW at **http://www.quote.com/**.

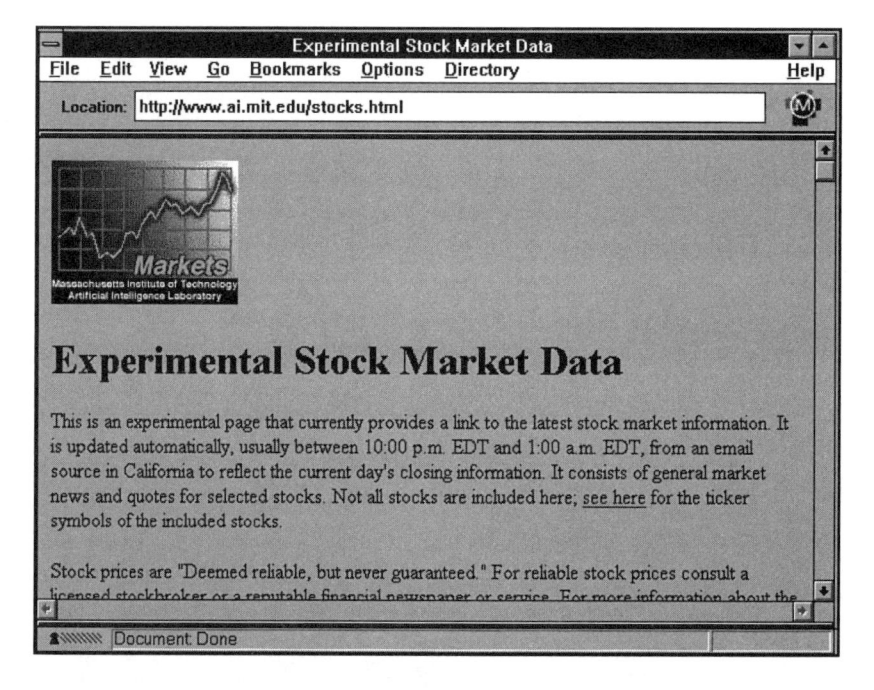

MIT's Experimental Stock Market Data Web page.

Chapter 16 ➤ *Getting Advice in the Business and Consumer Newsgroups*

For other kinds of investment advice, check out the following newsgroups:

➤ People with low risk thresholds have been flocking to the mutual fund market in recent years. What they usually find, however, is hundreds of different funds, each with its own peculiar mix of small cap, high cap, domestic, and foreign companies. How can a poor investor make sense of it all? A good place to start is the newsgroup **misc.invest.funds**. Experienced fund jockeys offer suggestions on which funds to buy, as well as strategies for building a well-rounded mutual fund portfolio.

➤ An old saw tells us that, since they're not making any more land, real estate values will always go up. Of course, the Reichmanns and Trumps of the world who got burned in the late-eighties real estate flameout would tell you that saw *is* a bit rusty. But if you haven't been scared off by investment opportunities in real estate, you can find prospective deals and some good advice in the group **misc.invest.real-estate**.

➤ Looking to turn a thousand dollars into a hundred thousand dollars just like a certain First Lady, but you can't tell a soybean from a pork belly? Before diving into the cutthroat world of futures trading, pay a visit to the pits at **misc.invest.futures**. You'll find Netizens who've survived the wars giving tips on current contracts, fundamentals, spreads, and other arcana of the futures market.

➤ Much of today's stock, options, and futures trading is based on obscenely complex mathematical models that rely on past patterns holding true in future dealings. This so-called *technical analysis* is the topic on everyone's mind in the newsgroup **misc.invest.technical**. You'll find lots of Type-A types holding intense discussions of the relative merits of Candlestick charts, stochastics, and RSI indices. Definitely not for the faint of heart or the mathematically challenged.

➤ Nobody likes to pay more taxes than they have to, but with tax forms getting ever more complicated, it's easy to miss out on crucial deductions and loopholes. To get help, subscribe to the newsgroup **misc.taxes**. You'll find lots of Q&A about personal tax stuff.

> Did you know that some of the world's most successful software shops come from Canada? Or that one of the biggest telecommunications companies on the planet is Canadian? The huge area north of the world's longest undefended border has more to offer than just Mounties, back bacon, and hockey. To learn about Canada's unique investment opportunities, hang out with the hosers in **misc.invest.canada**.

Checking Out the USENET Classifieds

USENET types certainly have lots to say, but it seems they have lots to sell, as well. There are dozens of groups devoted exclusively to buying and selling merchandise, memorabilia, collectibles, and old junk lying around the house.

> Finding the exact VCR you need is of no use if the current owner lives in Mauritius, or somewhere else equally inconvenient. For transactions a little closer to home, be sure to check your local hierarchies to see if they have any "forsale" groups. Toronto residents, for example, could browse the group **tor.forsale** for nearby bargains.

If you're looking to buy or sell something not related to computers, the place to be is the group **misc.forsale**. Here you'll find deals on sports equipment, electronics, videos, cars, houses, you name it. If you know what you want, but you don't see an ad for it in **misc.forsale**, post a request in **misc.wanted**.

USENET has over two dozen "forsale" groups that act as electronic yard sales for people peddling their possessions and browsing for bargains. Most of these groups deal only with computer-related items, especially for the Macintosh and IBM PC (including PC clones). To get in on the action, check out the various **misc.forsale.computers.*** newsgroups.

Job-Hunting on the Net

This section looks at several groups that feature want ads and job postings for computer professionals, sales and marketing positions, and even entry-level jobs:

> The group **misc.jobs.offered** contains ads for professional positions in programming, engineering, sales, and marketing. Most of the ads are posted by headhunters and executive-search firms.

FAQ Info:
> Article:
>> Welcome to misc.jobs! READ BEFORE POSTING
>
> RTFM.MIT.EDU Directory:
>> /pub/usenet-by-group/misc.jobs.offered

➤ If you're looking for a short-term or medium-term contract for programming, writing, and consulting, pore over the ads posted in **misc.jobs.contract**.

FAQ Info:
> Article:
>> Misc.jobs.contract: Frequently Asked Questions (FAQs)
>
> RTFM.MIT.EDU Directory:
>> /pub/usenet-by-group/misc.jobs.contract

➤ If you're just starting out in the workforce or in a particular field, try the newsgroup **misc.jobs.offered.entry**. You'll find ground-floor opportunities for things like sales reps, data entry clerks, part-time workers, and more.

FAQ Info:
> Article:
>> *** READ BEFORE POSTING: SPECIAL FAQ on using
>>   m.j.o.e***
>
> RTFM.MIT.EDU Directory:
>> /pub/usenet-by-group/misc.jobs.offered.entry

➤ Need tips on writing a résumé or cover letter? Feeling discouraged about the whole job-search thing? Then pay a visit to **misc.jobs.misc**. This group is the place to go to upgrade your job-hunting skills and pick up your spirits by communing with lots of other people who are in the same leaky boat.

➤ Once you've got a nice, shiny, impressive résumé, don't keep it to yourself; post it! Lots of personnel types, recruiters, and head-hunters scour **misc.jobs.resumes** looking for that perfect applicant. It might be you!

One final note: one of the Net's best sources for employment counseling and info is the Online Career Center (see the figure that follows). To check it out, gopher to **garnet.msen.com** (port 9062). This service has online books you can read, career assistance, a job-search section, a place to leave your résumé, and lots more.

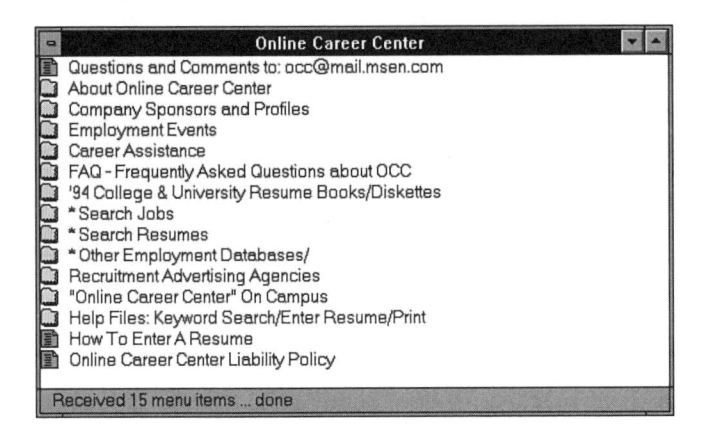

The main Gopher menu at the Online Career Center.

Chapter 17

From Antiques to Videos: The Hobby Newsgroups

> **In This Chapter**
> - Crafts, collectibles, and cooking newsgroups
> - Transportation groups
> - Audio and video groups
> - Pet groups, photography groups, and a whole lot more

What do you do during those leisure hours when you're not Net surfing or channel surfing? Well, if you're like many people, you probably have some kind of hobby. If so, whether it's collecting exotic stamps or traveling to exotic places, there's probably a newsgroup chock full of like-minded folk. This chapter presents a selection of USENET's extensive collection of hobby newsgroups.

Audio, Video, and Radio

Ever wonder what happened to that kid in class who always knew how to work the audio-visual equipment? Well, he (they were almost always guys) probably grew up to become an audiophile, video jockey, or ham radio operator. He also probably hangs out in the audio, video, or radio newsgroups that we'll look at in this section.

Big Audio Dynamite

The **rec** hierarchy has several newsgroups that cater to both the serious audiophile and regular Joes looking for the best deal in stereo equipment. Here's the rundown:

➤ When accessorizing your car, most of the available options really are optional: bucket seats, cruise control, fuzzy dice. But the one "option" that's an absolute must for the ultimate driving experience is a good sound system. To make sure you get the most awesome tunes for your vehicle, be sure to tune in to the newsgroup **rec.audio.car** for discussions of the best systems, do-it-yourself installations, and more.

```
FAQ Info:
    Articles: rec.audio.car FAQ (part 1/3)
              rec.audio.car FAQ (part 2/3)
              rec.audio.car FAQ (part 3/3)
    RTFM.MIT.EDU Directory: /pub/usenet-by-group/rec.audio.car
```

➤ If you're looking for advice on audio equipment, reviews of products, or technical help, check out both **rec.audio.opinion** and **rec.audio.tech**. These groups are populated with knowledgeable audio enthusiasts who seem only too happy to help out with troubleshooting, setup, and pre-purchase questions.

```
FAQ Info:
    Articles: FAQ: rec.audio.* (part 1 of 4)
              FAQ: rec.audio.* (part 2 of 4)
              FAQ: rec.audio.* (part 3 of 4)
              FAQ: rec.audio.* (part 4 of 4)
    RTFM.MIT.EDU Directory: /pub/usenet-by-group/rec.audio.tech
```

➤ If you're serious about your audio and don't want to waste time talking to the merely competent, then you'll enjoy the rarefied air of the group **rec.audio.high-end**. The denizens of this group only deal with either top-of-the-line equipment or homemade receivers and speakers.

➤ To round out our look at USENET audio, let's check out a few more groups. If you're looking to buy or sell audio equipment, pay a visit to **rec.audio.marketplace**. If you're a recording engineer or other audio professional, you'll find your peers in the group

Chapter 17 ➤ *From Antiques to Videos: The Hobby Newsgroups*

rec.audio.pro. Finally, if the groups I've mentioned don't quite fit your needs, you can always try the group **rec.audio.misc** as a last resort.

The USENET Village Vidiots

If video is your thing, whether it's just watching videos or actually making them, there's bound to be a newsgroup that suits your needs.

If you're looking to buy a new VCR or camcorder, or if you can't figure out your current machine (especially if your VCR sports that scarlet letter of the technically challenged: the flashing 12:00), program your newsreader to pick up the newsgroup **rec.video**. If you're a true vidiot and want to keep on top of all the latest releases, then the place to be is the group **rec.video.releases**. Finally, if you've pooh-poohed the whole VCR industry as archaic and obsolete, you must be a laserdisc aficionado. In that case, you can loiter with fellow laserdisc jockeys in the group **alt.video.laserdisc** to get the scoop on the latest machines and movie releases.

One of the most exciting new fields in the computer industry these days is desktop video production, where you actually edit and add special effects to videos right from your computer. In particular, *nonlinear* video editing lets you cut and paste video clips with the same ease that you now cut and paste text in your word processor. To keep abreast of happenings in this happening field, check out the group **rec.video.desktop**. If traditional video production is more your style, then you may prefer to read the newsgroup **rec.video.production**.

Finally, many TV junkies are too impatient to wait for the 500-channel universe that's allegedly on its way "real soon now." So, instead, they fork out the big bucks for a satellite dish so they can watch Brazilian sitcoms and Italian soap operas. If you've taken that particular plunge, here's a list of newsgroups you may find interesting:

rec.video.satellite	General confabs about satellites and dishes.
rec.video.satellite.dbs	Direct Broadcast Satellite (for example, DirecTV) discussions.
rec.video.satellite.misc	Q&A about other satellite systems.
rec.video.satellite.tvro	Talk about Television Receive Only systems.

Part 3 ➤ *All the News That's Fit to Surf*

```
FAQ Info:
    Article:  Satellite TV Frequently Asked Questions List
    RTFM.MIT.EDU Directory: /pub/usenet-by-group/rec.video.satellite
```

Amateur Radio Hamsters

Amateur radio buffs are among the most enthusiastic of hobbyists. They seem to love technology, too (not surprisingly), so there are many thriving amateur radio newsgroups on USENET.

> A number of documents of interest to amateur radio enthusiasts are available via anonymous FTP at **ftp.cs.tamu.edu**. Look in the directory **/pub/hamradio**. You can also gopher the documents by tunneling to **gopher.cs.tamu.edu**, selecting **Access to TAMU CS Anonymous FTP Files** from the main menu, and then choosing **hamradio**.

You should start your USENET ham radio tour in the newsgroup **rec.radio.info**. This group contains many periodic postings that include FAQ lists, daily solar and geophysical reports, information sources, and other articles that only an amateur radio addict could love.

```
FAQ Info:
    Articles: Amateur Radio: Elmers Resource Directory [A-M]
       Amateur Radio: Elmers Resource Directory [N-Z]
       FCC License Data Sources
       Internet Guide to International Broadcasters
       IPS Daily Report
       Welcome to rec.radio.info!
    RTFM.MIT.EDU Directory: /pub/usenet-by-group/rec.radio.info
```

Most of the amateur radio action occurs in the newsgroup **rec.radio.amateur.misc**. You'll find lots of periodic postings, as well as articles about equipment, dealing with the FCC, and helpful advice for those just getting started.

204

FAQ Info:
```
Articles: rec.amateur.radio.misc Frequently Asked Questions (Part 1 of 3)
          rec.amateur.radio.misc Frequently Asked Questions (Part 2 of 3)
          rec.amateur.radio.misc Frequently Asked Questions (Part 3 of 3)
RTFM.MIT.EDU Directory: /pub/usenet-by-group/rec.radio.amateur.misc
```

There's even a CB group, good buddy! You can find tips and old war stories about "bears in the air" in the newsgroup **rec.radio.cb**.

FAQ Info:
```
Articles: rec.radio.cb Frequently Asked Questions (Part 1 of 4)
          rec.radio.cb Frequently Asked Questions (Part 2 of 4)
          rec.radio.cb Frequently Asked Questions (Part 3 of 4)
          rec.radio.cb Frequently Asked Questions (Part 4 of 4)
RTFM.MIT.EDU Directory: /pub/usenet-by-group/rec.radio.cb
```

If shortwave radio is your thing, you'll want to dial in to the group **rec.radio.shortwave**. You'll find articles about shortwave gear, shortwave broadcasts, and more.

FAQ Info:
```
Articles: Handy Shortwave Chart
          Welcome to rec.radio.shortwave
RTFM.MIT.EDU Directory: /pub/usenet-by-group/rec.radio.shortwave
```

Scanner radio enthusiasts get quite a kick out of listening in to police, fire, and airline frequencies. For info about this popular hobby, the correct USENET frequency is **rec.radio.scanner**.

FAQ Info:
```
Articles: Buying a Used Scanner Radio
          How to Find Scanner Frequencies
          Introduction to Scanning
RTFM.MIT.EDU Directory: /pub/usenet-by-group/rec.radio.scanning
```

Conversing with Collectors

What is it with this mania that homo sapiens have for collecting stuff? Stamps, coins, cards, matchbooks, spoons, kitschy Elvis memorabilia. You name it, someone collects it. USENET, too, has its own collection of collectibles newsgroups, which we'll mount for display in this section.

As you'll soon see, there are newsgroups covering antiques, trading cards, sports merchandise, coins, and stamps. For all other collectibles, the place to be is the newsgroup **rec.collecting**. This group conducts online auctions (where potential buyers post bids for specific items), and offers lots of collecting info and opportunities to buy and sell just about any kind of collectible under the sun.

Antiques

One person's old piece of junk is often another person's precious work of art. If you believe that older is better, you'll probably enjoy the newsgroup **rec.antiques**. The people who participate in this group just love to discuss *fin-de-siéle* furniture, paintings, and anything else that's used but not used up. You'll also find lots of advice on restoring antiques to their original luster.

If your tastes run more toward ancient radios, telephones, and phonographic equipment, then you'll want to pay a visit to the group **rec.antiques.radio+phono**.

Trading Cards

There's plenty of action in trading card collecting, as you can see in this list of newsgroups devoted to card collectibles:

rec.collecting.cards	Cards of all kinds.
rec.collecting.cards.discuss	Discussions about trading card collectibles.
rec.collecting.cards.non-sports	Cards with non-sport motifs (movies, comics, serial killers).
rec.collecting.sport.baseball	Baseball cards.
rec.collecting.sport.basketball	Basketball cards.
rec.collecting.sport.football	Football cards.
rec.collecting.sport.hockey	Hockey cards.

Coins

Coins are one of the most popular of all collectibles. If you're looking to hang out with your fellow numismatists, sign up for the newsgroup **rec.collecting.coins**.

Stamps

Stamp collectors have a vocabulary all their own. If you know the difference between hinged and unhinged stamps (or would like to), you should subscribe to **rec.collecting.stamps** and see what all the philatelic fun is about.

An Online Banquet: Food and Cooking Newsgroups

Humans truly seem to enjoy talking about the things they love. Food is no exception, as writers from Epicurus to Margaret Visser have shown. So, of course, USENET has a number of groups that cater (sorry about that) to our desire to talk about food and drink:

➤ Looking for a good seafood restaurant in a city you'll be visiting in the near future? Then just post a question in the newsgroup **rec.food.restaurants**. Some kind gourmand from the city in question will probably be able to recommend someplace nice.

➤ If you're interested in old-style recipes from days gone by, or if you're wondering about, say, the history of the tamale, then you should check out the group **rec.food.historic**.

➤ The Net's vegetarian community hangs out in the group **rec.food.veg**. You'll find lots of discussion (mostly pro, but some con) about the vegetarian lifestyle, some recipes, cooking techniques, and sources of vegetarian info (such as books to read).

> **FAQ Info:**
> Articles: rec.food.veg Frequently Asked Questions LIST (FAQ)
> rec.food.veg World Guide to Vegetarianism - *
> RTFM.MIT.EDU Directory: /pub/usenet-by-group/rec.food.veg

A Round of Drink Newsgroups

Food is only half of the gustatory equation. The other half, of course, are the drinks we use to wash everything down (or imbibe by themselves). Here's a list of USENET's drink-related newsgroups:

rec.food.drink	Discussions of favorite wines, teas, and other beverages.
rec.food.drink.coffee	Everybody's favorite caffeine fix.
rec.food.drink.beer	Debates about the best beer—which, as everyone knows, comes from Canada ;-).
alt.beer	More wobbly pop palavering.
alt.food.cocacola	Do things really go better with Coke?
rec.crafts.brewing	How to brew your own brew.
alt.food.wine	In vino veritas.
rec.crafts.winemaking	Expert grape-stomping techniques.

More Food Topics to Chew On

The **alt** hierarchy has a few newsgroups that celebrate particular foods. Here's a rundown of the more popular ones:

alt.food.chocolate	Delicious, decadent, zit-creating.
alt.food.fat-free	The bland eating the bland.
alt.food.ice-cream	I scream, you scream, we all scream for ice cream!
alt.food.mcdonalds	Would you like fries with that?
alt.food.sushi	A Net joke: If IBM invented sushi, they'd market it as "raw, dead fish."

A Pinch of Cooking Groups

Eating food is a guaranteed good time, but some of us enjoy cooking food almost as much. This section looks at a few newsgroups that specialize in recipes and cooking techniques.

Chapter 17 ➤ *From Antiques to Videos: The Hobby Newsgroups*

In addition to the newsgroups, you also might want to check out the searchable database of recipes on the Net. Using your WAIS software, search the database **RECIPES.SRC**. If you're more a Web wanderer, head for the Einet Galaxy site at **http://www.einet.net/**. Find the **Leisure and Recreation** section and click on the **Recipes** link. The Recipes page has extensive recipe collections from around the world (including—yuck!—insect recipes).

➤ One of the most popular groups in all of USENET is **rec.food.cooking**. Every day, hundreds of articles pour in with favorite family recipes, cooking tips and techniques, food facts, and equipment recommendations. It's a great newsgroup for chefs of all persuasions.

```
FAQ Info:
    Articles: rec.food.cooking Commonly Discussed Topics
              rec.food.cooking FAQ and conversation file
    RTFM.MIT.EDU Directory: /pub/usenet-by-group/rec.food.cooking
```

➤ If all you're looking for is a new recipe for tonight's feast, then try **rec.food.recipes**. This is a moderated, recipes-only group, which cuts down on the noise and makes it easier to find what you want. You can also send requests for recipes to this group.

```
FAQ Info:
    Article:  ADMINISTRIVIA: Posting Guidelines
    RTFM.MIT.EDU Directory: /pub/usenet-by-group/rec.food.recipes
```

➤ Looking for a new way to prepare bean sprouts and rice? Then check out **rec.food.veg.cooking**, the newsgroup devoted exclusively to vegetarian recipes.

Chatting in the Crafts Groups

While the rest of us are idly surfing the Net or vegetating in front of our TVs, millions of skillful hands are working to create beautiful examples of modern folk art. This section looks at the various newsgroups devoted to crafts and the artisans who practice them.

➤ Many people have discovered that you can make jewelry as good as what you see in fancy-schmancy jewelry stores, but for a fraction of the price. To find out how, read the articles in

rec.crafts.jewelry. If you lack the talent or the inclination for such pursuits, this group is also the place to go for advice on buying jewelry.

➤ If you work with metals, whether as a blacksmith, silversmith, welder, or whatever, check out **rec.crafts.metalworking**. You'll find lots of advice on techniques and equipment.

➤ Working with textiles—be it sewing, needlepoint, or quilting—is one of the most popular categories of crafts. Check out **rec.crafts.textiles** for general discussions and some periodic postings (including FAQs). Cross-stitching is covered in **rec.crafts.textiles.needlework**. If you're a quilter, take a look at **rec.crafts.textiles.quilting** or **rec.crafts.quilting**. You can get (or give) general advice on sewing in **rec.crafts.textiles.sewing** and **alt.sewing**. If you like to knit (or purl), **rec.crafts.textiles.yarn** is the newsgroup for you.

```
FAQ Info:
    Articles: Textile Related Books FAQ: Part 1 of 2
              Textile Related Books FAQ: Part 2 of 2
              Textiles FAQ
    RTFM.MIT.EDU Directory: /pub/usenet-by-group/rec.crafts.textiles
```

Parleying in the Pet Newsgroups

USENET, as you'll see in a sec, has dedicated pet newsgroups for birds, cats, dogs, fish, and even reptiles and snakes. If your pet doesn't fall into one of these categories, then the place to go is the group **rec.pets**. Here you'll find advice on the care and feeding of ferrets, hamsters, rabbits, even the odd hedgehog.

```
FAQ Info:
    Articles:  rec.pets.*: Fleas, Ticks, and Your Pet FAQ
               rec.pets.*: Grief and Pet Loss FAQ
    RTFM.MIT.EDU Directory: /pub/usenet-by-group/rec.pets
```

Avian Avocations: The Bird Newsgroups

If you have a bird as a pet, you can flock with your fellow bird owners in **rec.pets.birds**. This active group provides lots of tips on bird care, info on the various bird varieties, and much more.

Chapter 17 ➤ *From Antiques to Videos: The Hobby Newsgroups*

```
FAQ Info:
   Articles: rec.pets.birds FAQ: (1/3) Monthly Posting
             rec.pets.birds FAQ: (2/3) Monthly Posting
             rec.pets.birds FAQ: (3/3) Monthly Posting
   RTFM.MIT.EDU Directory: /pub/usenet-by-group/rec.pets.birds
```

If you're more into watching birds than owning them, you can compare life lists with your fellow birders in the newsgroup **rec.birds**.

```
FAQ Info:
   Articles: rec.birds Frequently Asked Questions (FAQ) (Part 1/2)
             rec.birds Frequently Asked Questions (FAQ) (Part 2/2)
             rec.birds Monthly Optics for Birding FAQ
   RTFM.MIT.EDU Directory: /pub/usenet-by-group/rec.birds
```

A Feline Forum: The Cat Newsgroup

One of the most active newsgroups in all of USENET is **rec.pets.cats**. This group is loaded with dedicated cat fanciers of all persuasions. You'll find hundreds of useful posts that cover the basics of care and feeding, dealing with behavioral crises, medical advice, and suggestions for appropriate cat toys.

```
FAQ Info:
   Articles: rec.pets.cats: Basic Health Care FAQ
             rec.pets.cats: Cats and the Outside World FAQ
             rec.pets.cats: General Cat Care FAQ
             rec.pets.cats: Medical Information FAQ
             rec.pets.cats: Miscellaneous Information FAQ
             rec.pets.cats: Problem Behaviours in Cats FAQ
             rec.pets.cats: Resources FAQ
   RTFM.MIT.EDU Directory: /pub/usenet-by-group/rec.pets.cats
```

Bow-Wow Powwows: The Dog Newsgroups

Until recently, there was only one group for articles on man's (and woman's) best friend: **rec.pets.dogs**. This group was (and still is) extremely popular, and each day brought hundreds of articles on dog breeds, care and feeding, training advice, and lots more. This group was so popular that the participants decided to break it up into smaller, more specific newsgroups. Sure, much of the action still happens in

Part 3 ➤ *All the News That's Fit to Surf*

rec.pets.dogs, but the subgroups will be used more often as people get used to the new setup. Here's a summary of the new **rec.pets.dogs.*** groups:

rec.pets.dogs.activities	Basic training, dog shows, agility work, tracking, and other doggy fun.
rec.pets.dogs.behaviour	Correcting canine misdemeanors.
rec.pets.dogs.breeds	Breed basics and advice.
rec.pets.dogs.health	Medical miracles for mutts, mongrels, and more.
rec.pets.dogs.info	Dog info, lists, and FAQs—lots of FAQs.
rec.pets.dogs.misc	Miscellaneous dog doo-doo.
rec.pets.dogs.rescue	Training dogs for rescue work.

```
FAQ Info:
   Article:   rec.pets.dogs: Behavior: Understanding and Modifying FAQ
              rec.pets.dogs: Canine Activities: Flyball FAQ
              rec.pets.dogs: Complete List of Dog-Related Email Lists
              rec.pets.dogs: Complete List of Dog-Related Web Sites
              rec.pets.dogs: Getting a Dog FAQ
              rec.pets.dogs: Introduction FAQ
              rec.pets.dogs: Your New Dog FAQ
              rec.pets.dogs: Your New Puppy FAQ
   RTFM.MIT.EDU Directory: /pub/usenet-by-group/rec.pets.dogs
```

Transportation Tête-à-Têtes

People gotta move, as the song says, and the proof is the large number of newsgroups related to transportation topics. This section looks at the groups that deal with aviation, boating, and cars.

Earning Your Wings in the Aviation Newsgroups

Pilots and pilot wannabes will enjoy the dozen or so newsgroups devoted to aviation. You'll find discussions on everything from antique planes to modern fighter jets and from piloting instructions to advice for students. Here's the list:

Chapter 17 ➤ *From Antiques to Videos: The Hobby Newsgroups*

rec.aviation.answers	FAQ lists and periodic postings.
rec.aviation.homebuilt	Advice on plane DIY projects.
rec.aviation.ifr	Tips and advice on preparing for an IFR (Instrument Flight Rules) examination.
rec.aviation.military	Military aircraft, from Stuka to Stealth.
rec.aviation.misc	Blimps, commercial airlines, crashes, and whatever else doesn't fit in the other groups.
rec.aviation.owning	The ups and downs of owning a plane.
rec.aviation.piloting	Advice from pilots, for pilots.
rec.aviation.products	Reviews and opinions about plane gear.
rec.aviation.simulators	Flight Simulator and other computer flight simulation software.
rec.aviation.soaring	The gliders and hang-gliders group.
rec.aviation.student	Tips and advice for student pilots.
rec.aviation.ultralight	Heavyweight discussions of ultralight planes.

```
FAQ Info:
   Articles: Netiquette on rec.aviation (regular posting)
             rec.aviation FAQ
   RTFM.MIT.EDU Directory:
         /pub/usenet-by-group/rec.aviation.answers/aviation
```

Becoming Seaworthy in the Boat Newsgroups

If you're a boating buff—whether you travel the waters under your own steam, with sails unfurled, or with a fat Johnson outboard—you'll like the cut of the following newsgroups' jibs:

rec.boats	Catch-all group for those into sailing and power boating.
rec.boats.building	I's the b'y that builds the boat…

213

> **Part 3** ➤ *All the News That's Fit to Surf*

rec.boats.paddle	Conversations with canoe and kayak connoisseurs.
rec.boats.racing	Sailing for sport.

```
FAQ Info:
   Articles: rec.boats Frequently Asked Questions (Part 1 of 5)
             rec.boats Frequently Asked Questions (Part 2 of 5)
             rec.boats Frequently Asked Questions (Part 3 of 5)
             rec.boats Frequently Asked Questions (Part 4 of 5)
             rec.boats Frequently Asked Questions (Part 5 of 5)
   RTFM.MIT.EDU Directory: /pub/usenet-by-group/rec.boats
```

Traveling the Infobahn in the Car Newsgroups

North America's unending love affair with the car is evident from the popularity of the various newsgroups that exist for automobile nuts. Here's a compendium:

alt.autos.camaro.firebird	Z-28 and Trans-Am enthusiasts reminisce about the good old days.
rec.autos.antique	Vintage automobile aficionados.
alt.autos.antique	More of the same.
rec.autos.driving	Driving tips and complaints about bad drivers.
rec.autos.makers.chrysler	The Mopar fan club.
rec.autos.makers.saturn	A different kind of newsgroup?
rec.autos.marketplace	Buying and selling lemons.
rec.autos.misc	Miscellaneous car conversations (parts, repair questions, and so on).
rec.autos.rod-n-custom	Hot rods, custom cars, and other sublimations.
alt.autos.rod-n-custom	Me too!
rec.autos.simulators	Computer car simulation software.
rec.autos.tech	The science of cars.
rec.autos.vw	Beetles and other people wagons.

Chapter 17 ➤ *From Antiques to Videos: The Hobby Newsgroups*

Car enthusiasts will also want to check out the online magazine *AutoPages of the Internet.* This World Wide Web site is ostensibly for car dealers and those looking to buy a car, but anyone can enjoy the great pictures and info. Set your browser to the following URL:

http://www.clark.net/pub/networx/autopage/autopage.html

A Hodgepodge of Hobbies

We've covered most of the major hobbies so far in this chapter, but our tour has been by no means comprehensive. So, just to add a bit of an exclamation point to things, here's a list of a few miscellaneous hobby groups that might appeal to you:

rec.arts.bonsai	Shaping trees in your own image.
rec.gardens	A grab-bag of gardening goodies.
rec.gardens.orchids	Orchid fanciers trade secrets.
rec.gardens.roses	A newsgroup by any other name…
rec.folk-dancing	Clogging, polkas, and other quaint dance steps.
rec.gambling	Odds and sods about wagering.
alt.genealogy	Rooting around in your roots.
rec.heraldry	The pomp and circumstance surrounding armorial trappings.
rec.juggling	Bring out the chainsaws and flaming torches!
rec.kites	How to get legally strung out.
rec.models.railroad	Model railroad enthusiasts.
rec.models.rc	Radio-controlled cars, planes, boats.
rec.models.rockets	Do-it-yourself rocket science.
rec.models.scale	Building scale models of ships, vehicles, and planes.
rec.photo.advanced	For the photo cognoscenti only.
rec.photo.darkroom	Photographic darkroom techniques.

215

rec.photo.help	Q&A about photography.
rec.photo.marketplace	Buying and selling photographic equipment.
rec.photo.misc	Miscellaneous photo stuff.
rec.puzzles	Logic puzzles, math conundrums, and such. Sharpen your brain before entering.
rec.puzzles.crosswords	Mostly the cryptic-style crosswords that make my head hurt.
alt.anagrams	If USENET is making U tense, exercise your mind with a few anagrams.

Chapter 18

Newsgroups for the Games People Play

In This Chapter
- ➤ Computer game newsgroups
- ➤ Groups dedicated to multi-user dungeons (MUDs)
- ➤ Fantasy and role-playing game groups
- ➤ Newsgroups for video and arcade games
- ➤ Game groups galore

If you're like many Netizens, after you've mailed your e-mail, FTPed your files, waded through the Web pages, and surfed the serious Netnews, you like to reward yourself with a few rounds of your favorite game. What do you do, though, if you have a question about a particular game, or if you just feel like communing with other game groupies? Why, you head for USENET, of course. This chapter tells all.

Computer Games

We'll begin our tour of the game newsgroups with a look at the groups dedicated to computer games for the PC, Amiga, Macintosh, and other systems.

Playing on the PC

USENET has no less than nine newsgroups devoted to PC games (not including the groups that cover specific games such as *DOOM* and *Ultima*). Most of these groups offer game hints, cheat sheets, Q&A about technical problems, arguments about the best games, and lots of game gushing and giggling. Here's the list:

comp.sys.ibm.pc.games.action	Arcade-style games such as *Wolfenstein 3-D* and *Tie Fighter*.
comp.sys.ibm.pc.games.adventure	Adventure games such as *King's Quest* and *Myst*.
comp.sys.ibm.pc.games.announce	FAQs and announcements about new games (moderated).
comp.sys.ibm.pc.games.flight-sim	Flight simulator games.
comp.sys.ibm.pc.games.marketplace	Buying, selling, and trading games.
comp.sys.ibm.pc.games.misc	Miscellaneous games not covered by the other PC groups.
comp.sys.ibm.pc.games.rpg	Role-playing games such as *Dark Sun*, *Star Trail*, and *Xeen*.
comp.sys.ibm.pc.games.strategic	Strategy/planning games such as *Galactic Civilization* and *SimCity*.
comp.sys.ibm.pc.soundcard.games	Help using sound cards with games.

```
FAQ Info:
    Articles: PC GAMES FAQ <- Guide to the Gaming World (Part 1 of 2)
              PC GAMES FAQ <- Guide to the Gaming World (Part 2 of 2)
                *** NET PC GAMES TOP 100 * DOCUMENT ***
    RTFM.MIT.EDU Directory:
       /pub/usenet-by-group/comp.answers/PC-games-faq
```

Chapter 18 ➤ *Newsgroups for the Games People Play*

Playing on Other Systems

MS-DOS and Windows PCs are not, of course, the only game machines in town. There are plenty of leisure programs available for the Amiga, Macintosh, and OS/2 systems.

If the Amiga is your machine of choice, try the newsgroup **comp.sys.amiga.games** for announcements, game hints, and tech help.

You can join other Mac game mavens in **comp.sys.mac.games**. Be forewarned, however, this is one of the most popular groups on USENET.

FAQ Info:
```
Article:  comp.sys.mac.games FAQ
RTFM.MIT.EDU Directory: /pub/usenet-by-group/comp.sys.mac.games
```

If you're looking for info on OS/2 games, or if you have a question about making game hardware (such as a sound card) work with OS/2, check out the newsgroup **comp.os.os2.games**.

Death and Destruction with DOOM

If you count yourself among *DOOM*'s rabid followers, you'll want to check out the various newsgroups that cater to *DOOM* devotees:

rec.games.computer.doom.announce	Announcements about *DOOM* stuff (moderated).
rec.games.computer.doom.help	Q&A about getting *DOOM* up and running, getting to new levels, and so on.
rec.games.computer.doom.misc	Miscellaneous *DOOM* and gloom.
rec.games.computer.doom.editing	Creating new *DOOM* landscapes and scenarios.
rec.games.computer.doom.playing	Strategies for more efficient alien-wasting.
alt.binaries.doom	*DOOM* files and add-ons.

DOOM diehards will want to check out the *DOOM* World Wide Web site at the following location:

```
http://www.cs.indiana.edu/games/doom/doom-home.html
```

This site gives you a brief history of *DOOM*, tells you where to get the program and add-ons, how to play over a network, and lots more.

Multi-Player Games

One of the most popular game categories on the Internet is the multi-player genre. In these games, two or more players participate at the same time, usually competitively, but occasionally cooperatively. This section looks at the USENET newsgroups devoted to multi-player games.

➤ *Air Warrior* is a World War II flight simulation game. You can get *Air Warrior* tips and info from your fellow flyboys and flygirls in the group **alt.games.air-warrior**.

➤ When Macintosh users need to relax, one of the networked games they turn to most often is *Bolo*. This is a strategy war game where you, the allies playing with you, and the enemies playing against you, all control tanks. You can get *Bolo* hints and help in the group **rec.games.bolo**.

```
FAQ Info:
   Articles: FAQ: rec.games.bolo (1/2)
             FAQ: rec.games.bolo (2/2)
   RTFM.MIT.EDU Directory: /pub/usenet-by-group/rec.games.bolo
```

➤ *Diplomacy* is one of the Net's many "play-by-mail" games. Based on the original board game, *Diplomacy* players perform geo-political machinations from the pre-World War I era. The Net version of *Diplomacy* progresses through deals and alliances struck via e-mail messages. Fans of the game, and those with questions about rules and strategies, congregate in the newsgroup **rec.games.diplomacy**.

```
FAQ Info:
   Articles: rec.games.diplomacy FAQ (1/2)
             rec.games.diplomacy FAQ (2/2)
   RTFM.MIT.EDU Directory: /pub/usenet-by-group/rec.games.diplomacy
```

Chapter 18 ➤ *Newsgroups for the Games People Play*

➤ *Empire* is like a cross between *SimCity* and *Diplomacy*. You're the leader of a nation, and you have to build your empire by designating hexagonal squares to produce raw materials and thereby create durable goods. Game tips and strategies from fellow empire builders can be found in the newsgroup **rec.games.empire**.

>   **FAQ Info:**
>   Article: rec.games.empire FAQ
>   RTFM.MIT.EDU Directory: /pub/usenet-by-group/rec.games.empire

➤ In the game *BattleTech*, huge mechanical robots battle each other in the 31st century. These battles can attract dozens of players and, once the smoke clears, many of them meet in the newsgroup **rec.games.mecha** to rehash the main events.

➤ *Netrek* is one of the oldest of the multi-player games. Based on the original *Star Trek* series, *Netrek* players divide into teams of eight or less and try to blow each other out of space and conquer the other team's planet. You can chat with other *Netrek* nabobs in the group **rec.games.netrek**.

>   **FAQ Info:**
>   Article: rec.games.netrek FAQ List
>   RTFM.MIT.EDU Directory: /pub/usenet-by-group/rec.games.netrek

➤ *VGA Planets* is another play-by-mail game. In this case, the clashes occur in space as you and 10 other players vie for supremacy. You'll find mid-battle discussions going on in the group **alt.games.vga-planets**.

A *MUD* (*multi-user dungeon* or, sometimes, *multi-user dimension*) is a game that creates a virtual world in which you can move around and explore. Each player controls a specific character and interacts (read: has fights) with characters controlled by other players. There are lots of MUD variations with names like DikuMUD, LPMUD, and the non-violent Tiny MUDs (such as MUSH, MUSE, MUCK, and MOO). Here's a list of the USENET groups where you can interact with your fellow MUDheads:

rec.games.mud.admin	For MUD administrators and programmers.
rec.games.mud.announce	MUD notices and FAQs (moderated).

rec.games.mud.diku	The ins and outs of DikuMUDs.
rec.games.mud.lp	LPMUD discussions.
rec.games.mud.misc	MUD miscellany.
rec.games.mud.tiny	Tiny MUD topics.

```
FAQ Info:
   Articles: [rec.games.mud]: FAQ #1/3: MUDs and MUDding
             [rec.games.mud]: FAQ #2/3: MUD Clients and Servers
             [rec.games.mud]: FAQ #3/3: RWHO and mudwho
   RTFM.MIT.EDU Directory:
      /pub/usenet-by-group rec.games.mud.announce
```

Fantasy and Role-Playing Games

Many people get their kicks by entering fantasy worlds populated by dwarfs, sorcerers, and monsters of various sizes and killing abilities. These *fantasy and role-playing (FRP)* games can be extremely realistic, and players have been known to spend days, even weeks, exploring nooks and crannies, searching for treasure, and, of course, battling the creatures who inhabit these worlds. This section does some exploring of its own by looking at the extensive collection of FRP game groups on USENET.

Groups for Specific FRP Games

Most FRP games are offshoots and rip-offs of either the original *Dungeons and Dragons* game or the game *Rogue* (whose descendants are called "roguelike" games).

For announcements about roguelike games and events, keep an eye on the moderated group **rec.games.roguelike.announce**. For FAQs and info on other roguelike games, enter the newsgroup **rec.games.roguelike.misc**.

```
FAQ Info:
   Article:  Roguelike Games Info and FTP Sites (FAQ)
   RTFM.MIT.EDU Directory:
      /pub/usenet-by-group/rec.games.roguelike.misc
```

Here's a rundown of the newsgroups that cater to specific games:

rec.games.frp.dnd	*Dungeons and Dragons*: for diehards only.
alt.games.frp.dnd-util	*Dungeons and Dragons*: computer utilities.
rec.games.roguelike.angband	*Angband*: FRP with a distinctly Tolkien feel.
rec.games.roguelike.moria	*Moria*: anyone up for a battle with the Balrog?
rec.games.roguelike.nethack	*Nethack*: meandering in the Mazes of Menace.
rec.games.roguelike.rogue	*Rogue*: gone (almost), but not forgotten.
alt.games.torg	*Torg*: find out what's happening in the Infiniverse.

General FRP Stuff

No matter which game (or games) they play, FRP fiends are a passionate community. When they're not hanging out in the game-specific groups, you'll usually find them in one of the following FRP newsgroups:

rec.games.frp.advocacy	Which-game-is-best arguments and previews of new games.
rec.games.frp.announce	Announcements of happenings in the FRP world (moderated).
rec.games.frp.archives	Archivable stories, lists, and resources (moderated).
rec.games.frp.cyber	Discussion of cyberpunk-related FRP games.
rec.games.frp.live-action	Live-action FRP games.
rec.games.frp.marketplace	FRP game materials wanted and for sale.

rec.games.frp.misc   General discussion of FRP
                          games.

alt.games.whitewolf   Discussion of WhiteWolf's
                          line of gothic/horror FRP
                          games.

> **FAQ Info:**
>   Articles: [rec.games.frp.*]: Frequently Asked Questions Part 1
>   [rec.games.frp.*]: Frequently Asked Questions Part 2
>   [rec.games.frp.*]: Welcome to the roleplaying
>   discussion groups!
>   RTFM.MIT.EDU Directory:
>   /pub/usenet-by-group/rec.games.frp.announce

Board Games

This section looks at the USENET newsgroups that cater to the Net's board game buffs. If your favorite board game doesn't have its own group (see following list), you can use the newsgroup **rec.games.board** to get hints and info from fellow gamesters.

> **FAQ Info:**
>   Articles: Scrabble FAQ - Club and Tournament Supplement
>   Scrabble FAQ - General Information
>   rec.games.board FAQ and intro
>   RTFM.MIT.EDU Directory: /pub/usenet-by-group/rec.games.board

Here's a sampling of the board game newsgroups:

➤ If you're addicted to backgammon, be sure to subscribe to the newsgroup **rec.games.backgammon**. You'll find game strategies, tournament announcements, and locations of Net sites with more backgammon info and computer backgammon games.

> **FAQ Info:**
>   Article: Backgammon — Frequently Asked Questions. (monthly)
>   RTFM.MIT.EDU Directory:
>   /pub/usenet-by-group/rec.games.backgammon

➤ If you prefer the challenge of Chinese chess (xiangqi), you'll find hints, strategies, and info in the group **rec.games.chinese-chess**.

Chapter 18 ➤ *Newsgroups for the Games People Play*

```
FAQ Info:
   Article: rec.games.chinese-chess FAQ
   RTFM.MIT.EDU Directory:
      /pub/usenet-by-group/rec.games.chinese-chess
```

➤ Go is one of the oldest board games, but it's probably more popular today than ever. Whether you're a nine-dan master studying the game's subtleties, or a rookie trying to understand basic strategies and moves, be sure to check out the group **rec.games.go**.

```
FAQ Info:
   Article: The Game Go-Frequently Asked Questions
   RTFM.MIT.EDU Directory: /pub/usenet-by-group/rec.games.go
```

➤ If chess is your board game of choice, you'll definitely want to move to the newsgroup **rec.games.chess**. This busy site offers lots of chess strategies, chess news from around the world, and reviews/opinions/complaints about the multitude of computer chess programs available.

```
FAQ Info:
   Articles:
      rec.games.chess Answers to Frequently Asked Questions (1/2)
      rec.games.chess Answers to Frequently Asked Questions (2/2)
   RTFM.MIT.EDU Directory: /pub/usenet-by-group/rec.games.chess
```

The Internet Chess Server lets you play real-time chess with actual flesh-and-blood opponents. To check it out, telnet to **ics.uoknor.edu 5000** and login with your name or some snappy chess handle. Graphical interfaces for the Internet Chess Server are available from the Internet Chess Library. FTP anonymously to **chess.uoknor.edu** and look in the directory **/pub/chess**. You can also get there via the World Wide Web by browsing the following location:

```
http://caissa.onenet.net/chess/HTML/homepage.html
```

Video and Arcade Games

With the power of the new systems rising and their prices falling, it seems *everyone* plays video games. So it will come as no surprise that USENET has a thriving collection of groups devoted to video game topics. This section plugs you in.

225

Specific Systems

Here's the scoop on the newsgroups that deal with specific game systems or companies:

rec.games.video.3do	See what all the 3DO hype is about.
rec.games.video.atari	Atari systems, including the 2600 and Jaguar.
alt.games.lynx	The Atari Lynx system.
rec.games.video.cd32	Amiga CD32 game info and tips.
rec.games.video.nintendo	Talk about systems from NES to Project Reality, and much Sega-bashing.
rec.games.video.sega	Talk about systems from Genesis to Saturn, and much Nintendo-bashing.

Arcade Games

The arcade spirit lives on in the following newsgroups:

rec.games.video.arcade	High-volume group specializing in arcade arcana.
rec.games.video.arcade.collecting	Arcade game auctions, buying, selling, and repairs.
rec.games.pinball	Pinball wizards bounce around ideas and favorite machines.
alt.games.sf2	Discussions about *Street Fighter 2*.

FAQ Info:
```
    Articles: general pinball Frequently Asked Questions
              monthly rec.games.pinball FAQ, one of two
              monthly rec.games.pinball FAQ, two of two
    RTFM.MIT.EDU Directory: /pub/usenet-by-group/rec.games.pinball
```

Play-by-Mail Games

Earlier in this chapter, I told you about *Diplomacy* and *VGA Planets*, two of the Net's *play-by-mail (PBM)* games. There are, in fact, dozens of games you can play via e-mail, with more being added all the time. PBMers congregate in the newsgroup **rec.games.pbm** to talk about the games, announce new ones, and ask questions.

> **FAQ Info:**
> Article: rec.games.pbm Frequently Asked Questions (FAQ) List
> RTFM.MIT.EDU Directory: /pub/usenet-by-group/rec.games.pbm

If you're interested in the rapidly growing play-by-mail movement, be sure to check out the World Wide Web's *Play by Mail (PBM) Games Homepage* at the following location:

> http://fermi.clas.virginia.edu/~gl8f/pbm.html

A Grab Bag of Game Groups

This section presents a regular motley crew of groups with game themes that didn't fit into any of the other categories. Have fun!

➤ If you have a question that just doesn't seem to fit anywhere else, give the group **rec.games.misc** a try.

➤ If games of pure strategy and logic turn your crank, you'll find info about them in the group **rec.games.abstract**.

➤ If you're one of the bridge cognoscenti, or would like to be, then subscribing to the newsgroup **rec.games.bridge** is a must.

> **FAQ Info:**
> Article: rec.games.bridge style guide
> RTFM.MIT.EDU Directory: /pub/usenet-by-group/rec.games.bridge

➤ If a good time for you is a rousing game of *Trivial Pursuit*, you'll feel right at home in **rec.games.trivia**. Posters try to stump each other with questions, and there's usually a quiz in progress in which you can match memories with other Netizens.

➤ If you're into tabletop wargaming with miniatures, be sure to make the group **rec.games.miniatures** a regular stop. You'll find painting tips, advice on tactics, rule clarifications, and more.

> **FAQ Info:**
> Article: Miniatures Painting Guide and FAQ
> RTFM.MIT.EDU Directory:
> /pub/usenet-by-group/rec.games.miniatures

➤ Games such as *Zork* and *Adventure* take you through elaborate worlds that are described to you with only a few lines of text. You can then interact with these worlds by entering your own text commands. These types of games may have been superseded by newer games with flashy graphics and sounds, but the simplicity of the original interactive fiction adventures is still appealing to many people. Those of them that are on the Net can probably be found trading hints and secrets in the group **rec.games.int-fiction**.

Chapter 19

Left Versus Right: The Politics Newsgroups

In This Chapter

➤ Newsgroups that track current events
➤ Civil liberties groups
➤ Groups that cover war and history
➤ Conservative and liberal groups
➤ A plethora of political newsgroups

Back in Chapter 4, "Jargon, Acronyms, Smileys, and More," I defined a *holy war* as "a never-ending, unchanging argument where the opinions of combatants on both sides of the issue never budge an inch." Although most holy wars can be deadly dull for people who don't care much about the topic at hand, they can be quite exhilarating for the participants doing the proselytizing. If you're spoiling for a holy war or two yourself, you can do no better than to look in any of the various political newsgroups. Here you'll find ongoing battles about abortion, the environment, health care, civil liberties, and much more. This chapter will be your guide to these political arenas.

Keeping Abreast of Current Events

How can busy mouse potatoes like us keep up with the issues *du jour* so we can toss in our two cents' worth at cocktail parties? Well, yeah, reading the paper would be a good idea, but you can also get your fix and hone your arguments in the newsgroups devoted to current events. The next few sections give you the scoop.

Debating in the Issues-Oriented Groups

For starters, let's take a look at a few groups that cover the burning issues of the day: abortion, the environment, health care, guns, and more.

➤ In the newsgroup **talk.abortion**, pro-choice and pro-life proponents lob emotionally charged bombs at each other. And if you don't get your fill in this group, there's always **alt.abortion.inequity**.

```
FAQ Info:
    Article:
        Freedom of Access to Clinic Entrances Act
        (FACE) FAQ
    RTFM.MIT.EDU Directory:
        /pub/usenet-by-group/talk.abortion
```

➤ Most people agree the environment should be one of our major concerns, but everybody has a different plan on how to go about it. If you're looking to hash out these kinds of concerns, and if you want a truckload of local actions to go along with your global thoughts, check out the groups **talk.environment** and **alt.save.the.earth**. If your environmental activism takes on a political hue, you might want to read **alt.politics.greens** to see what the Green Party is up to these days.

➤ There's currently a hot debate going on about using encryption to send secure messages on the Net. On the one hand, privacy advocates want a method that will allow them to keep their e-mail and other correspondence out of the hands of snoops. On the other hand, the government wants to be able to "tap" into e-mail to prevent criminals and other undesirables from hatching their nefarious plots. The USENET battleground for this debate is the group **talk.politics.crypto**.

Chapter 19 ➤ *Left Versus Right: The Politics Newsgroups*

```
FAQ Info:
    Articles: Crytpography FAQ (01/10: Overview)
              Crytpography FAQ (02/10: Net Etiquette)
              Crytpography FAQ (03/10: Basic Cryptology)
              Crytpography FAQ (04/10: Mathematical Cryptology)
              Crytpography FAQ (05/10: Product Ciphers)
              Crytpography FAQ (06/10: Public Key Cryptography)
              Crytpography FAQ (07/10: Digital Signatures)
              Crytpography FAQ (08/10: Technical Miscellany)
              Crytpography FAQ (09/10: Other Miscellany)
              Crytpography FAQ (10/10: References)
    RTFM.MIT.EDU Directory:
        /pub/usenet-by-group/talk.politics.crypto
```

➤ Gun nuts and anti-gun zealots take up arms against each other in the group **talk.politics.guns**.

➤ The Clinton administration's desire to reform health care has created a firestorm of controversy. On one side, you have those who think basic health care should be available to all; on the other, you have those who think anything that increases the size of government is a bad idea. The inevitable clashes occur in the group **talk.politics.medicine**.

➤ In the group **alt.politics.correct**, you'll find ongoing debates about the merits of political correctness, as well arguments about issues that can be divided along correct/incorrect political fault lines.

➤ To keep up with the latest news on human rights, including reports of violations and info on organizations such as Amnesty International, subscribe to the newsgroup **soc.rights.human**.

Drug Discussions

Has the government gone too far in its crackdown on crack, or not far enough? The dispute rages on in the following groups:

talk.politics.drugs	This is where most of the heavy arguing takes place.
alt.drugs	This group has more general conversations about drugs.

alt.drugs.culture	Drugs as a cultural phenomenon.
alt.drugs.pot	Cannabis conversations and calls for the legalization of hemp.

```
FAQ Info:
    Article: alt.drugs Frequently Asked Questions (FAQ)
    RTFM.MIT.EDU Directory: /pub/usenet-by-group/alt.drugs
```

Miscellaneous Causes

Here's a list of a few more newsgroups that tackle the burning issues of the day:

alt.politics.datahighway	Planning the Infobahn.
alt.politics.homosexuality	The rights of same-sex couples.
alt.politics.sex	Gives new meaning to the phrase "political bedfellows."
alt.prisons	Are there too many prisons or not enough?
soc.feminism	Discussion of feminism and feminist issues (moderated).
talk.politics.animals	The use and/or abuse of animals.

Discussing Current Events in the U.S.

Most Internet traffic is based in the United States, so it's not surprising that most of the current-affairs talk has a distinctly American feel. Over and above that, however, there are quite a few USENET groups devoted exclusively to U.S. topics, and we'll check them out in this section.

If you've got something to say to the President or the Vice President, you can always drop them a line via e-mail. The President's e-mail address is **president@whitehouse.gov**. For the Vice President, send your missives to **vice.president@whitehouse.gov**. For more White House documents and info, be sure to browse the White House World Wide Web site at the location **http://www.whitehouse.gov/**.

Chapter 19 ▶ Left Versus Right: The Politics Newsgroups

▶ The newsgroup **alt.politics.usa.misc** is supposed to be a catch-all forum for discussing political concerns that don't fit anywhere else. A good chunk of the posts are press releases and statement transcripts direct from the White House.

```
FAQ Info:
    Articles:
        Government Information on the Internet
            (1/4, Gumprecht)
        Government Information on the Internet
            (2/4, Gumprecht)
        U.S. Government Information on the Internet
            (3/4, Parhamovish)
        U.S. Government Information on the Internet
            (4/4, Parhamovich)
        The Balanced Budget Amendment FAQ
    RTFM.MIT.EDU Directory:
        /pub/usenet-by-group/alt.politics.usa.misc
```

▶ If you've got something to say about term limits, lobbyists, pork, or the line-item veto, you can vent your spleen in the groups **alt.politics.elections** and **alt.politics.reform**.

▶ In the groups **alt.politics.clinton** and **alt.president.clinton**, the President's supporters and enemies quarrel over the latest policy initiatives and scandals.

```
FAQ Info:
    Article: FAQ: E-Access to Wash, DC (Beltway FAQ)
    RTFM.MIT.EDU Directory:
        /pub/usenet-by-group/alt.politics.clinton
```

▶ If you're interested in the Constitution, you have the right to subscribe to the group **alt.politics.usa.constitution**.

▶ If you're wondering what the CIA is up to now that the Cold War is long over, you'll want to read **alt.politics.org.cia**.

▶ If you want the scoop on the super-secret National Security Agency, be sure to take a look at **alt.politics.org.nsa**.

Part 3 ➤ *All the News That's Fit to Surf*

Current Events Everywhere Else

The U.S. may sometimes feel (and act) like it's the center of the universe, but of course there's plenty of strife happening in other parts of the world. For proof, just read any of the following newsgroups:

misc.news.bosnia	News, articles, reports and information on Bosnia (moderated).
alt.politics.british	Scandals of the stiff upper lip variety.
talk.politics.china	Trade versus human rights in China.
alt.politics.ec	Confabs about the European Economic Community.
alt.politics.europe.misc	Miscellaneous discussions about European politics.
alt.current-events.haiti	What's happening in Haiti.
talk.politics.mideast	Rabid debates over Mideast events.
alt.current-events.russia	The mess in Russia.
alt.current-events.ukraine	What's happening in the "breadbasket of the world."

Freedom and Civil Liberties

The lack of central authority makes the Net a fundamentally free place (subject to the constraints of netiquette, of course), so it tends to attract its share of civil libertarians and individualists. These people, in turn, agree with Eisenhower that "history does not long entrust the care of freedom to the weak or the timid." So, strongly and boldly, they seek to preserve their freedom by, among other things, participating in the newsgroups we'll discuss in this section.

➤ Is our society becoming less concerned with civil liberties as we try to make things "safer?" How do we reconcile civil rights and the common good? For the answers to these questions and many more, join the discussion in the newsgroup

Chapter 19 ➤ Left Versus Right: The Politics Newsgroups

alt.society.civil-liberty. (There's also a group called **alt.society.civil-liberties** that has substantially less traffic.)

➤ The philosophy of *individualism* posits a belief in self-reliance, personal independence, and that the interests of the individual take precedence over those of the community or state. Sounds good to me. If you, too, find this appealing, you can hang with like-minded individuals in the group **alt.individualism**.

➤ With hundreds of messages being posted every day, **alt.politics.libertarian** is one of USENET's most active groups. The participants discuss current events from a libertarian perspective, debate libertarian principles, and discuss individual freedom, in general.

```
FAQ Info:
    Articles:
        Libertarian FAQ: Frequently Asked Questions
        Libertarian FAQ: Organizations
        Libertarian FAQ: World's Smallest Political Quiz
    RTFM.MIT.EDU Directory:
        /pub/usenet-by-group/alt.politics.libertarian
```

If you want to learn more about libertarianism, check out the Libertarian Party's World Wide Web site. This site is chock full of libertarian info, documents, history, and more. Set your favorite browser to the following location:

```
http://www.lp.org/lp/
```

➤ While libertarians believe in minimizing government intrusions into the lives of individuals, anarchists believe in eliminating government altogether! What, then, becomes of things like private property, health care, and lobbyists? To find out, join the debate in the every-man-or-woman-for-him-or-herself newsgroup **alt.society.anarchy**.

➤ Do you worry about possible invasions of privacy each time you give out your Social Security number? Do you wonder if a cracker with nothing better to do is intercepting your fax or e-mail messages? For these and many other privacy issues, turn to the newsgroup **alt.privacy** for advice. There tends to be a hint of paranoia to the posts but, hey, if everyone is out to get you, then paranoia is just good thinking.

```
FAQ Info:
    Article:
        Junk Mail FAQ PRIVACY Info Source
        (credit,medical,personal,etc)
        Social Security Number FAQ
    RTFM.MIT.EDU Directory: /pub/usenet-by-group/alt.privacy
```

➤ There's been a disturbing trend in recent years to "solve" problems by banning the materials that cause them, be they books, TV shows, or cigarettes. Are the powers that be who are enforcing these bans guardians of the public good or censors? You can plead your case, pro or con, in the newsgroup **alt.censorship**.

```
FAQ Info:
    Article:
        How to Receive Banned Newsgroups
        FAQ Libernet: an electronic forum
    RTFM.MIT.EDU Directory:
        /pub/usenet-by-group/alt.censorship
```

Skirmishes Between Conservatives and Liberals

USENET's political arguments always seem to degenerate into the age-old camps of conservative versus liberal, right versus left, reactionary versus radical. So it makes some sense that there'd be a few newsgroups that cater specifically to either end of the political spectrum. In this section, we'll check out the greenness of the grass on both sides of the fence.

Rooting for the Right

Not long before I wrote this, the American voters gave control of the House of Representatives and the Senate to the Republicans. Does this signal a fundamental shift to the right for the American public, or was it mere anti-incumbency that turfed out the Democrats? You can debate such questions in the following newsgroups devoted to conservative causes:

➤ I once heard George Will (a famous conservative pundit and baseball fan) say that conservatism begins when the children need orthodontic work. I don't know if that's true or not (I don't have

Chapter 19 ▶ Left Versus Right: The Politics Newsgroups

kids), but you can debate it all you want in the newsgroup that caters to the philosophy of conservatism: **alt.society.conservatism**.

▶ These days, most economic and social conservatives congregate under the "Big Tent" of the Republican Party. And those Republicans that are wired congregate in **alt.politics.usa.republican**. When I tuned in to this busy group, most posters were crowing over the new Republican majorities in the House and Senate. But I also saw some messages speculating about the race for the 1996 Republican nomination, and I'd expect this theme to dominate as primary season draws closer.

▶ The newsgroup devoted to former President George Bush (**alt.politics.bush**) is dead in the water, but the one devoted to Dan Quayle, his much-maligned Vice President, is thriving. Hmmm. However, when you check out **alt.fan.dan-quayle**, you'll soon see why: half the articles are from Quayle bashers who can't resist such an obvious target, and the other half are from Quayle fans who'd love to see old J. Danforth throw his hat into the ring in '96.

▶ The group **alt.fan.rush-limbaugh** (part of what Rush fans call RushNet) contains transcripts of Rush Limbaugh's daily radio show, discussions about Limbaugh's pet peeves of that day, and much talk about "feminazis" and other Rushisms. (Just so you know, there's also a group named **alt.rush-limbaugh** that has a much lower volume of traffic.)

```
FAQ Info:
    Articles:
        FYI: VISITOR'S GUIDE TO RUSHNET
        02:FYI: VISITOR'S GUIDE TO RUSHNET
        03:FYI: VISITOR'S GUIDE TO RUSHNET
        04:FYI: VISITOR'S GUIDE TO RUSHNET
        05:FYI: VISITOR'S GUIDE TO RUSHNET
    RTFM.MIT.EDU Directory:
        /pub/usenet-by-group/alt.fan.rush-limbaugh
```

Leaning Toward the Left

One thing you'll notice about USENET's political groups is that there are no groups devoted to "centrist" organizations or positions. Everyone and every issue seems to get polarized into the usual right and left camps and, more often than not, these positions become hardened into the radical right and the radical left. This is most obvious in the newsgroups that cater to left-wing politics. As you'll see, some of these groups are so far left, they're right:

➤ The group **alt.activism** is extremely busy with articles trumpeting liberal ideas, info about activist organizations, and rallying cries for left-wing causes. The group **alt.activism.d** is supposed to be a discussion group about the issues raised in **alt.activism**, but there doesn't seem to be much traffic.

> **FAQ Info:**
> Article: GROUPS: Anti War-on-Drugs Activists List
> RTFM.MIT.EDU Directory:
> /pub/usenet-by-group/alt.activism

➤ If you're violently opposed to the death penalty, pay a visit to **alt.activism.death-penalty**.

➤ If your political instincts begin with Marxism and then head left, you'll feel at home in the newsgroup **alt.politics.radical-left**. This surprisingly active group covers current events with a decidedly left-wing slant, but it does include the odd post by some brave conservative.

➤ If your appetite for Marxist dogma still isn't satisfied, you can fill up on the articles in the group **alt.society.revolution**. Again, you get more opinions on current goings-on from the point of view of the almost-defunct radical left.

Trading Old War Stories in the War and History Groups

The Internet may be the wave of the future, but there's a sizable component of people still fascinated by, and still trying to understand, the past. Many of these folks turn to the various war and history newsgroups to satisfy their curiosity and to learn what they can about the people and events that preceded us.

Crying "Havoc!" in the War Newsgroups

If you're a war buff, you'll find lots of other interesting discussions in the following war newsgroups:

Chapter 19 ➤ *Left Versus Right: The Politics Newsgroups*

alt.war	General discussions about warfare.
soc.history.war.misc	Miscellaneous talk of wars not covered elsewhere.
alt.war.civil.usa	A popular group that discusses all aspects of the U.S. Civil War.
alt.war.vietnam	The Vietnam War (includes posts by many vets).
soc.history.war.world-war-ii	The history and events of WW II (moderated).

FAQ Info:
Articles: U.S. Civil War FAQ
         U.S. Civil War Reading List
RTFM.MIT.EDU Directory: /pub/usenet-by-group/alt.war.civil.usa

FAQ Info:
Article:
   [soc.history.war.world-war-ii] Frequently Asked Questions
RTFM.MIT.EDU Directory:
   /pub/usenet-by-group/soc.history. war.world-war-ii

If you're a Civil War buff looking for more info about Grant, Lee, and the boys, I suggest pointing your Web browser to the following URL:

http://www.digimark.net/bdboyle/cw.html

This site is loaded to the rafters with documents, orders of battle, and info on Civil War groups.

If you're interested in Civil War photographs, the Library of Congress has set up a Web site with hundreds of rare pics. Here's the address to enter into your browser:

http://rs6.loc.gov/cwphome.html

What's Past Is Prologue: The History Newsgroups

If it's true that those who don't learn from history are condemned to repeat it, then the USENETers who frequent the various history newsgroups will have nothing to worry about:

soc.history	Discussions of things historical.
soc.history.living	Living history and reenactment, issues, and info.
soc.history.moderated	All aspects of history (moderated).
soc.history.science	History of science and related areas.

>   **FAQ Info:**
>   Articles:
>   HOLOCAUST FAQ: Willis Canto & The Institute for
>   Historical Review (1/2)
>   HOLOCAUST FAQ: Willis Canto & The Institute for
>   Historical Review (2/2)
>   RTFM.MIT.EDU Directory: /pub/usenet-by-group/
>   soc.history
>   **FAQ Info:**
>   Article: Poor Gabriel's Almanac FAQ
>   RTFM.MIT.EDU Directory:
>   /pub/usenet-by-group/soc.history.moderated

Miscellaneous Political Stuff

Our political newsgroups campaign has almost run its course. For the home stretch, let's look at a few groups that cover more general topics:

➤ If you're looking to post a general political polemic, or if you'd just like to read some political ranting and raving, the place to be is the newsgroup **talk.politics.misc**.

➤ What's the difference between socialism and communism? Is a two-party system a good thing? For the answers to these and other political posers, subscribe to the newsgroup **talk.politics.theory**.

➤ In the newsgroup **alt.politics.economics**, posters of all political persuasions provide their formulas for balancing the budget and encouraging world trade, and explain things like trickle-down economics in 25 lines or less.

➤ Join the Net's resident paranoiacs in the group **alt.conspiracy** to talk about UFO cover-ups, White House Masonic rituals, and what the pyramid on the dollar bill *really* means.

Chapter 20

Psychology, Sex, and More: The Social Newsgroups

In This Chapter

- ➤ Psychology and support groups
- ➤ Sex, sex, and more sex
- ➤ Religion and philosophy newsgroups
- ➤ Newsgroups for education and kids' concerns
- ➤ More social newsgroups than you can shake a stick at

Man is a social animal.
—Baruch Spinoza

For proof of Spinoza's famous dictum, we need look no further than USENET itself. All that chatting and chinwagging and chewing the fat is sociability taken to its highest level. As you read USENET, it becomes obvious that these people *crave* social contact (and, for some of the nerdier Netniks, it may be the *only* social contact they have). Yes, man (and woman) is a social animal, so, naturally, there are lots of newsgroups devoted to social concerns such as psychology, education, religion, philosophy, modern life, and sex (which is, of course, where the "animal" part of "social animal" comes in).

Psychology and Support Groups

Whether you have epilepsy or an eating disorder, whether you're suffering through a depression or a divorce, you'll be able to find people online who've been through (or who are going through) the same thing.

➤ Want to know more about Primal Scream therapy? Looking for source material on Seasonal Affective Disorder (SAD), the cause of the "winter blues?" For these and other psychology posers, turn to the newsgroup **alt.psychology.help**.

FAQ Info:
```
Articles:
    Psychology & Support Groups Newsgroup Pointer
    Suicide - Frequently Asked Questions
RTFM.MIT.EDU Directory:
    /pub/usenet-by-group/alt.psychology.help
```

➤ Over the years, philosophers, psychologists, and other students of human nature have tried to classify people into various personality types. If this subject interests you, be sure to check out the group **alt.psychology.personality**.

➤ Self-help mania has carried over into USENET and has found a home in the newsgroup **alt.self-improve**. Here you'll find reviews of the latest self-help screeds, feedback from the followers of Anthony Robbins, Stephen Covey, and others, and success stories from the new and improved.

FAQ Info:
```
Article:
    alt.self-improve FAQ (Part 1 of 2)
    alt.self-improve FAQ (Part 1 of 2)
RTFM.MIT.EDU Directory:
    /pub/usenet-by-group/alt.self-improve
```

➤ Did you have a particularly strange, powerful, or scary dream last night? Are you interested in dream work but don't know where to begin? Look no further than the newsgroup **alt.dreams**, where you'll find dreamers posting their nocturnal dramas for interpretation, advice on how to remember dreams and start a dream journal, and info on good books to read. "Lucid" dreaming is when you know you're dreaming while a dream is in progress. You can find out more about it in the group **alt.dreams.lucid**.

```
FAQ Info:
Article:
      Dreams FAQ Pt.1/4: General information, dream interpretation
      Dreams FAQ Pt.2/4: Nightmares, OOBEs, paranormal issues
      Dreams FAQ Pt.3/4: About Lucid Dreaming
      Dreams FAQ Pt.4/4: Research, Help, reading recommendations
RTFM.MIT.EDU Directory: /pub/usenet-by-group/alt.dreams
```

Support Groups for Physical Ailments

Diseases and other physical problems are an unfortunate fact of human life, but they don't have to be faced alone. Sure, their family and friends will be there for them, but disease sufferers often need to connect with others who've faced the same ailment, or with professionals who are experts in the treatment of the disease. One way to get this kind of support is to subscribe to one of the following newsgroups:

alt.support.arthritis	Arthritis advice and remedies.
alt.support.asthma	Dealing with labored breathing.
alt.support.cancer	Emotional aid for people with cancer (FAQ available).
alt.support.cerebral-palsy	Cerebral Palsy support.
alt.support.diabetes.kids	Support for kids with diabetes and their families.
alt.support.eating-disord	Anorexia and bulimia support.
alt.support.epilepsy	Support group for epileptics.
alt.support.headaches.migraine	Discussion of migraine headaches.
alt.support.mult-sclerosis	Living with multiple sclerosis.
alt.support.obesity	Support and resources to treat obesity (moderated).
alt.support.stuttering	Support for people who stutter.
alt.support.tinnitus	Coping with ringing ears and other head noises (FAQ available).

Support Groups for Mental Ailments

Physical diseases are, unfortunately, not the only afflictions we humans are prey to. There are plenty of mental ailments that can be just as debilitating. For help, here are some support groups you can turn to:

alt.abuse.recovery	Helping victims of abuse to recover.
alt.recovery	For people in recovery programs (for example, AA, ACA).
alt.sexual.abuse.recovery	Helping others deal with experiences of sexual abuse (FAQ available).
alt.suicide.holiday	Talk of why suicides increase at holidays (FAQ available).
alt.support	Catch-all group dealing with emotional situations and experiences.
alt.support.abuse-partners	For people who have been abused by their spouses.
alt.support.depression	Dealing with depression and mood disorders (FAQs available).
alt.support.diet	Weight loss advice and cautionary tales (FAQs available).
alt.support.divorce	Discussion of marital breakups.
alt.support.loneliness	Support for the lonely.
alt.support.shyness	Overcoming shyness.
alt.support.stop-smoking	Getting over the nicotine addiction.

Pillow Talk: Sex and Sexuality Newsgroups

Internauts, it seems, will talk about sex at the drop of a hat. For proof, just tune into one of USENET's many groups dealing with relationships, sex of all kinds, and sexuality.

Chapter 20 ➤ *Psychology, Sex, and More: The Social Newsgroups*

Men ask, "What do women really want?" Women ask, "What do men really want?" And the answer is: who the heck knows! Still, this doesn't stop people from trying to figure out what makes the opposite sex tick in the newsgroup **soc.couples**. You'll find advice on relationships, insights into coupledom, and reports from the frontlines of the battle between the sexes.

The **alt.sex.*** newsgroups cater to just about every sexual preference under the sheets, from bestiality to voyeurism. You'll find advice, stories, and lots of heavy breathing by hot and bothered Netizens.

Gay men and women can commune with like-minded surfers in the following groups:

alt.homosexual	Discussing the gay lifestyle (FAQ available).
soc.bi	Bisexuality from a sociological point of view.
soc.motss	Issues pertaining to homosexuality.

Traveling the World in the soc.culture.* Groups

Want to learn more about the culture and politics of some faraway land or ethnic group? Got a hankering to go to Africa but both time and money are in short supply? Planning a trip to Canada and want to know what a "hoser" is? Got some questions about Japanese customs? You can get news, info, and traveling advice for dozens of countries in the **soc.culture.*** newsgroups. Happy trails!

Heavy Thinking in the Philosophy Forums

Philosophers have been wracking their brains trying to fathom the mysteries of existence for thousands of years. The tradition continues here in the '90s in the USENET groups devoted to philosophical concerns:

➤ Wondering about the meaning of life? Sounds like you need a good dose of **talk.philosophy.misc**. This highly literate group discusses various philosophical concerns and conundrums. A lot of it is pretty heavy going, and many of the posts have a how-many-angels-can-fit-on-the-head-of-a-pin quality, but the philosophically inclined should enjoy themselves.

- ► Humanists, as opposed to mystics or theologians, are primarily concerned with human rather than supernatural or divine matters. They emphasize rational thought, ethics, and intelligent compassion as an approach to life. The Net's humanist community meets—and occasionally clashes with the mystic/religious factions—in the newsgroup **talk.philosophy.humanism**.

- ► Semioticians, deconstructionists, and other pointy-headed postmodernists blather on in the newsgroup **alt.postmodern**. If you can figure it all out, let me know.

- ► The nature of conciousness which is one of the oldest and most mysterious of philosophical issues. If you have an insight you'd like to share, or if you're just trying to come to grips with this whole consciousness thing, you'll want to tune into the group **alt.consciousness**.

USENET's Religious Round Tables

Although technology is probably the religion of choice for many Net citizens, there are still plenty of people online who follow one of the more traditional religions. Whatever you're into, be it Christianity or Islam, Paganism or Shamanism, you'll likely find a USENET group where fellow believers congregate. We'll check them out in this section.

We'll start our tour of the religious newsgroups by looking at two groups that cater to people who don't subscribe to any religious beliefs at all. In **alt.atheism** and the moderated group **alt.atheism.moderated**, heathens of all kinds debunk religious dogma, campaign against things like prayer in public schools, and generally wear their skepticism on their sleeves.

```
FAQ Info:
    Articles:
        Alt.Atheism FAQ: Introduction to Atheism
        Alt.Atheism FAQ: Overview for New Readers
    RTFM.MIT.EDU Directory: /pub/usenet-by-group/alt.atheism
```

If Buddhism is your path, you'll want to check out the various groups devoted to Buddhism itself, or to Zen Buddhism, in particular. Or not. If you do, you'll find posts on how to approach modern issues from a

Buddhist perspective, requests for info on Buddhist temples and organizations, and lots of *koan*-like meditations that may or may not be profound. Here's a couple of newsgroups to check out:

alt.philosophy.zen	Zen flesh, Zen bones, Zen posts, Zen follow-ups.
talk.religion.buddhism	Discussing Buddhism's place in the modern world.
alt.buddha.short.fat.guy	Buddhism. Not Buddhism. Both. Neither.

FAQ Info:
>   Article:
>   alt.buddha.short.fat.guy Frequently Asked Questions (FAQ)
>   RTFM.MIT.EDU Directory:
>   /pub/usenet-by-group/alt.buddha.short.fat.guy

Today's Christian has more on his or her mind than faith, hope, and charity. Why is church attendance dropping steadily? What effect do the radical Fundamentalists have on people's attitude toward Christianity? Should we expect some kind of apocalyptic dénouement when the new millennium hits? These are big questions, and you'll find them (and lots more) discussed at length in the following newsgroups:

alt.religion.christian	Haphazard theological debates and Bible interpretations.
soc.religion.christian	A more focused (read: moderated) look at Christianity.
soc.religion.christian.bible-study	Examining the Holy Bible (moderated).
soc.religion.christian.youth-work	Christians working with young people (moderated).

FAQ Info:
>   Article: Bible Software FAQ
>   RTFM.MIT.EDU Directory:
>   /pub/usenet-by-group/soc.religion.christian

If God is good, then why is there evil in the world? What is evil, anyway? Who among us is evil incarnate? Murderers? Despots? Smokers? Junk bond salesmen? If you're brave enough, the place to explore the nature of evil is the newsgroup **alt.evil**. And if Satan worship is either your goal or your deepest fear, you might want to keep an eye on the group **alt.satanism**.

The Net's Muslims have a couple of forums they can use to discuss Islam, the Qur'an, and the teachings of the Prophet Mohammed. For general subjects, check out the newsgroup **alt.religion.islam**. For moderated discussions, subscribe to the group **soc.religion.islam**.

FAQ Info:
    Article:
        [alt.religion.islam] Frequently Asked Questions
    RTFM.MIT.EDU Directory:
        /pub/usenet-by-group/alt.religion.islam

If your faith flows in directions other than those previously listed, don't worry. USENET has quite a few other groups devoted to religion and specific religious faiths:

talk.religion.misc	Debating religious, ethical, and moral issues.
soc.religion.eastern	Eastern religions such as Taoism, Sufism, and Hinduism (moderated).
soc.religion.gnosis	Gnosis, marifat, jnana and direct sacred experience (moderated; FAQ available).
soc.culture.jewish	Jewish culture and religion (FAQs available).
soc.religion.quaker	The Religious Society of Friends (FAQ available).
alt.religion.mormon	The Mormon religion.
alt.mythology	Zeus, Hera, and the gods and goddesses within and without.
talk.religion.newage	Theosophy and other New Age religions.

alt.out-of-body	Speculations about the out-of-body experience (OOBE).
alt.pagan	Paganism, Wicca, and the Great Mystery (FAQ available).
alt.religion.scientology	L. Ron Hubbard's Church of Scientology (FAQs available).
alt.religion.shamanism	The shamanic experience.
soc.religion.shamanism	More on shamanism (moderated; FAQs available).

Confabs on Kids and Education

Whether your kids are rug rats or moody adolescents, you'll find a USENET newsgroup that helps you through. And if education is your primary concern, there are plenty of education-related newsgroups, too. Here's a list of newsgroups that specifically cater to kid concerns:

misc.kids	Children, their behavior, and activities (FAQs available).
misc.kids.computer	They're never too young to be wired.
misc.kids.consumers	Reviews and opinions on products related to kids.
misc.kids.health	Info, advice, and discussions on children's health.
misc.kids.info	FAQs and periodic postings related to kids (moderated).
misc.kids.pregnancy	Pre-pregnancy planning, pregnancy, childbirth (FAQs available).
misc.kids.vacation	Discussion on all forms of family-oriented vacationing.
alt.infertility	Info on infertility causes and treatments.
alt.adoption	Tips and advice on adoption.

Why Johnny Can't Post: The Education Groups

If you're concerned about education—either as a teacher, parent, or student—be sure to attend any of the following education newsgroups:

alt.education.research	Studying about studying.
misc.education	General discussions about the educational system.
misc.education.adult	Adult education and adult literacy programs.
misc.education.home-school.christian	Christian home-schooling.
misc.education.home-school.misc	Home-schooling: what, why, and how.
misc.education.language.english	ESL info and programs.
misc.education.medical	Med-school info and MCAT advice.
misc.education.multimedia	Advice on using multi-media in the classroom (moderated).
misc.education.science	Issues related to science education.

USENET's College Courses

If you're in college or graduate school, or are thinking about it, USENET has several newsgroups that provide info on schools, programs, and college life:

soc.college	Miscellaneous college info.
soc.college.grad	General issues related to graduate schools.
soc.college.gradinfo	Information about graduate schools.
soc.college.org.aiesec	The International Association of Business and Commerce Students.
alt.fraternity.sorority	Discussions of fraternity and sorority life and what to wear to a toga party.

A Selection of Social Newsgroups

This section finishes off our look at the social newsgroups by examining a selection of groups that don't fit into the previous categories. We'll look at folklore, feminism, women, men, and more.

Sewer Alligators and Other Modern Folk Tales

In ancient times, people would huddle around a fire after a hard day's hunting and gathering and tell each other stories and tales of men and deeds from the dim past. Nowadays, people hunker down in front of computer screens and relate urban legends, old-wives tales, and modern myths to the various **alt.folklore.*** newsgroups. Others attempt to refute or confirm these stories, and much fun is had by all. Here's the list:

alt.folklore.college	Collegiate pranks and high-jinks.
alt.folklore.computers	Stories and anecdotes about computers (some true!).
alt.folklore.ghost-stories	Ooh, that's scary, kids!
alt.folklore.herbs	Herbal cures and other aspects of folk medicine.
alt.folklore.military	Rumors about new military weapons and past military experiments.
alt.folklore.science	Lore and legends from the scientific community.
alt.folklore.suburban	Same as **alt.folkore.urban**, but with a higher signal-to-noise ratio (moderated).
alt.folklore.urban	Urban legends, à la Jan Harold Brunvand.

```
FAQ Info:
    Articles:
        alt.folklore.urban  Frequently Asked Questions  (Part 1 of 4)
        alt.folklore.urban  Frequently Asked Questions  (Part 2 of 4)
        alt.folklore.urban  Frequently Asked Questions  (Part 3 of 4)
        alt.folklore.urban  Frequently Asked Questions  (Part 4 of 4)
    RTFM.MIT.EDU Directory:
        /pub/usenet-by-group/alt.folklore.urban
```

The Battle of the Sexes Goes Online

The Women's Movement and the nascent Men's Movement have no shortage of proponents on the Net. For posts that go beyond the usual can't-live-with-'em-and-can't-live-without-'em polemics, tune in to any of the following groups:

alt.feminism	Feminist discussions and debates.
soc.feminism	Same as **alt.feminism**, but less noise (moderated; FAQs available).
alt.feminism.individualism	Relating feminism and individualism.
soc.women	Women's issues from a not-necessarily-feminist point of view.
soc.men	Men's issues with attempts to go beyond Iron John.

Chapter 21

Monday Morning Quarterbacking in the Sports Newsgroups

In This Chapter

➤ Swinging for the fences in the baseball newsgroups

➤ Taking it to the hoop in the basketball groups

➤ Going long in the football groups

➤ Picking the top corner in the hockey groups

➤ A smorgasbord of other sports groups

An old sports saw says that "those who can, do; those who can't, teach." But whether you can or you can't, whether you play sports or teach them, it seems *everybody* loves to talk about sports. It could be in the local watering hole after the game, around the office water cooler on Monday morning, or in any of the dozens of USENET sports newsgroups that we'll check out in this chapter.

Groups for Baseball Buffs

The 1994 baseball season may have been a washout thanks to the strike, but that hasn't stopped USENET's baseball fans from posting to the various newsgroups devoted to America's national pastime. This section fills out the lineup card for the baseball-related groups.

For general baseball conversations, subscribe to the newsgroup **rec.sport.baseball**. Most of the current posting action has been strike-related (a recent Subject line: "AAAAAAHHHHHH! I've had it!!!"), but there are still plenty of baseball purists discussing stats, favorite players, recent trades, and more.

If you prefer your newsgroups to have more signal and less noise, you'll enjoy the moderated group **rec.sport.baseball.analysis**. Instead of the "That player sucks," "No, he doesn't" threads that **rec.sports.baseball** sometimes degenerates into, **rec.sport.baseball.analysis** serves up intelligent, thoughtful articles on various aspects of the game. A must for true fans.

```
FAQ Info:
    Articles:
        rec.sport.baseball FAQ: Part 0: Index
        rec.sport.baseball FAQ: Part 1: General Information
        rec.sport.baseball FAQ: Part 2: Rules
        rec.sport.baseball FAQ: Part 3: Scoring and Awards
        rec.sport.baseball FAQ: Part 4: Books and Movies
        rec.sport.baseball FAQ: Part 5: Glossary
    RTFM.MIT.EDU Directory:
        /pub/usenet-by-group/rec.sport.baseball
```

Looking for baseball data on the World Wide Web? Well, there's certainly no shortage. One of the best sites is the Nando X Baseball Server. This site has a searchable index of data, tons of stats, analyses, standings, and lots more. Point your favorite Web browser to the following location:

> http://www.nando.net/baseball/bbmain.html

The World Wide Web Virtual Library has a baseball page that features lots of links to other baseball sites. To try it out, surf to the following URL:

> http://www.atm.ch.cam.ac.uk/sports/baseball.html

For more baseball talk, check out the following newsgroups:

➤ Baseball, more than any other sport, is a game of numbers. You've got your batting averages, slugging percentages, strikeouts, saves, and more TLAs (three-letter acronyms) than you can spit a wad of chewing tobacco at (ERA, RBI, OBP, and so on). To get all the raw baseball data you can handle, grab your scorecard and head for **rec.sport.baseball.data**. You'll get not only the players' stats, but also team schedules, Hall of Fame balloting and results, player birthdays, and more.

➤ Few sports fans are as rabid and as intense as those who play in baseball's fantasy leagues. And after hanging off every pitch in whatever game is on TV or radio, after poring over the box scores with their morning coffee, and after carefully checking the team injury reports, they head for **rec.sport.baseball.fantasy**. Here, fellow fantasy league fans discuss player stats and trades, and make league announcements.

➤ Professional baseball players may be greedy, overpaid bums, but the sport is still pure at the college level. (Unless, of course, you happen to think aluminum bats are blasphemous.) College baseball fans meet in the newsgroup **rec.sport.baseball.college** to discuss their favorite teams and argue over who'll make it to this year's College World Series.

➤ If you have a baseball team you love (or one you love to hate), be sure to pay a visit to the newsgroup devoted to that team. Head for the **alt.sports.baseball.*** groups for discussions on all the teams from the Atlanta Braves to the Toronto Blue Jays.

Hoops, There It Is: The Basketball Groups

Michael Jordan may have retired, but thanks to the likes of Shaquille O'Neal, Charles Barkley, and Hakeem Olajuwon, basketball remains one of the world's most popular sports. This section looks at USENET's small (but popular) collection of basketball newsgroups.

➤ If you think the NBA is "fan-tastic," then you'll definitely want to subscribe to the newsgroup **rec.sport.basketball.pro**. Here you'll find game boxscores, debates about the best teams, player dissing and adulation, and more.

```
    FAQ Info:
        Articles: faq
                  index
        RTFM.MIT.EDU Directory:
            /pub/usenet-by-group/rec.sport.basketball.pro
```

> Many basketball fans pass on the pros entirely and prefer to focus on college basketball. This is reflected in USENET, where the newsgroup **rec.sport.basketball.college** is hugely popular. Fans debate the current Top 25 teams, discuss their favorite players, and argue over which team is going to blow what other team out of the building. If you're a college hoops fan, YOU'LL LOVE THIS GROUP, BAYBEE!

> To keep up with the latest in women's basketball (mostly at the U.S. college level), be sure to include **rec.sport.basketball.women** in your list of favorite groups.

> Most of the basketball newsgroups are decidedly American-oriented, and that's as it should be. But the game thrives in Europe and many other hoop hot spots around the world, so international fans need to get their fix, as well. They can if they subscribe to the newsgroup **rec.sport.basketball.misc**. This group features articles about the European leagues, news of overseas championships, and talk about Olympic basketball.

> To find out the latest and greatest about your favorite NBA team, subscribe to one of the **alt.sports.basketball.*** groups set up for boosters of specific teams.

The Net is loaded with data for basketball addicts. For starters, try out the World Wide Web's Basketball Server. It has complete coverage of both the NBA and NCAA. To try it out, point your Web browser to the following site:

http://www.nando.net/sports/bkb/1994/bkserv.html

If college hoops turns your crank, one of the best sites is the College Basketball Page at the following URL:

http://www.cs.cmu.edu:8001/afs/cs.cmu.edu/user/wsr/Web/bball/bball.html

---

Huddling in the Football Newsgroups

If you're a football fan and you think the game is more than just "violence punctuated by committee meetings," as George Will has said, you'll definitely want to get involved in any of USENET's football newsgroups.

Chapter 21 ▸ *Monday Morning Quarterbacking in the Sports Newsgroups*

> There's no shortage of info on the Net for football fanatics. One of my favorite sites is Eric Richard's Professional Football Server. You'll find game summaries, current stats, draft info, and NFL history. This is a World-Wide Web site located at the following URL:
>
> `http://www.mit.edu:8001/services/sis/NFL/NFL.html`
>
> College gridiron groupies will definitely want to check out the College Football Home Page on the Web. This page include summaries of recent game action (including pictures!), conference standings, the latest poll results, and more. Point your browser to the following location:
>
> `http://www.nando.net/football/1994/college/college.html`

▶ Aficionados of the National Football League meet in the newsgroup **rec.sport.football.pro**. This busy group features lots of post-game crowing by fans of winning teams (and plenty of excuses and wait-until-next-times by fans of the losers), stats, player compliments and criticisms, and tips for picking this week's winners against the spread. You can even put your gridiron knowledge to the test in the weekly pool that runs during the season.

```
FAQ Info:
     Article:  NFL Pool - Instructions
     RTFM.MIT.EDU Directory:
          /pub/usenet-by-group/rec.sport.football.pro
```

▶ Got an opinion on the number one college football team in the nation? Got a prediction on who'll win this year's Heisman Trophy? Got a beef or an axe to grind about a particular college football program? Then you should definitely attend the newsgroup devoted to NCAA football: **rec.sport.football.college**.

▶ If you prefer your football to have three downs and to be played on a field 110 yards long, then you're obviously a fan of the Canadian Football League (or whatever they're going to call it in 1995). In that case, you should definitely head north and see what's happening in the newsgroup **rec.sport.football.canadian**. CFL fans discuss their favorite teams, expansion, realignment, and explain the "rouge" (the single point often awarded after punts and missed field goals) to newcomers.

> ➤ If you're part of a football Rotisserie league, be sure to include the newsgroup **rec.sport.football.fantasy** in your Net surfing plans. Participants in this forum discuss player trades, league strategies, and more.

> ➤ All other football topics are covered in the newsgroup **rec.sport.football.misc**. This catch-all group covers Pop Warner football and discussions of other leagues (such as the defunct USFL); it's also the best place for football neophytes to ask questions about the game.

> ➤ If you live and die with the exploits of a particular NFL team, you can keep abreast of the latest goings-on by subscribing to the team's newsgroup in **alt.sports.football.pro.***.

Hockey Night in USENET

Whether you're a fan of the NHL, NCAA, or any of the junior or European hockey leagues, the place to hang out with your hockey cohorts is the newsgroup **rec.sport.hockey**. Fans discuss their favorite teams and players, make predictions about upcoming games and playoff series, and trade hockey lore and info of all kinds.

```
FAQ Info:
    Articles: rec.sport.hockey FAQ Part 1 of 2
              rec.sport.hockey FAQ Part 2 of 2
    RTFM.MIT.EDU Directory: /pub/usenet-by-group/rec.sport.hockey
```

If you're part of a hockey fantasy league, or are thinking about it, you can get more info and trade player stats with fellow fantasists in the newsgroup **alt.sports.hockey.fantasy**.

Hockey lovers tend to be fans of the game as a whole, and will often watch whichever teams happen to be playing on TV. However, when it comes to their favorite teams, hockey fans become rabidly partisan and will defend their local heroes tooth and nail. For proof, just read any of the **alt.sports.hockey.nhl.*** newsgroups devoted to specific NHL teams.

Finally, it may sound strange, but one of the Net's best sites for hockey info is located in Hawaii! The Professional Hockey Server is jammed to the rafters with stats, info on standings and awards, images, and links to the home pages of NHL teams and other hockey sites. To see for yourself, skate to the following World Wide Web locale:

    http://maxwell.uhh.hawaii.edu/hockey/hockey.html

Other Sports Groups

There is, of course, more to sports than just the Big Four of baseball, basketball, football, and hockey. Lots more, in fact. USENET recognizes this with groups that cater to everything from auto racing to windsurfing. We'll check them all out in the following sections.

By the way, sports fans of all stripes will love the World Wide Web of Sports page. This Web site has links to all kinds of sports info on the Net. It covers not only baseball, basketball, football, and hockey, but also the Olympics, soccer, cycling, golf, running, rowing, and even Frisbee. You can also customize the page to view only those sports you're interested in. To check it out, point your Web browser to the following URL:

    http://tns-www.lcs.mit.edu/cgi-bin/sports

Auto Racing

The speed demons in the crowd will love the USENET newsgroups devoted to auto racing. You'll find race results and schedules, technical info, and lots of arguing over who's the best driver.

rec.autos.sport.f1	The Formula 1 circuit.
rec.autos.sport.indy	Indy car racing.
rec.autos.sport.info	Racing news, results, and announcements (moderated).
rec.autos.sport.misc	Racing stuff that doesn't fit anywhere else.
rec.autos.sport.nascar	NASCAR and other professional stock car racing.
rec.autos.sport.tech	The technology of auto racing.
rec.motorcycles.racing	Racing motorcycles. Wear your leathers!

```
FAQ Info:
    Articles:
        rec.autos.sport FAQ 1/7: Introduction Frequently
            Asked Questions
        rec.autos.sport FAQ 2/7: Race Schedule Frequently
            Asked Questions
        rec.autos.sport FAQ 3/7: Single Seater Frequently
            Asked Questions
        rec.autos.sport FAQ 4/7: NASCAR Frequently Asked
            Questions
        rec.autos.sport FAQ 5/7: General Autosport
            Frequently Asked Questions
        rec.autos.sport FAQ 6/7: Other Race Series
            Frequently Asked Questions
        rec.autos.sport FAQ 7/7: Autosport Addresses
    RTFM.MIT.EDU Directory: /pub/usenet-by-group/rec.autos.sport
```

Bowling

Whether you're an occasional bowler, you play in a bowling league, or you follow the Pro Bowler's Tour, you'll want to strike out for the newsgroup **alt.sport.bowling**. Bowling buffs trade tips about techniques and equipment and brag about their averages.

Boxing

Fans of the "sweet science" meet in the newsgroup **rec.sport.boxing**. Here, pugilistic pundits predict the winners of upcoming bouts and argue over who's the best fighter in various weight classes.

Cricket

Cricket is one of those sports where half the people in the world are avid followers and the other half haven't the faintest idea what's going on. If you're in the latter category, don't bother with **rec.sport.cricket**. In this group, the cricket cognoscenti discuss the latest test match results, trade stats, and the world's best players. It's all a bit incomprehensible for the layman. If you're just interested in cricket scores and averages, check out the moderated newsgroup **rec.sport.cricket.info**.

Chapter 21 ➤ *Monday Morning Quarterbacking in the Sports Newsgroups*

```
FAQ Info:
    Articles:
        Weekly FAQ - CricInfo via Email, (Cricket Info Server)
        Weekly FAQ - CricInfo via Gopher, (Cricket Info Server)
        Weekly FAQ - CricInfo via IRC, (Cricket Info Server)
        Weekly FAQ - CricInfo via Telnet, (Cricket Info Server)
    RTFM.MIT.EDU Directory:
        /pub/usenet-by-group/rec.sport.cricket FOO
```

Fishing

If happiness for you is a rod and reel, a boat and some bait, and a few hours to kill, then you'll love the fishing newsgroups. Anglers of all ages and abilities exchange tips, debate the effectiveness of various lures, and trade stories about the one that got away.

rec.outdoors.fishing	All aspects of sport and commercial fishing.
alt.fishing	An alternative look at fishing.
rec.outdoors.fishing.fly	Fly fishing tips and techniques.
rec.outdoors.fishing.saltwater	Saltwater fishing, methods, gear, Q&A.

Golf

If there's one thing golfers enjoy more than playing the game, it's talking about it. It seems everyone is looking for that one tip that will shave 10 strokes off their game. That may never happen, but people sure try, especially in the newsgroup **rec.sport.golf**. This popular group has lots of golfing tips, of course, but there are also discussions about favorite golf courses, the latest news from the PGA and LPGA tours, equipment reviews, course strategy advice, and lots more.

```
FAQ Info:
    Article:  rec.sport.golf Golf FAQ
    RTFM.MIT.EDU Directory: /pub/usenet-by-group/rec.sport.golf
```

Martial Arts

If you participate in any of the martial arts—whether it's karate, kung fu, jujitsu, or judo—be sure to take a bow in the group **rec.martial-arts**. The *senseis* in this group provide advice on techniques and fighting strategies, news on upcoming tournaments, and reviews of martial arts films.

Running

The running craze may have come and gone a few years ago, but all kinds of fanatics became addicted to the "runner's high" and have stuck with it over the years. Those that are online meet in the newsgroup **rec.running** to trade advice about shoes, training regimens, stretching, and how best to deal with ill-tempered dogs on your daily jaunt.

```
FAQ Info:
    Articles:   rec.running FAQ part 1 of 6
                rec.running FAQ part 2 of 6
                rec.running FAQ part 3 of 6
                rec.running FAQ part 4 of 6
                rec.running FAQ part 5 of 6
                rec.running FAQ part 6 of 6
    RTFM.MIT.EDU Directory: /pub/usenet-by-group/rec.running
```

Skating (In-Line, Ice, and Roller)

The latest fad to hit our streets and parks is in-line skating. This cross between ice skating and roller skating is great exercise and just plain fun, to boot. If you're looking for in-line info about skates, safety equipment, or any of the roller hockey leagues that have started up, the place to be is the newsgroup **rec.skate**. But there's more to this group than in-line skating. You'll also find lots of articles on ice skating (especially figure skating) and roller skating.

```
FAQ Info:
    Articles:
        Rec.skate FAQ: (Roller)Hockey (3/11)
        Rec.skate FAQ: In-Line Skate and Product Reviews (5/11)
        Rec.skate FAQ: Skating Clubs and Organizations (9/11)
```

```
                    Rec.skate FAQ: Skating Tricks and Moves Sec. 1 (10/11)
                    Rec.skate FAQ: Skating Tricks and Moves Sec. 2 (11/11)
                    Rec.skate FAQ: What and Where to Buy (4/11)
                    Rec.skate FAQ: Wheels and Bearings (2/11)
                    Rec.skate FAQ: Where to Skate (Indoors) (6/11)
                    Rec.skate FAQ: Where to Skate (Outdoors) Sec. 1 (7/11)
                    Rec.skate FAQ: Where to Skate (Outdoors) Sec. 2 (8/11)
                    Rec.skate Frequently Asked Questions: General Info (1/11)
           RTFM.MIT.EDU Directory: /pub/usenet-by-group/rec.skate
```

Skiing

The Net's skiers can get advice, info about ski resorts, and reviews of equipment in the following newsgroups:

rec.skiing.alpine	Discussions on downhill skiing.
rec.skiing.announce	Competition results, snow reports, and more (moderated).
rec.skiing.nordic	Cross-country skiing conversations.
rec.skiing.snowboard	How best to annoy regular skiers on a snowboard.

Skydiving

If you're an avid skydiver, or are screwing up the courage to try it, jump to the newsgroup **rec.skydiving**. This surprisingly popular group has articles on jump schools, tips on buying equipment, and good advice for newcomers.

```
FAQ Info:
    Article: rec.skydiving FAQ (Frequently Asked Questions)
    RTFM.MIT.EDU Directory: /pub/usenet-by-group/rec.skydiving
```

Soccer

The 1994 World Cup proved to us North Americans that a well-played game of soccer (or "association football," as the rest of the world calls it) can be both beautiful and exciting. If you caught the fever (or already had it in spades to begin with), then you'll get a kick (sorry about that) out of the newsgroup **rec.sport.soccer**. Here you'll find all the latest results from leagues around the world and plenty of partisan support from fans and hooligans alike.

Tennis and Other Racquet Sports

Tennis is one of the most popular participation sports in North America. If you count yourself among the legions of tennis enthusiasts, you'll want to subscribe to the newsgroup **rec.sport.tennis**. You'll find tennis tips to help your game, equipment advice, and lots of talk about professional tennis.

```
FAQ Info:
    Articles:
        FAQ for rec.sport.tennis (1/6) - Tournaments
        FAQ for rec.sport.tennis (2/6) - Rankings
        FAQ for rec.sport.tennis (3/6) - Player Information
        FAQ for rec.sport.tennis (4/6) - Equipment
        FAQ for rec.sport.tennis (5/6) - Tennis Media
        FAQ for rec.sport.tennis (6/6) - Miscellaneous
    RTFM.MIT.EDU Directory: /pub/usenet-by-group/rec.sport.tennis
```

Many of the same people who love tennis also enjoy other racquet sports such as racquetball, squash, and table tennis. The good news for them is that there are also USENET newsgroups for each of these sports:

alt.sport.racquetball	All aspects of indoor racquetball.
alt.sport.squash	Squash advice, tips, and strategies.
rec.sport.table-tennis	Things related to table tennis (a.k.a. Ping-Pong; FAQs are available).

Triathlon

Triathlons of various lengths and degrees of craziness required have become amazingly popular with fitness freaks the world over. If you count yourself in this hardy group, you can meet with your peers in the newsgroup **rec.sport.triathlon** to discuss training methods, competitions, and more.

```
FAQ Info:
    Article:  FAQ [updated]
    RTFM.MIT.EDU Directory:
        /pub/usenet-by-group/rec.sport.triathlon
```

Chapter 21 ➤ *Monday Morning Quarterbacking in the Sports Newsgroups*

Water Sports

There's a water sport for all occasions, and many of them have their own newsgroup:

rec.scuba	Scuba diving advice and info.
rec.sport.water-polo	Water polo discussions.
rec.sport.waterski	Waterskiing and other boat-towed activities.
rec.windsurfing	Surfing the waves instead of the Net.
alt.sport.jet-ski	Those annoying personal watercraft.
rec.sport.swimming	Training for and competing in swimming events.
rec.sport.rowing	Crew for competition or fitness.

FAQ Info:
```
    Article:
        [rec.scuba] FAQ: Frequently Asked Questions about Scuba,
            Monthly Posting
    RTFM.MIT.EDU Directory: /pub/usenet-by-group/rec.scuba
```

Some Sport Shorts

Okay, we've covered the most popular of USENET's sporting newsgroups, but there are still plenty more where those came from. I don't have the room to cover the remaining groups in depth, but the following list will at least let you know what's available:

rec.sport.misc	Sports not covered in any other group.
alt.archery	Doing the William Tell thing (FAQ available).
rec.sport.billiard	Billiards and snooker (FAQ available).
rec.sport.disc	Flat Frisbee flips fly straight (FAQ available).
rec.equestrian	Horsie rides of all kinds (FAQ available).

rec.sport.fencing	All aspects of epeé and swordplay (FAQ available).
misc.fitness	Physical fitness and exercise.
rec.sport.football.australian	The insanity of Aussie Rules Football.
rec.gambling	Articles on games of chance and betting (FAQ available).
alt.gambling	Like rec.gambling, only different.
rec.sport.hockey.field	Discussion of the sport of field hockey.
alt.sport.horse-racing	Running for the roses: breeding, betting on, and racing horses.
rec.hunting	Discussions about hunting (moderated).
alt.sport.lacrosse	Canada's national game. No, really.
alt.sport.officiating	On being a referee.
rec.sport.olympics	All aspects of the Olympic Games.
rec.sport.volleyball	Discussions about volleyball.

Chapter 22

Geek Heaven: The Computer Newsgroups

In This Chapter
- ➤ Newsgroups that deal with software
- ➤ Operating systems newsgroups
- ➤ Hardware newsgroups for PCs, Macs, and UNIX boxes
- ➤ Groups for artificial intelligence, multimedia, and more

The Net is, of course, a giant computer network, so I think it's safe to say that most Netizens have at least a passing interest in some aspect of computers. Otherwise, they'd be getting their info/news/jollies using some other medium. It makes sense, then, that computers represent USENET's largest category of newsgroups. There are, in fact, hundreds of computer-related newsgroups. Many of these groups cover mainstream subjects such as databases and Macintosh computer systems, but lots of them cover absurdly obscure topics such as cognitive engineering and Field Programmable Gate Arrays (don't ask me). I don't have even remotely enough room in a single chapter to give full coverage to all the computer newsgroups, so we'll only look at the most popular, the most accessible, and the most useful.

Artificial Intelligence

Artificial intelligence (AI) is considered by some to be the Holy Grail of computer science. The goal of AI researchers is to use computers to model the behavioral aspects of human intelligence. USENET has a number of AI groups that are quite popular with both researchers and amateurs in the field.

If you're looking for more information on AI (and on computers in general), the EINet Galaxy World Wide Web site should be your first stop. The Computer Technology page has links for all kinds of AI stuff such as fuzzy logic, genetic algorithms, and neural nets. There's also a truckload of links for other computer topics. To get there, send your Web browser software to the following spot:

```
http://www.einet.net/galaxy/Engineering-and-Technology/
Computer-Technology.html
```

General AI Discussions

For discussions on just about any aspect of AI, tune in to the newsgroup **comp.ai**. You'll find researchers discussing technical problems, AI book reviews, job postings, symposium announcements, and much more.

FAQ Info:

```
Articles:
    FAQ: AI Associations and Journals 3/6 [Monthly Posting]
    FAQ: AI Newsgroups and Mailing Lists 2/6 [Monthly Posting]
    FAQ: Artificial Intelligence Bibliography 4 [Monthly Posting]
    FAQ: Artificial Intelligence FTP Resources 5/6 [Monthly Posting]
    FAQ: Artificial Intelligence FTP Resources 6/6 [Monthly Posting]
    FAQ: Artificial Intelligence Questions and Answers 1/6
      [Monthly Posting]
RTFM.MIT.EDU Directory: /pub/usenet-by-group/comp.ai
```

Fuzzy Logic: The Fuzzification of a System

With fuzzy logic, the idea is to make computers go beyond their normal black-and-white way of processing information to allow them to handle "shades of gray" in meaning and natural language. Fuzzy logicians put forth new theories and hash out different approaches in the newsgroup **comp.ai.fuzzy**.

```
FAQ Info:
    Article:

        FAQ: Fuzzy Logic and Fuzzy Expert Systems 1/1 [Monthly Posting]
    RTFM.MIT.EDU Directory: /pub/usenet-by-group/comp.ai.fuzzy
```

Building a Better Robot

The promise of intelligent robots has thus far been fulfilled only in science fiction. Still, robotics researchers soldier on, and many of them can be found exchanging ideas in the newsgroup **comp.robotics**.

```
FAQ Info:
    Articles:
        comp.robotics Frequently Asked Questions (FAQ) part 1/3
        comp.robotics Frequently Asked Questions (FAQ) part 2/3
        comp.robotics Frequently Asked Questions (FAQ) part 3/3
    RTFM.MIT.EDU Directory: /pub/usenet-by-group/comp.robotics
```

Discussions About Data Communications

Data communications—the slinging of bits from machine to machine—is a hot topic these days. Whether it's low-tech like fax transmissions, medium-tech like modem connections and local area network transfers, or high-tech like ISDN and ATM lines, everybody wants to get the most out of their communications. This section looks at the USENET groups devoted to all aspects of data communications.

USENET's Fax Forum

It's almost certain that e-mail will someday send fax machines into the same pile as computer punch card readers and eight-track tape machines. For now, though, faxing is alive and well, and you can discuss fax software, hardware, and transmission techspeak with fellow fax freaks in the newsgroup **comp.dcom.fax**.

```
FAQ Info:
    Article:
        Fax (comp.dcom.fax) Frequently Asked Questions (FAQ) [Part 1/2]
        Fax (comp.dcom.fax) Frequently Asked Questions (FAQ) [Part 2/2]
    RTFM.MIT.EDU Directory: /pub/usenet-by-group/comp.dcom.fax
```

Mastering Your Modem

If your modem is making a mess of things, you should be able to get some expert help in the newsgroup **comp.dcom.modems**. This is also the place to be to get reviews of new modems and ask questions about the confusing alphabet soup of modem standards (V.32, V.32bis, V.34, and so on).

The (as yet) Unfulfilled Promise of ISDN

Integrated Services Digital Network (ISDN) is a telecommunications service that turns a phone line into an all-digital affair. In its basic guise (called the *Basic Rate Interface*, or *BRI*), the upgraded digital line can carry two signals—one for data and one for voice—at 64Kbps (kilobits per second), compared to only 14.4Kbps for most of today's modems. Despite this obvious advantage, the pace of ISDN implementation has been glacial, at best, either because the local phone companies have been slow to jump on the bandwagon, or because the prices have been prohibitive. But the massive numbers of people getting online has created a need for extra bandwidth, so more businesses and even individuals are starting to give ISDN a closer look. To check things out for yourself, be sure to dial into the newsgroup **comp.dcom.isdn** for the latest ISDN info and news.

FAQ Info:
```
Article: comp.dcom.isdn Frequently Asked Questions (FAQ)
RTFM.MIT.EDU Directory: /pub/usenet-by-group/comp.dcom.isdn
```

ATM: The Shape of Things to Come?

You'll probably be hearing a lot more about *Asynchronous Transfer Mode (ATM)* in the months to come. Why? Well, because ATM promises data transfer rates measured in *megabits* per second (that's *millions* of bits per second), which will make today's fastest modems, and even ISDN, look like tricycles on the Infobahn. There's still a long way to go, but you can keep up with the latest developments (and other stuff about Cell Relay products) by reading the newsgroup **comp.dcom.cell-relay**.

```
FAQ Info:
    Articles:
        comp.dcom.cell-relay FAQ: ATM, SMDS, and related technologies
          (part 1/2)
        comp.dcom.cell-relay FAQ: ATM, SMDS, and related technologies
          (part 2/2)
    RTFM.MIT.EDU Directory: /pub/usenet-by-group/comp.dcom.cell-relay
```

Conversations About Local Area Networks

If your data communicating occurs over a *local area network (LAN)*, then you'll want to keep your eye on the following newsgroups for tips, advice, and product reviews:

comp.dcom.lans.ethernet	Discussions of the Ethernet/IEEE 802.3 protocols (FAQs available).
comp.dcom.lans.fddi	Discussions of the FDDI protocol suite.
comp.dcom.lans.misc	Local area network hardware and software.
comp.dcom.lans.token-ring	Installing and using token ring networks.

Multimedia Madness Online

Everywhere you turn nowadays, it's multimedia this, multimedia that. USENET, of course, isn't immune to the multimedia trend, as you'll see in this section when we look at newsgroups related to various facets of multimedia.

Miscellaneous Multimedia Musings

Got a silent sound card? Looking for some savvy scanner advice before taking the plunge? Wondering what this desktop video malarkey is all about? For answers to these and a multitude of other multimedia questions, turn to the newsgroup **comp.multimedia**.

CD-ROM: Hardware and Software

In USENET, the bulk of the CD-ROM action occurs in the newsgroup **alt.cd-rom**. This popular group is loaded with CD-ROM advice, technical Q&A, and posts advertising CD-ROM drives and discs for sale.

> In computer lingo, CD-ROMs that are jam-packed with second-rate pictures, sounds, and programs are called **multimediocrities**.

As everybody and his uncle tries to cash in on the CD-ROM craze, it's inevitable that there will be people trying to foist low-end drives and discs on unsuspecting buyers. My advice? Well, *caveat emptor*, for starters, and be sure to check out the newsgroup **alt.cd-rom.reviews**. This group features nothing but reviews of the latest drives and discs from Net guinea pigs.

If an IBM PC or a PC clone is your multimedia machine of choice, you might prefer to use **comp.sys.ibm.pc.hardware. cd-rom** to get PC-specific advice on CD-ROM stuff.

Making Beautiful Computer Music

If you're into *MIDI (Musical Instrument Digital Interface)* or any kind of electronic music, you'll find lots of like-minded e-music fans in the newsgroups **comp.music** and **alt.emusic**.

```
FAQ Info:
    Article:
        Electronic and Computer Music Frequently Asked Questions (FAQ)
    RTFM.MIT.EDU Directory: /pub/usenet-by-group/comp.music
```

USENET's Software Newsgroups

Software, of course, makes the computer world go 'round. Without it, our machines would just be noisy, worthless hunks of metal and plastic. We're definitely talking boat anchor material. Fortunately, there's been no shortage of pizza-and-cola-fueled programmers willing to spend long hours hacking out code for our benefit, so we have programs to run a-plenty. Unfortunately (and somewhat surprisingly to me), there aren't all that many USENET newsgroups that cover specific software packages. Oh sure, there are (as you'll see later on) umpteen groups for programming languages and operating systems, but relatively few for the word processors and spreadsheets the rest of us use every day. That will likely change in the future, but for now we're stuck with the groups covered in this section.

The Database Discussions Groups

Everyone knows we're up to our eyeballs in information, but what do we do with it all? Well, the most common route is to stick it in a database and hope it behaves itself. Then, after you've got your raw data safely ensconced, you need to tame it by using some kind of *database management system (DBMS)*. But which system do you choose? And after you've settled on the software, how do you get the most out of it? For the answers to these and other database queries, you'll need to read the following database newsgroups:

comp.databases	General database and data management issues and theory (FAQs available).
comp.databases.informix	Informix database management software discussions.
comp.databases.ingres	Issues relating to INGRES products.
comp.databases.ms-access	The Microsoft Access relational database system.
comp.databases.object	Object-oriented directions in database systems.
comp.databases.oracle	The SQL database products of the Oracle Corporation.
comp.databases.paradox	Borland's Paradox database software for DOS and Windows (FAQ available).
comp.databases.sybase	Discussions of SQL Server issues (FAQ available).
comp.databases.xbase.fox	Microsoft's FoxPro DBMS for DOS and Windows (FAQs available).
comp.databases.xbase.misc	Discussions of xBASE (dBASE-like) products.

alt.comp.databases.xbase.clipper	Tips and techniques for using Clipper.
comp.client-server	Setting up and maintaining client-server applications.
comp.lang.basic.visual.database	Programming database applications in Visual Basic.
comp.sys.mac.databases	Database systems for the Apple Macintosh.

Getting Help with E-Mail Software

By far the most widely used Internet service is e-mail. Many people rely on the convenience of e-mail in their daily routines, so it's all the more frustrating when that routine is upset by a mail program that won't read messages or send them. Before pulling out what remains of your hair, you may be able to get just the advice you need from one of the following newsgroups:

comp.mail.elm	Discussion and fixes for the Elm mail system (FAQs available).
comp.mail.mime	About the Multipurpose Internet Mail Extensions (FAQs available).
comp.mail.misc	General discussions about computer mail (FAQs available).
comp.mail.pine	Tips and advice for the Pine mail user agent (FAQs available).
comp.mail.sendmail	Configuring and using the BSD sendmail agent.
comp.mail.uucp	Mail in the UUCP network environment (FAQs available).

USENET's Graphics Groups

If you need help coming to grips with the realities of computer graphics, or if you need advice on a commercial graphics program, you can get the big picture in one of the following newsgroups:

comp.graphics	Computer graphics, art, animation, image processing (FAQs available).

comp.graphics.algorithms	Algorithms used in producing computer graphics.
comp.graphics.animation	Technical aspects of computer animation.
comp.graphics.opengl	The OpenGL 3-D application programming interface.
comp.graphics.packages.alias	Working with the graphics packages from Alias Research.
comp.graphics.packages.lightwave	Newtek's Lightwave 3-D.
comp.graphics.raytracing	Ray tracing software and tools.

If you're scouring the Net for more info on graphics, a good place to start is the Yahoo World Wide Web site. Set your browser to the following location:

```
http://akebono.stanford.edu/yahoo/Computers/
```

Select the **Graphics** link to get a wealth of great graphics pics, programs, and info.

The Shareware Shop

Looking for a shareware program that accomplishes a specific task? Got a shareware program you want to share with the world? For shareware requests, announcements, and help, check out the newsgroup **alt.comp.shareware**.

> **Shareware**, just so you know, is software that you can try out for free. If you decide to use the program regularly, however, you need to send in a small fee (usually between $5 and $25) to the author.

Spreadsheet Tips and Tricks

The world's number crunchers rely on spreadsheets to take the drudgery out of financial calculations, scientific modeling, and lots more. If you're a spreadsheet maven, you'll definitely want to subscribe to the newsgroup **comp.apps.spreadsheets**. Posters to this group present spreadsheet tips, solutions, and queries for various programs, including Excel, Lotus 1-2-3, and Quattro Pro.

Operating Systems

The importance of operating systems in our computer lives is reflected in the sheer wealth of USENET newsgroups devoted to them. In this section, we'll look at groups that cover the Big Four: DOS, OS/2, UNIX, and Windows.

DOS Discussions

Windows users have been sounding the DOS death knell for a few years now, but the old warrior refuses to go gently into that good night. If a daily dose of DOS is still a big part of your life, here are some newsgroups you might want to check out:

comp.os.msdos.apps	Tips and tricks for DOS applications.
comp.os.msdos.desqview	QuarterDeck's Desqview and related products.
comp.os.msdos.mail-news	Administering mail and network news systems under DOS.
comp.os.msdos.misc	Bits and pieces of DOS lore and advice.

Warping into the OS/2 Groups

OS/2 has always had a small, but intensely loyal, coterie of devotees. Now, with OS/2 Warp looking like a solid hit, the ranks are sure to grow substantially over the next year or two. For those of you who've already dipped your toes in the OS/2 waters, here are the groups you can subscribe to in order to hang out with your confrères:

comp.os.os2.advocacy	OS/2 arguments, pro and con.
comp.os.os2.announce	Notable news and announcements related to OS/2 (moderated).
comp.os.os2.apps	Running applications under OS/2.
comp.os.os2.bugs	OS/2 bug reports, fixes, and work-arounds.

Chapter 22 ▶ *Geek Heaven: The Computer Newsgroups*

comp.os.os2.misc	Miscellaneous topics about OS/2.
comp.os.os2.multimedia	Multimedia on OS/2 systems.
comp.os.os2.networking.misc	Miscellaneous OS/2 networking issues.
comp.os.os2.networking.tcp-ip	Configuring TCP/IP under OS/2.
comp.os.os2.setup	Installing and configuring OS/2.

Meditating with UNIX High Priests

UNIX is so pervasive in the Internet community that it's become a sort of *de facto* religion. Its practitioners speak in hushed tones of "shells" and "main pages," and pay obeisance to the wizards who can figure out commands such as `sed's/,''g'¦ grep-v $USER¦sort¦uniq`. And there are about as many different versions of UNIX as there are world religions, so there are all kinds of newsgroups set up for humble UNIX supplicants:

comp.unix.admin	Administering a UNIX-based system.
comp.unix.advocacy	UNIX flattery and flames.
comp.unix.aix	IBM's version of UNIX (FAQs available).
comp.unix.aux	Apple's version of UNIX (FAQs available).
comp.unix.bsd	Berkeley Software Distribution UNIX (FAQ available).
comp.unix.misc	Miscellaneous UNIX square pegs that don't fit in the other groups' round holes.
comp.unix.osf.misc	Various aspects of Open Software Foundation products.
comp.unix.osf.osf1	The Open Software Foundation's OSF/1.

comp.unix.pc-clone.32bit	UNIX on 386 and 486 machines.
comp.unix.questions	Q&A for UNIX neophytes (FAQs available).
comp.unix.shell	Using and programming the UNIX shell (FAQs available).
comp.unix.solaris	Sun Microsystem's Solaris UNIX.
comp.unix.sys5.r3	UNIX System V Release 3.
comp.unix.sys5.r4	UNIX System V Release 4.
comp.unix.ultrix	Discussions about DEC's Ultrix UNIX.
comp.unix.unixware	Novell's UNIXWare products.
comp.unix.user-friendly	UNIX user-friendliness—or lack thereof (FAQ available).
comp.unix.wizards	For UNIX pointy-heads only (moderated).
comp.windows.open-look	The ins and outs of the Open Look GUI.
comp.windows.x	Explanations of the X Window System.
comp.windows.x.announce	X Window System announcements (moderated).
comp.windows.x.apps	Working with applications in X.
comp.windows.x.i386unix	The XFree86 Window system and others.
comp.windows.x.motif	Mutterings about the Motif GUI (FAQs available).
comp.windows.x.pex	The PHIGS Extensions to the X Window System.

Chapter 22 ➤ *Geek Heaven: The Computer Newsgroups*

Wandering Through the Windows Newsgroups

Windows, thanks to its huge and ever-growing user base, is the reigning champ in the battle for operating system supremacy. Oh sure, it's still the new kid on the Internet block, but that'll change so fast it'll make your mouse spin. USENET celebrates Windows' emerging dominance with a passel of newsgroups for all of Windows' incarnations (Windows 3.1, Windows for Workgroups, Windows NT, and Windows 95):

comp.os.ms-windows.advocacy	Windows boosting and bashing.
comp.os.ms-windows.announce	Announcements relating to Windows (moderated).
comp.os.ms-windows.apps.comm	Windows communication software.
comp.os.ms-windows.apps.financial	Windows financial and tax software.
comp.os.ms-windows.apps.misc	Other Windows applications.
comp.os.ms-windows.apps.utilities	Windows utilities.
comp.os.ms-windows.apps.word-proc	Windows word-processing applications.
comp.os.ms-windows.misc	General discussions about Windows issues.
comp.os.ms-windows.networking.misc	Windows and other networks.
comp.os.ms-windows.networking.tcp-ip	Windows and TCP/IP networking.
comp.os.ms-windows.networking.windows	Networking with NT and WfW.
comp.os.ms-windows.nt.misc	Windows NT miscellany.

Part 3 ➤ *All the News That's Fit to Surf*

comp.os.ms-windows.nt.setup	Configuring Windows NT systems.
comp.os.ms-windows.setup	Installing and configuring Windows.
comp.os.ms-windows.video	Video adapters and drivers for Windows.

Computer Systems' User Groups

USENET has dozens of newsgroups that cater to the users of specific computer systems. In this section, we'll look at the groups for users of IBM PCs and PC clones, Macintosh, Silicon Graphics, Sun, and more.

IBM PCs and Their Clone Cousins

If you're one of the billions and billions of people who use an IBM PC or a clone as your main machine, you'll be happy to know that USENET is bound to have a newsgroup that can handle whatever ailment your computer is suffering from this week:

comp.sys.ibm.pc.demos	Demonstration programs that showcase programmer skill.
comp.sys.ibm.pc.hardware.chips	Processors, memory, and more.
comp.sys.ibm.pc.hardware.comm	PC modems and communication cards.
comp.sys.ibm.pc.hardware.misc	Miscellaneous PC hardware topics.
comp.sys.ibm.pc.hardware.networking	Hardware and equipment for PC networking.
comp.sys.ibm.pc.hardware.storage	Hard drives and other PC storage devices.
comp.sys.ibm.pc.hardware.systems	IBM PC computer and clone systems.

comp.sys.ibm.pc.hardware.video	Video cards and monitors.
comp.sys.ibm.pc.misc	Whatever strikes your fancy.
comp.sys.ibm.pc.soundcard.advocacy	Sound card pros and cons.
comp.sys.ibm.pc.soundcard.misc	General sound card stuff.
comp.sys.ibm.pc.soundcard.music	Making sound cards make music.
comp.sys.ibm.pc.soundcard.tech	Technical questions about sound cards.
comp.sys.ibm.ps2.hardware	Ruminations on the IBM PS/2.
alt.sys.pc-clone.dell	Discussions about Dell computers.
alt.sys.pc-clone.gateway2000	Complaints about Gateway 2000's technical support.

The Core Macintosh Newsgroups

For those of you who have a Mac, here are the newsgroups where you can commune with your Mac mates:

comp.sys.mac.advocacy	Mac advocates and adversaries square off.
comp.sys.mac.announce	Important notices for Mac users (moderated).
comp.sys.mac.apps	Tips and tricks for Mac applications.
comp.sys.mac.comm	Data communications on the Mac.
comp.sys.mac.databases	Database systems for the Mac.
comp.sys.mac.digest	Macintosh info and uses (moderated).

Part 3 ➤ *All the News That's Fit to Surf*

comp.sys.mac.graphics	Mac graphics: paint, draw, 3D, CAD, animation.
comp.sys.mac.hardware	Macintosh hardware issues and discussions.
comp.sys.mac.hypercard	Stuff on Hypercard stacks.
comp.sys.mac.misc	General discussions about the Macintosh.
comp.sys.mac.portables	Powerbooks and other portable Macs.
comp.sys.mac.scitech	Using the Mac in scientific and technological work.
comp.sys.mac.system	Discussions of Macintosh system software.
comp.sys.mac.wanted	Postings of the "I want such-and-such for my Mac" variety.

The Silicon Graphics Valley of Newsgroups

If you're into graphics, few machines inspire pure techno-lust the way the workstations of Silicon Graphics International (SGI) do. Whether you use a low-end Indy desktop machine, a six-figure Onyx beast, or, like me, just drool at the thought of owning one, here are the places where the Silicon Graphics groupies loiter:

comp.sys.sgi.admin	System administration for SGI machines.
comp.sys.sgi.announce	Announcements for the SGI community (moderated).
comp.sys.sgi.apps	Applications that run on SGI computers.
comp.sys.sgi.audio	Audio on SGI systems.
comp.sys.sgi.bugs	Bugs found in the IRIX operating system.
comp.sys.sgi.graphics	Tips and advice for graphics packages.

Chapter 22 ➤ *Geek Heaven: The Computer Newsgroups*

comp.sys.sgi.hardware	SGI hardware and peripherals.
comp.sys.sgi.misc	General discussions about SGI machines.

Here Come the Sun Newsgroups

Sun Microsystems is the market leader in high-end workstations, so they've built up an enthusiastic following of people who really know how to put a computer through its paces. Here's a list of the newsgroups that deal with Sun workstations:

comp.sys.sun.admin	Sun system administration issues and questions.
comp.sys.sun.announce	Sun announcements and Sunergy mailings (moderated).
comp.sys.sun.apps	Software applications for Sun computer systems.
comp.sys.sun.hardware	Sun Microsystems hardware.
comp.sys.sun.misc	Miscellaneous discussions about Sun products.
comp.sys.sun.wanted	People looking for Sun products and support.

USENET's Computer Marketplace

Looking to buy or sell a computer system or peripheral? No problem. Just drop by any of the **misc.forsale.computers.*** newsgroups to get in on the action. You'll find people selling stuff for Macs, IBM PCs, and lots more.

Miscellaneous Hardware

To finish our tour of duty in the hardware forums, here's a grab bag of newsgroups that cater to various hardware subjects:

comp.arch.storage	Storage system issues, both hardware and software (FAQs available).
comp.periphs	Peripheral devices such as keyboards, tape drives, and scanners.

283

comp.periphs.printers	Help with printer problems.
comp.periphs.scsi	Discussions of SCSI-based peripheral devices (FAQs available).
comp.sys.intel	According to my Pentium, this group averages 999.9468 posts a day (FAQs available).
comp.sys.laptops	Laptop and notebook computers.
comp.sys.mips	Talk about systems based on MIPS chips.
comp.sys.misc	Discussions about computers of all kinds.
comp.sys.palmtops	Super-powered calculators in the palm of your hand (FAQ available).
comp.sys.pen	The pros and cons of pen-based computing.
comp.sys.powerpc	General PowerPC discussions (FAQs available).

Chapter 23

Talking with Tall-Forehead Types in the Science Groups

In This Chapter
- Newsgroups dealing with biology and medicine
- The physics forums
- Groups for the mathematically unchallenged
- Space and astronomy newsgroups
- A superabundance of groups from the social sciences, chemistry, and more

The Net is now home to many different species, but scientists retain a special place in the Net's heart as both its progenitors and its most ardent users. This is reflected in the scads of science newsgroups that USENET has in its coffers. This chapter gives you the lowdown on the most popular of the hundreds of groups available.

Dissecting the Biology Newsgroups

Whether you're into ecology, ethology, or evolution you should find a newsgroup that covers your area of expertise. The newsgroup **sci.bio** handles biology posts, questions, and announcements that have a more general nature. The Net has lots of sites that provide good biology info and data. To help you find what you're looking for, watch out for a periodic post in the **sci.bio** group with the Subject line "A Biologist's Guide to Internet Resources." This section looks at a few of the most heavily traveled biology newsgroups.

➤ Scientists and professional breeders interested in aquariums exchange advice and info in the newsgroup **sci.aquaria**. Note that this group is for scientific postings only. If you're a hobbyist, you'll find calmer waters in the group **rec.aquaria**.

```
FAQ Info:
    Articles:
        AQUARIA FAQ: Filters (3/6)
        AQUARIA FAQ: Introduction to the *.aquaria FAQ (1/6)
        AQUARIA FAQ: Magazines and Mail Order Information (4/6)
        AQUARIA FAQ: Plants (5/6)
        AQUARIA FAQ: Water (6/6)
    RTFM.MIT.EDU Directory: /pub/usenet-by-group/sci.aquaria/
        general-faq
```

➤ If you're interested in ecological activism, check out the groups **talk.environment**, **alt.save.the.earth** and **alt.politics.greens** (described in Chapter 19, "Left Versus Right: The Politics Newsgroups"). However, if your daily labors concern the *science* of ecology, then you'll find the newsgroup **sci.bio.ecology** more to your liking.

➤ As a dog lover, I'm always puzzled (and, if truth be told, a bit embarrassed) when I see dogs "greeting" one another by smelling each other's backsides. I haven't the faintest idea why they do it, but I'm sure at least some of the *ethologists* (people who study animal behavior) who hang out in the newsgroup **sci.bio.ethology** would know.

➤ Evolution, at least in the scientific community, is the accepted explanation for how we (and everything else on the planet) became what we are today. But many questions still remain. For example, do species evolve gradually over time, or in wholesale bursts? Can we explain behavior such as altruism in evolutionary terms? For discussions on these and other evolutionary concerns with a scientific bent, tune in to the moderated newsgroup **sci.bio.evolution**. If you're looking for something a little more up-tempo and flame-filled, you can join in the never-ending holy war between creationists and evolutionists in the group **talk.origins**.

➤ If amphibians and reptiles of every stripe, hue, and degree of sliminess are your thing, you're sure to find the herpetological discussions in the newsgroup **sci.bio.herp** of interest.

➤ The Net's microbiology community gets together in the newsgroup **sci.bio.microbiology** to discuss *E.coli* and other hard-to-see fauna.

➤ What do you do if you're looking for a particular piece of lab equipment or software for a biology project? Well, if you're on the Net (and what self-respecting biologist isn't?), then you post a request to the newsgroup **sci.bio.technology**.

➤ Although I won't cover it in any detail here, you should also know about USENET's **bionet** hierarchy. This collection of newsgroups caters to biology pros from all fields. The **bionet** guidelines state that posts should be "research-related only," so the groups tend to be mostly signal with very little noise.

Conversations with Chemists

If chemistry is your bag, USENET has a small collection of newsgroups where you'll find like-minded souls. This section gives you the rundown.

➤ If you have a general chemical query, the place to post it is the newsgroup **sci.chem**. Recent threads in this group include why some soaps have honey in them (!), and the composition of Diet Coke.

➤ You'll find more specialized discussions on the field of electrochemistry in the newsgroup **sci.chem.electrochem**.

Part 3 ➤ *All the News That's Fit to Surf*

```
FAQ Info:
    Article:
        sci.chem.electrochem Frequently Asked Questions (FAQ)
    RTFM.MIT.EDU Directory:
        /pub/usenet-by-group sci.chem. electro chem
```

➤ What do cellulose, proteins, silk, plastic, and synthetic fibers all have in common? Well, I didn't know either, but I looked it up, and it turns out they're all polymers. How about that. For discussions on all aspects of polymer science, subscribe to the newsgroup **sci.polymers**.

```
FAQ Info:
    Article:   FAQ: sci.Polymers
    RTFM.MIT.EDU Directory: /pub/usenet-by-group/sci.polymers
```

Groups for Geology and Other Earth Sciences

This section looks at newsgroups that cover earth sciences such as geology, meteorology, and oceanography.

➤ Geologists concern themselves with ancient things like the origin and history of the earth, and with modern things such as earthquakes and tectonic plates. When they've got a question or something to share with their peers, the Net's geologists head for the newsgroup **sci.geo.geology**.

```
FAQ Info:
    Articles:
        sci.geo.geology FAQ 1/5 Introduction
        sci.geo.geology FAQ 2/5 Contents
        sci.geo.geology FAQ 3/5 faq
        sci.geo.geology FAQ 4/5 Glossary
        sci.geo.geology FAQ 5/5 Appendices
    RTFM.MIT.EDU Directory: /pub/usenet-by-group/sci.geo.geology
```

➤ For discussions about atmospheric, surface, and groundwater hydrology, submerge yourself in the newsgroup **sci.geo.hydrology**.

➤ We just had a big snowstorm here a day or two ago, and the skies are threatening more of the nasty white stuff, so my personal interest in meteorology is a bit pedestrian. If your interests are

Chapter 23 ➤ *Talking with Tall-Forehead Types in the Science Groups*

more scientific, however, then you can take shelter in the newsgroup **sci.geo.meteorology**.

```
FAQ Info:
    Article:
        Meteorology Resources FAQ
        Sources of Meteorological Data FAQ Part 1/2
        Sources of Meteorological Data FAQ Part 2/2
    RTFM.MIT.EDU Directory:
        /pub/usenet-by-group/sci.geo.meteorology
```

➤ If you're an oceanographer looking to make waves or just study them, the place to be is the newsgroup **sci.geo.oceanography** for posts on all aspects of oceanography and marine science.

USENET's Medical Science Newsgroups

All the sciences are important in their own way, but medical science in particular has an urgency that the others lack. The reason is obvious: The stakes—life and limb—are higher. Perhaps this is why the medical science newsgroups that we'll look at in this section are among the busiest of USENET's science forums.

General Medical Discussions

If you have questions or concerns about medical science that don't fit into any of the other groups, then try **sci.med**.

```
FAQ Info:
    Articles:
        alt.supoort.asthma FAQ: Asthma--General Information
        Tinnitus Frequently Answered Questions v1.0
    RTFM.MIT.EDU Directory: /pub/usenet-by-group/sci.med
```

Researching the AIDS Epidemic

The threat of AIDS has scared the bejeezus out of any sexually active person who hasn't been safely ensconced in a monogamous relationship for the past dozen years or so. But the race is on to find a cure for this plague-in-the-making, and you can keep up with the latest findings by reading the moderated newsgroup **sci.med.aids**. Most of the posts deal with the pathology and biology of the HIV virus, but

> Please remember that the **sci.med.*** newsgroups are for scientific research and medical professionals only. If you have something to say about the health care crisis, take it to **talk.politics.medicine**. If you have some symptoms you want to be diagnosed, try one of the **alt.support.*** groups (see Chapter 20, "Psychology, Sex, and More: The Social Newsgroups").

there's also a handy "AIDS Daily Summary" published by the Center for Disease Control (CDC) with the latest news from the battlefront. If you're looking for AIDS discussions with a less technical bent, try **misc.health.aids**.

```
FAQ Info:
  Articles:
      Sci.Med.AIDS FAQ part 1 of 10
      Sci.Med.AIDS FAQ part 2 of 10
      Sci.Med.AIDS FAQ part 3 of 10
      Sci.Med.AIDS FAQ part 4 of 10
      Sci.Med.AIDS FAQ part 5 of 10
      Sci.Med.AIDS FAQ part 6 of 10
      Sci.Med.AIDS FAQ part 7 of 10
      Sci.Med.AIDS FAQ part 8 of 10
      Sci.Med.AIDS FAQ part 9 of 10
      Sci.Med.AIDS FAQ part 10 of 10
  RTFM.MIT.EDU Directory: /pub/usenet-by-group/
      sci.med.aids
```

Seeking a Cure for Cancer

AIDS may get most of the attention in the popular press, but there's still much work to be done before we can cross cancer off the list of deadly diseases. Researchers discuss drugs, treatments, and new therapies in the newsgroup **sci.med.diseases.cancer**.

```
FAQ Info:
    Article: Cancer - Online Information Sources FAQ
    RTFM.MIT.EDU Directory:
       /pub/usenet-by-group/sci.med.diseases.cancer
```

Dentistry Deliberations

Wired dentists will no doubt want to spend some time in the newsgroup **sci.med.dentistry**. Posters here discuss dentistry jobs, new dental treatments, the ins and outs of teeth, and how to calm dental patients experiencing The Fear. No appointment necessary.

Chapter 23 ➤ *Talking with Tall-Forehead Types in the Science Groups*

The Nursing Newsgroup

If you think health care is in some sort of crisis, imagine what things would be like if we didn't have nurses! I shudder to even think about it. In the newsgroup **sci.med.nursing**, nurses discuss techniques, medical info, and career opportunities.

```
FAQ Info:
    Article:  sci.med.nursing FAQ
    RTFM.MIT.EDU Directory: /pub/usenet-by-group/sci.med.nursing
```

Carpal Tunnel Syndrome and Other Occupational Hazards

A few years ago, while working particularly long hours to meet a book deadline, I felt an ominous ache in my wrists that I took to be the first symptoms of Carpal Tunnel Syndrome (CTS). I jumped on the Net and was able to track down lots of good info on the prevention of CTS and other repetitive strain injuries (RSI), and I've been pain-free ever since. If you're experiencing some kind RSI problem, or if you're a professional investigating occupational hazards of all kinds, the newsgroup **sci.med.occupational** is the place to be for talk about prevention, detection, and treatment.

```
FAQ Info:
    Articles:
        FAQ: Typing Injuries (1/5): Recent Changes [monthly posting]
        FAQ: Typing Injuries (2/5): General Info [monthly posting]
        FAQ: Typing Injuries (3/5): Keyboard Alternatives
            [monthly posting]
        FAQ: Typing Injuries (4/5): Software Monitoring Tools
            [monthly posting]
        FAQ: Typing Injuries (5/5): Furniture Information
            [monthly posting]
    RTFM.MIT.EDU Directory: /pub/usenet-by-group/sci.med
```

More Medical Newsgroups

To round out our look at the medical science newsgroups, here are a few more to keep an eye out for:

Part 3 ▶ *All the News That's Fit to Surf*

alt.med.allergy	Helping allergy sufferers (FAQs available).
alt.med.cfs	Chronic Fatigue Syndrome information.
alt.med.equipment	Discussions about medical equipment.
misc.health.alternative	Alternative and holistic health care.
misc.health.diabetes	Coping with diabetes in day-to-day life.
sci.med.immunology	Medical and scientific aspects of immune system illnesses.
sci.med.nutrition	The physiological impacts of diet.
sci.med.pharmacy	The teaching and practice of pharmacy.
sci.med.physics	Issues of physics in medical testing and care.
sci.med.psychobiology	Dialog and news in psychiatry and psychobiology.
sci.med.radiology	All aspects of radiology.
alt.image.medical	Medical image exchange discussions.

Mathematical Mystery Tours

The Net's amateur and professional mathematicians head for the newsgroup **sci.math** when they have a hard math nut they need help cracking, or if they've come up with an elegant solution to a problem, or if they just want to shoot the breeze about, say, Fermat's Last Theorem.

```
FAQ Info:
    Articles:
        sci.math: Frequently Asked Questions [1/3]
        sci.math: Frequently Asked Questions [2/3]
        sci.math: Frequently Asked Questions [3/3]
```

Chapter 23 ▸ Talking with Tall-Forehead Types in the Science Groups

```
           Introduction to Frequently Asked Questions
           RTFM.MIT.EDU Directory: /pub/usenet-by-group/sci.math
```

Fractals have captured the imaginations of math and non-math types ever since Benoit Mandelbrot's unlikely bestseller *The Fractal Geometry of Nature* appeared. You can indulge your interest in chaos theory, Julia sets, Lorenz attractors, and other objects of fractional dimension in the newsgroup **sci.fractals**. (You may also want to check out the newsgroup **sci.nonlinear**.)

> **FAQ Info:**
> Article: Fractal Questions and Answers
> RTFM.MIT.EDU Directory: /pub/usenet-by-group/sci.fractals

Doing heavy math on a computer—such as solving nonlinear equations and differentiating functions—has always been problematic thanks to the inevitable truncation and rounding errors that arise. The field of numerical analysis investigates not only algorithms to perform the math, but also ways to reduce the errors (such as demanding a Pentium chip that works properly!). The Net's numerical analysts meet in the newsgroup **sci.math.num-analysis** to trade code snippets and computational tricks.

> **FAQ Info:**
> Articles:
>   Part 1 of 3: Free C,C++ for numerical computation
>   Part 2 of 3: Free C,C++ for numerical computation
>   Part 3 of 3: Free C,C++ for numerical computation
> RTFM.MIT.EDU Directory: /pub/usenet-by-group/sci.math.num-analysis

The moderated newsgroup **sci.math.research** is the place where mathematicians doing leading-edge research report their results and request advice on sticky problems.

If you use mathematics software packages such as *Mathematica* or *Maple V*, or if you're trying to develop programs for doing symbolic algebra, you can get advice and tips in the newsgroup **sci.math.symbolic**.

If you believe Wittgenstein when he says "the logic of the world is prior to all truth and falsehood," then you'll definitely want to hang out with your fellow logicians in the newsgroup **sci.logic**.

If you're interested in operations research—whether you're researching it, teaching it, or applying it in the real world—you can exchange ideas in the newsgroup **sci.op-research**.

```
FAQ Info:
    Article:
        Linear Programming FAQ
        Nonlinear Programming FAQ
    RTFM.MIT.EDU Directory: /pub/usenet-by-group/sci.op-research
```

Here's a list of the USENET newsgroups that devote their lives to the study and application of statistics:

newsgroup sci.stat.consult	Statistical consulting.
newsgroup sci.stat.edu	Statistics education.
newsgroup sci.stat.math	Statistics from a strictly mathematical viewpoint.

USENET's Forums for Physicists

If you're into physics—either doing full-blown, cutting-edge research, or as an avid reader of books like *The Dancing Wu-Li Masters* and *The Tao of Physics*—USENET probably has a newsgroup that suits your interests.

Random Walks in the Physics Neighborhood

Wondering what Schrodinger's cat is up to these days? Need some info on black holes or quantum physics? Got some technical or theoretical data you'd like to share? The place for these and other general physics articles is the popular newsgroup **sci.physics**.

```
FAQ Info:
    Articles:
        Sci.Physics Frequently Asked Questions (1/4) - Administrivia
        Sci.Physics Frequently Asked Questions (2/4) - Cosmology/
          Astrophysics
        Sci.Physics Frequently Asked Questions (3/4) - General Physics
        Sci.Physics Frequently Asked Questions (4/4) - Particles/SR/
Quantum
    RTFM.MIT.EDU Directory: /pub/usenet-by-group/sci.physics
```

Physics: The Way-Out and Wacky

Few sciences provoke such wildly speculative theories as physics. From the Many Worlds Interpretation of Quantum Mechanics to faster-than-light travel to black holes, physics on the edge can be a pretty way-out affair. The Net's physicists—professional and amateur—get their "what-if" ya-yas out in the newsgroup **alt.sci.physics.new-theories**.

USENET's Electronics Circuit

If topics such as circuits, capacitance, and microcontrollers make your eyes light up, you want to solder a connection to the newsgroup **sci.electronics**. You'll find articles on constructing and connecting electronic devices (including—yikes!—homemade lasers), electronics theory, and electronics equipment.

If schematic drafting, printed circuit layout, and other electronics CAD issues are more your style, check out the group **sci.electronics.cad**. And if you're looking for tips and advice on repairing electronic equipment, try **sci.electronics.repair**.

```
FAQ Info:
    Articles:
        68hc11 microcontroller FAQ
        8051 microcontroller FAQ
        Electrical Wiring FAQ [Part 1/2]
        Electrical Wiring FAQ [Part 2/2]
        Microcontroller primer and FAQ
    RTFM.MIT.EDU Directory: /pub/usenet-by-group/sci.electronics
```

Energetic Energy Discussions

If you're looking to keep up with the latest developments in alternative energy sources, the ideal place to do it is the newsgroup **sci.energy**. There are articles on wind and solar power, electric cars, battery breakthroughs, and lots of debates on where we should be spending our money and time on energy R and D.

Keeping an Eye on Optics

sci.optics is a highly technical group that covers optics topics such as lasers, lenses, and holography.

A Medley of Physics Newsgroups

I don't have the space to cover all of USENET's physics groups in detail, but many of them are at least worth mentioning. Here's a list of some other newsgroups where the Net's physics community congregates:

sci.physics.accelerators	Particle accelerators and the physics of beams.
alt.sci.physics.acoustics	The soundness of the science of sound.
sci.physics.electromag	Electromagnetic theory and applications.
sci.physics.fusion	Info on fusion, especially "cold" fusion (FAQ available).
sci.energy.hydrogen	All about hydrogen as an alternative fuel.
sci.physics.particle	Particle physics discussions (FAQ available).
sci.physics.plasma	Plasma Science and Technology community exchange (moderated).
alt.sci.physics.plutonium	How to build your own thermonuclear device?
sci.physics.research	Current physics research (moderated).

Newsgroups for the Social Sciences

This section looks at the USENET newsgroups that are devoted to the social sciences of anthropology, archaeology, psychology, and linguistics.

Anthropology Assemblies

If you enjoy poking your nose into other people's cultures, beliefs, and traditions, you must be an anthropologist either in fact or in spirit. Whatever your interest in humankind, check out the newsgroup **sci.anthropology** for articles on all aspects of anthropological study.

If your anthropological interests lie more toward cultures that are pre-*Homo sapiens*, head for **sci.anthropology.paleo**, instead.

Digging in the Dirt: Archaeology Newsgroups

Archaeologists and other people who like to examine really old things and don't mind a bit of dirt under their fingernails exchange theories, finds, announcements, and advice in the group **sci.archaeology**.

If your antiquities research is centered on Mesoamerican peoples such as the Mayans, you'll find many kindred souls in the newsgroup **sci.archaeology.mesoamerican**.

Meetings of the Minds in the Psychology Groups

Psychology has been in the news a lot recently as academics and pundits of all political persuasions weigh in with their two cents worth about the controversial book *The Bell Curve*. If you've got some insights into IQ, or if you've got something to say about any other aspect of psychology, the place to be is the newsgroup **sci.psychology**.

```
FAQ Info:
    Article:
        sci.psychology FAQ (Answers to Frequently Asked Questions)
    RTFM.MIT.EDU Directory: /pub/usenet-by-group/sci.psychology
```

Psychology professionals can publish their research (or can ask for help solving a research problem) in the moderated newsgroup **sci.psychology.research**.

If your psychological crank is turned by the cognitive functions of perception, memory, judgment, and reasoning, take a look at the newsgroup **sci.cognitive**.

Linguistic Gabfests

In a Tower of Babel world that boasts hundreds of languages and dialects, the study of language is no trivial task. The Net's linguists use the newsgroup **sci.lang** to examine natural languages, understand communications, and analyze alphabets and other linguistic building blocks.

```
FAQ Info:
    Article:   sci.lang FAQ (Frequently Asked Questions)
    RTFM.MIT.EDU Directory: /pub/usenet-by-group/sci.lang
```

The Space and Astronomy Groups

The Apollo moon landings instilled in me (and, I have no doubt, many other people as well) a deep interest in space exploration and astronomy. So I quite enjoy many of the less technical debates and controversies that erupt in USENET's various space and astronomy groups. Whether you're a passionate amateur, like me, or a dedicated professional, you're bound to find one of the following groups of interest.

The very busy newsgroup **sci.astro** is home to astronomy aficionados of all stripes. You'll find musings on faster-than-light travel, news about current NASA missions, advance notice of meteor showers, and lots, lots more.

```
FAQ Info:
    Articles:
       Astro/Space Frequently Seen Acronyms
       Purchasing Amateur Telescopes FAQ (part 1/2)
       Purchasing Amateur Telescopes FAQ (part 2/2)
    RTFM.MIT.EDU Directory: /pub/usenet-by-group/sci.astro
```

Amateur astronomers have their own newsgroup: **sci.astro.amateur**. The articles in this group discuss telescope construction and collimation, reviews of equipment, and suggestions for celestial objects to inspect.

Should we build a space station? Should we plan any more manned space missions to the moon or even to Mars? Is NASA's budget too much or too little? For debates on these and other thorny issues in space exploration, turn to the newsgroup **sci.space.policy**. If you like to keep up with the latest shuttle news, the newsgroup **sci.space.shuttle** is a must read.

To bring our discussion of space and astronomy newsgroups to a safe landing here on earth, the following list presents a selection of groups that you may find interesting:

sci.astro.hubble	Processing Hubble Space Telescope data (moderated).
sci.astro.planetarium	Discussion of planetariums.
sci.astro.research	Forum for astronomy/astrophysics research (moderated).
alt.sci.planetary	Studies in planetary science.
sci.space.news	Announcements of space-related news items (moderated).
newsgroup sci.space.science	Space and planetary science and related technical work (moderated; FAQs available).
sci.space.tech	Technical issues related to space flight (moderated).

More Science Stuff

It's time to close out our discussion of the USENET's science forums, but not before mentioning a few other science groups that you might want to try out:

sci.cryonics	The latest in human deep-freeze technology (FAQs available).
sci.crypt	The science and politics of data encryption (FAQs available).
sci.crypt.research	Research issues in cryptography and cryptanalysis (moderated).
sci.econ	The science of the dismal science.
sci.engr	Technical discussions about engineering tasks.
sci.engr.advanced-tv	HDTV/DATV standards, formats, and equipment.
sci.engr.biomed	Discussing the field of biomedical engineering.

sci.engr.chem	All aspects of chemical engineering.
sci.engr.civil	Topics related to civil engineering.
sci.engr.control	The engineering of control systems.
sci.engr.lighting	Light, vision and color in architecture, the media, and more.
sci.engr.manufacturing	Manufacturing technology.
sci.engr.mech	The field of mechanical engineering.
sci.engr.semiconductors	Semiconductor devices, processes, materials, and physics.
sci.environment	Scientific discussions about the environment.
sci.military	Discussions about science and the military (moderated).
sci.misc	Miscellaneous musings on a smorgasbord of science subjects.
sci.nanotech	The science of self-reproducing molecular-scale machines (moderated).
sci.philosophy.meta	The scientific slant on metaphysics.
sci.philosophy.tech	Technical philosophy: math, science, and logic.
sci.research	Research methods, funding, ethics, and whatever.
sci.research.careers	Issues relevant to careers in scientific research.
sci.research.postdoc	Anything about postdoctoral studies, including offers.
sci.skeptic	Skeptics discuss and debunk pseudo-science (FAQ available).
sci.virtual-worlds	Virtual reality technology and culture (moderated).
sci.virtual-worlds.apps	Current and future uses of virtual-worlds technology (moderated).

Chapter 24

News About the Net: Internet-Related Newsgroups

In This Chapter

➤ USENET's Internet newsgroups
➤ Newsgroups for Gopher, the World Wide Web, and other services
➤ A new look at the **news** hierarchy
➤ Groups for USENET newbies, addicts, and kooks

There's one thing many Net users enjoy talking about the most: the Net itself! Most of the time, we just need more info to help us navigate the Net morass: advice on newsreaders, World Wide Web Q&A, that kind of thing. The rest of the Net conversations are true *jumps-out-of-the-system (JOOTS)* in which we talk about things like the impact of the Internet on society, the traditions, rituals, and customs of Internet culture, and why so many Netizens are so, well, strange. I call it "net.navel-gazing," and it's the subject of this chapter.

Random Internet Interactions

We'll begin our look at USENET's Internet forums with a collection of newsgroups that have nothing whatsoever in common other than that they have some aspect of the Net as their reason for being.

Is "Internet Culture" an Oxymoron?

The group **alt.culture.internet** is perhaps the best example of the JOOTSing I mentioned at the beginning of the chapter. This group's posters take a step or two back from their daily Net chores to gaze unrelentingly at the Big Picture. Typical topics include the psychology (and psychopathology) of flaming, how best to welcome newbies, the impact of the Net's rapid growth, and speculations about the future of the Net.

```
FAQ Info:
    Articles:
        ONLINE OUTPOSTS--Cyberspatial Community Groups--Local,
            Nat'l, Internat'l
        Online Activism Resource List
    RTFM.MIT.EDU Directory:
        /pub/usenet-by-group/alt.culture.internet
```

Helping the Access-Deprived

Many people's online connections offer only limited access to the vast resources of the Internet. They get e-mail, FTP, maybe Telnet, and perhaps a few newsgroups. This often only whets their appetites, and they start looking around for an access provider who can supply them with a full-course Net meal. The best place to find a provider in your area is to post a request to the newsgroup **alt.internet.access.wanted**. Make sure you mention where you live (your area code is even better) and what kind of service you need.

```
FAQ Info:
    Articles:
        Internet access in New Zealand FAQ
        Network Access in Australia FAQ
        Summary list of Internet access providers in the UK
    RTFM.MIT.EDU Directory:
        /pub/usenet-by-group/alt.internet.access.wanted
```

Chapter 24 ➤ *News About the Net: Internet-Related Newsgroups*

Knocking the Net Down to Size

The Internet is so vast that a thriving cottage industry has evolved for letting people know what kinds of services are available and where to find them. Documents such as Kevin Savetz's *Internet Press* give you reams of information on sites that cater to specific subjects. You can find these articles and more in the newsgroup **alt.internet.services**.

```
FAQ Info:
    Articles:
        Accessing the Internet by E-Mail FAQ
        Bible of USENET FAQ
        FAQ: CSH Coke Machine Information
        FAQ: EFF's (Extended) Guide 2.3, Life, and Everything...
        FAQ: How can I send a fax from the Internet?
        FAQ: International E-mail accessibility
        Internet Mall: Shopping the Information Highway
        Internet Press
        Internet Services FAQ
        Net-Letter Guide
        Unofficial Internet Book List
        Updated Inter-Network Mail Guide
        Zines on the Internet (1/5)
        Zines on the Internet (2/5)
        Zines on the Internet (3/5)
        Zines on the Internet (4/5)
        Zines on the Internet (5/5)
    RTFM.MIT.EDU Directory:
        /pub/usenet-by-group/alt.internet.services
```

Scott Yanoff's list of *Special Internet Connections* is a great resource for finding things on the Net. It's organized by subject, so you can look up, say, Astronomy to get a list of Net sites with astronomical info. I find that this list is much easier to navigate in its World Wide Web format because you can usually just click on the links you want. To try this out, set your Web browser to the following locale:

```
http://slacvx.slac.stanford.edu:80/misc/internet-services.html
```

Accessing Libraries from the Internet

One of the handiest of Internet services is the capability to telnet to a library and search its subject catalogues from the comfort of your den or office. To find out the latest news in Internet library access, read the moderated newsgroup **comp.internet.library**.

The Net Is a Happening Place

One of the Internet's most attractive features is that it's constantly changing. To keep up with all the new stuff, try reading the moderated newsgroup **comp.internet.net-happenings**. This group's keeper picks out interesting and useful additions to the Internet community and posts them for your browsing pleasure.

Looking for Long-Lost Net Folk

Got an old friend you've lost contact with over the years? Looking for that deadbeat you lent some money to last year? Got an obituary to pass on or an announcement about a class reunion? If the people involved are (or were) Netizens, you can post a request for information on their current whereabouts in the newsgroup **soc.net-people**.

FAQ Info:
```
Article:   Tips on using soc.net-people
RTFM.MIT.EDU Directory: /pub/usenet-by-group/soc.net-people
```

The Internet Welcome Wagon

Are you a Net neophyte looking for a safe haven for asking "square one" kinds of questions? Then look no further than the newsgroup **alt.newbie**. This group is designed so new users—*newbies*—can get the help and advice they need without imposing on one of the regular newsgroups. The good news is that it's a "no-flame zone," so you can post *any* question, no matter how silly or trivial it may seem, and get a thoughtful response from some patient Net vet.

An Internet Phone-In Radio Show (Sort Of)

Carl Malamud's Internet Talk Radio service runs various Internet-related talk shows and distributes them over the Net in multi-megabyte sound files. The listeners then talk about the shows' subjects in the newsgroup **alt.internet.talk-radio**.

> To find out more about Internet Talk Radio, send an e-mail message to **info@radio.com**.

Newsgroups for Specific Internet Services

The Internet's greatest weakness is the sheer wealth of services it provides for tracking down information. Huh? Well, all those services are great, but it means we have to learn a different program for every service we use; and, of course, each of these programs uses a different interface, has different commands, and has a different way of approaching the Net. To help us keep up, USENET has a few newsgroups that are devoted to specific Internet services, and we'll examine them in this section.

Gopher Groups

If your Gopher software isn't tunneling straight, you can get help by posting a question to the newsgroup **comp.infosystems.gopher**. This group is also the place to watch out for announcements of upgrades to Gopher programs, advice for running Veronica and Jughead searches, reviews of top Gopher sites, and lots more.

Where There's a Will, There's a WAIS

WAIS (Wide Area Information Server) is a great way to find information on the Net—when it works, that is. When it doesn't work, WAIS can be as frustrating as anything in cyberspace. If you're having trouble with your WAIS software, or if you'd like to improve your searching technique, try the newsgroup **comp.infosystems.wais**.

The Wonderful World of the World Wide Web

If you're wondering about the future of the Internet, look no further than the World Wide Web. There has been an explosion in the growth of Web sites and pages in the last year or two, and it shows no sign of slowing down any time soon. If you've got a question about a WWW browser (especially Netscape, one of the Mosaic flavors, or Lynx), or if you're looking for a particular Web site or page, try the newsgroup **comp.infosystems.www.users**.

FAQ Info:
    Articles:
       World Wide Web Frequently Asked Questions (FAQ), Part 1/2
       World Wide Web Frequently Asked Questions (FAQ), Part 2/2
       World Wide Web A Guide to Cyberspace
    RTFM.MIT.EDU Directory:
       /pub/usenet-by-group/comp.infosystems.www.users

If you provide information to the WWW, either as a server site or as the designer of your own Web pages, you can get technical help, advice, and all the info you need in **comp.infosystems.www.providers.**

FAQ Info:
    Article:
       What comp.infosystems.www.providers Is About - Read Before
          Posting (FAQ)
    RTFM.MIT.EDU Directory:
       /pub/usenet-by-group/comp.infosystems.www.providers

For all other Web issues, use the group **comp.infosystems.www.misc.** For example, this group would be the place to talk about the future of the Web, post Web stats, and discuss Web culture.

FAQ Info:
    Article:
       What comp.infosystems.www.misc Is About - Read Before
          Posting (FAQ)
    RTFM.MIT.EDU Directory:
       /pub/usenet-by-group/comp.infosystems.www.misc

As the World Wide Web becomes the standard interface for the Internet, more and more people will start doing their own Web publishing. If this interests you, the WWW Systems Engineering site is overflowing with all the info you need to create your own pages and set up your own server. To get there, send your favorite browser to the following URL:

    http://www.charm.net/~web/

Chapter 24 ➤ *News About the Net: Internet-Related Newsgroups*

The Internet Relay Chat

If you really want to reach out and touch someone on the Net, the best way to do this is via the *Internet Relay Chat (IRC)*. If you're one of the folks already addicted to this service, or if you're interested in joining an IRC channel but need more info, be sure to try out the following newsgroups:

alt.irc	General IRC material.
alt.irc.announce	Announcements about the IRC (moderated).
alt.irc.hottub	Discussions about the IRC channel **#hottub**.
alt.irc.ircii	Talking about IRCII.
alt.irc.questions	How-to questions for IRC.
alt.irc.recovery	Support group for IRC addicts.

```
FAQ Info:
    Articles:
        IRC Frequently Asked Questions (FAQ)
        IRC Undernet Frequently Asked Questions (FAQ) (Part 1 of 2)
        IRC Undernet Frequently Asked Questions (FAQ) (Part 2 of 2)
    RTFM.MIT.EDU Directory: /pub/usenet-by-group/alt.irc
```

USENET-Related Newsgroups

Back in Chapter 3, "Learning Netiquette: Minding Your USENET Ps and Qs," I told you about a couple of newsgroups designed for USENET newcomers: **news.announce.newusers** and **news.newusers.questions**. But there are actually two or three dozen groups that handle USENET-specific posts. This section looks at USENET's USENET newsgroups.

It Was the Best of News, It Was the Worst of News...

With newsgroups now numbered in the several thousands, there's no way for any mere mortal to read even a small percentage of the logorrhea that passes through the system each day. The result is usually a persistent, niggling sense of missing out on something.

Well, you'll be happy to know that the group **alt.best.of.internet** (*ABOI*) can lend a hand. The posts to this group are actually "re-posts" from other USENET groups. The idea is that if USENETers come across articles that are "funny, entertaining, intelligent, thought-provoking, or otherwise interesting," they should send them to ABOI. (You do this by following up the original article and changing the follow-up's Newsgroups line to **alt.best.of.internet**. See the FAQ for more details.) Yeah, sure, the articles aren't always funny, entertaining, and so on, but it's a good way to get a cross-section of what's happening in the USENET world.

```
FAQ Info:
    Article:   ABOI frequently answered questions (fun!)
    RTFM.MIT.EDU Directory:
        /pub/usenet-by-group/alt.best.of.internet
```

USENET Comedy Central

With tens of thousands of articles being posted to USENET every day, somebody's bound to say something humorous (intentionally or otherwise). When people come across something witty while reading the news, they send it in to the newsgroup **alt.humor.best-of-usenet**, and the group's moderators cull out the best ones (allegedly) and post them for everyone's enjoyment. If you want to discuss one of the **alt.humor.best-of-usenet** articles, or just berate the moderators, the place to post is the discussion group **alt.humor.best-of-usenet.d**.

A Review of the news Hierarchy

The **news** hierarchy is devoted to issues, info, and discussions about USENET news. Here's a rundown of some of the groups in the **news** hierarchy (I'll add a few more in the next couple of sections):

news.admin.misc	General topics of USENET news administration (FAQs available).
news.admin.policy	Policy issues of USENET.
news.admin.technical	Technical aspects of maintaining network news (moderated).
news.announce.conferences	Calls for papers and conference announcements (moderated).

Chapter 24 ➤ *News About the Net: Internet-Related Newsgroups*

news.announce.important	General announcements of interest to all USENETers (moderated).
news.announce.newusers	Explanatory postings for USENET neophytes (moderated).
news.answers	Repository for periodic USENET postings and FAQs (moderated).
news.lists	News-related statistics and lists (moderated).
news.lists.ps-maps	Maps relating to USENET traffic flows (moderated).
news.misc	Discussions of USENET itself.
news.newsites	Postings of new site announcements.
news.newusers.questions	Q&A for users new to USENET.

```
FAQ Info:
    Articles:
        FAQ on making and using a .signature file
        How to find the right place to post (FAQ)
        Internet Services FAQ (ver. 1.8)
        Signature and Finger FAQ
        Welcome to news.newusers.questions! (weekly posting)
    RTFM.MIT.EDU Directory:
        /pub/usenet-by-group/news.newsusers.questions
```

Groups About Groups

Newsgroups are what USENET is all about, so it makes sense that there'd be a few "meta-groups" devoted solely to discussing groups themselves. Here they are:

alt.config	Proposals for new **alt** newsgroups (FAQ available).
alt.newgroup	Lists of **alt** groups and new **alt** group announcements.

Part 3 ▸ *All the News That's Fit to Surf*

news.announce.newgroups	Calls for new groups and announcements of same (moderated).
news.config	Postings of system down times and interruptions.
news.future	The future technology of network news systems.
news.groups	RFDs and CFVs for proposed newsgroups.
news.groups.questions	"Where can I find talk about topic *X*?"
news.groups.reviews	"What is going on in the group or mailing list named *X*?" (moderated; FAQ available).

Newsreader Newsgroups

All the USENET reading and posting we do would be just about impossible if it weren't for our trusty newsreader sidekicks. But most newsreaders are imperfect beasts, at best, so advice and tips are always welcome. You can get newsreader news from any of the following groups:

news.software.anu-news	VMS B-news software from Australian National University (FAQ available).
news.software.b	Discussions about B-news-compatible software.
news.software.nn	Discussions about the **nn** news reader package (FAQ available).
news.software.nntp	Tips and tricks for Network News Transfer Protocol software (FAQs available).
news.software.notes	Notesfile software from the University of Illinois.
news.software.readers	Discussions of software used to read network news (FAQs available).
alt.usenet.offline-reader	Getting your fix offline.

310

Index

A

abortion newsgroups, 230
accessing-Internet newsgroups, 302
accessing-Internet-library newsgroups, 304
acronyms (articles), 40-43
addresses, domain names, 144, 156
advertising, 29
AI (artificial intelligence) newsgroups, 268-269
AIDS research newsgroups, 289-290
AIR newsreader
    articles
        posting, 120-121
        printing, 119
        reading, 118-119
    customizing, 121-122
    Newsgroup Browser, 113-114
    newsgroups
        finding, 114-115
        subscribing/unsubscribing, 115-117
    starting, 112-113
Air Warrior newsgroup, 220
alt hierarchy (USENET), 4
alternative music newsgroups, 188-189
amateur radio newsgroups, 204-205
America Online
    articles
        posting, 163-164
        posting follow-up articles, 162-163
        printing, 162
        reading, 161-162
        saving, 162
    newsgroups
        finding, 156-157
        subscribing/unsubscribing, 157-161
Amiga computer systems, games newsgroups, 219
anarchist newsgroup, 235
anonymous articles, posting via e-mail, 50-52

anthropology newsgroups, 296-297
antiques newsgroups, 206
aquariums newsgroups, 286
arcade game newsgroups, 225-226
archaeology newsgroups, 297
archiving articles, 105-107
articles, 4-7, 15-16
    acronyms, 40-43
    archiving (Trumpet newsreader), 105-107
    body, 5
    components, 16-19
    cross-posting, 28
    emphasizing, 45-46
    encoding, 19
    expired, 36
    filtering, 52
    flames, 6, 31, 36, 38-40
    folders, saving to, 105-107
    follow-up articles, posting, 4, 20-21
        AIR newsreader, 120
        America Online, 162-163
        Delphi, 173-174
        e-mail netiquette, 30-31
        Netscape newsreader, 131-132
        NewsWatcher newsreader, 140-141
        rn/trn newsreaders, 78
        tin newsreader, 93
        Trumpet newsreader, 107-108
    headers, 5
    kill files, 37
    navigating, 151
    netiquette, 5-6, 26-30
    posting, 4, 15, 109-110
        AIR newsreader, 120-121
        America Online, 163-164
        anonymous postings, 50-52
        CompuServe, 153-154
        Delphi, 174-175
        e-mail, 50-52
        netiquette, 26-30
        Netscape newsreader, 133
        newsreaders, testing, 29-30

        NewsWatcher newsreader, 141
        rn/trn newsreaders, 79
        tin newsreader, 93-94
        without newsreaders, 7
    printing
        AIR newsreader, 119
        America Online, 162
        Netscape newsreader, 131
        NewsWatcher newsreader, 140
    reading
        AIR newsreader, 118-119
        America Online, 161-162
        CompuServe, 150-151
        Delphi, 170-172
        Gopher, 6-7, 48-49
        Netscape newsreader, 128-130
        NewsWatcher newsreader, 139-140
        rn/trn newsreaders, 76-78
        tin newsreader, 91-92
        Trumpet newsreader, 102-104
    replying to, 152-153
        e-mail, 78, 108
    saving, 77-78, 119
        America Online, 162
        CompuServe, 152
        Delphi, 172
        Netscape newsreader, 131
        NewsWatcher newsreader, 140
        rn/trn newsreaders, 77-78
        tin newsreader, 92-93
        to files, 107
    selecting
        rn/trn newsreaders, 74-75
        tin newsreader, 89-91
    shouting, 27
    signatures, 5
    smileys, 6, 43-44
    special characters, 27
    Stanford Netnews Filtering Service, 7
    subject lines, 28

testing (rn/trn newsreaders), 29-30
threads, 4, 20-21
  selecting with tin newsreader, 89-91
  selecting with trn newsreader, 75-76
trolling, 38
artificial intelligence (AI) newsgroups, 268-269
asbestos longjohns, 39
asterisk (*), newsgroups, 46
astronomy newsgroups, 298-299
atheism newsgroups, 246
ATM (Asynchronous Transfer Mode) newsgroup, 270-271
audio newsgroups, 202-203
auto racing newsgroups, 259-260
automobile newsgroups, 214-215
aviation newsgroups, 212-213

B

backgammon newsgroup, 224
bandwidths, 34
banning (censorship) newsgroup, 236
bar placeholders, 36-37
baseball newsgroups, 253-255
basketball newsgroups, 255-256
BattleTech newsgroup, 221
baud rates, 35
beverage newsgroups, 208
biology newsgroups, 286-287
bionet newsgroups, 287
biotechnology newsgroups, 287
bird newsgroups, 210-211
bits per second (bps), 35
biz hierarchy, 5
  advertising, 29
board game newsgroups, 224-225
boats newsgroups, 213-214
body of articles, 5
Bolo newsgroup, 220
books newsgroups, 185
  science fiction, 192
bowling newsgroups, 260
boxing newsgroups, 260
bps (bits per second), 35
bridge game newsgroups, 227
Buddhism newsgroups, 246-247
burbles, 39
business newsgroups, 194

C

cancer research newsgroups, 290
car newsgroups, 214-215
carpal tunnel syndrome (CTS) newsgroup, 291
carpet bombs (newsgroups), 35
cat newsgroups, 211
CD-ROM newsgroups, 272
censorship newsgroup, 236
CFVs (Call For Votes) newsgroup RFDs, 61
charters (new group RFDs), 59
chemistry newsgroups, 287-288
chess newsgroups, 225
children newsgroups, 249
Chinese chess (xiangqi) newsgroup, 224-225
Christianity newsgroups, 247
civil liberties newsgroups, 234-236
classical music newsgroups, 189
classifieds newsgroups, 198
clone/PC newsgroups, 280-281
cognitive psychology newsgroups, 297
coins newsgroups, 207
collector newsgroups, 205-207
college newsgroups, 250
comic book newsgroups, 186-187
comp hierarchy (USENET), 4
CompuServe
  articles
    posting, 153-154
    reading, 150-151
    saving, 152
  newsgroups
    finding, 144-146
    subscribing/ unsubscribing, 147-150
  USENET options, 146-147
computer games newsgroups, 217-220
computer systems newsgroups, 280-284
computers for sale newsgroups, 283
conciousness philosophy newsgroup, 246
conservative politics newsgroups, 236-237
consumer newsgroups, 194-195

cooking newsgroups, 208-209
country newsgroups, 189
crafts newsgroups, 209-210
creating newsgroups, 57-62
cricket (sports) newsgroups, 260-261
cross-posting articles, 28
CTS (Carpal Tunnel Syndrome) newsgroup, 291
current event newsgroups, 230-234

D

data communications newsgroups, 269-271
DBMS (database management system) newsgroups, 273-274
death penalty newsgroup, 238
decoding graphics (newsgroups), 55
deleting
  articles from folders, 106
  folders (Trumpet newsreader), 107
  newsgroups from Personal Favorites lists (Delphi), 175
Delphi, 165-166
  articles
    posting, 174-175
    posting follow-up articles, 173-174
    reading, 170-172
    saving, 172
  Internet services, registering, 166
  newsgroups
    subscribing, 169-170
    unsubscribing, 175
  signature files, creating, 172-173
  starting, 166-169
  USENET Discussion Groups menu, 168-170
delurking (articles), 36
Democrat newsgroups, 237-238
dentistry newsgroups, 290
dictionary flames, 40
disease support-group newsgroups, 243-244
dog newsgroups, 211-212
domain names (addresses), 144, 156
DOOM newsgroups, 219-220
DOS newsgroups, 276
downloading
  GIF files, 54

Index

graphics from newsgroups, 54-55
NewsWatcher newsreader, 136
dream newsgroups, 242-243
drinks newsgroups, 208
drugs newsgroups, 231-232

E

e-mail
　articles
　　posting, 50-52
　　replying to, 78, 108
　　sending follow-up articles, 31
　mailing lists, 13
e-mail game newsgroups, 227
e-mail software newsgroups, 274
earth science newsgroups, 288-289
ecology newsgroups, 286
education newsgroups, 250
electrochemistry newsgroup, 287-288
electronics newsgroups, 295
Elliot, James, 13
emoticons
　non-smileys, 45
　smileys, 43-44
Empire newsgroup, 221
encoding articles, 19
encryption newsgroups, 230-231
energy newsgroups, 295
environmental newsgroups, 230
ethnic culture newsgroups, 245
ethology newsgroups, 286
evolution newsgroups, 286-287
exiting tin newsreader, 94
expired articles, 36

F

fantasy games newsgroups, 222-224
FAQ (Frequently Asked Question) lists, 3, 25-26
　tin newsreader, 82
fax forum (USENET) newsgroup, 269
feline newsgroups, 211
feminist newsgroups, 252
files
　GIF, downloading, 54-57
　JPEG, downloading, 54-57
　kill (articles), 37

.newsrc files, newsreaders, 69-72
　tin newsreader, 82-83
　signature (Delphi), 172-173
　Trumpet newsreader file, obtaining, 96-97
filtering articles, 52
finding newsgroups
　AIR newsreader, 114-115
　NewsWatcher newsreader, 137-138
firefighters, 40
fishing newsgroups, 261
flames (articles), 6, 31, 36, 38-40
folders
　deleting (Trumpet newsreader), 107
　saving articles to, 105-107
folk newsgroups, 189
folklore newsgroups, 251
follow-up articles, posting, 4, 20-21
　AIR newsreader, 120
　America Online, 162
　Delphi, 173-174
　e-mail netiquette, 30-31
　Netscape newsreader, 131-132
　newsreaders, 78
　NewsWatcher newsreader, 140-141
　tin newsreader, 93
　Trumpet newsreader, 107-108
foo placeholder, 36-37
foobar placeholders, 36-37
food newsgroups, 207-208
football newsgroups, 256-258
fractals newsgroups, 293
Frequently Asked Question (FAQ) lists, 3, 25-26
　tin newsreader, 82
FTP (File Transfer Protocol), 11-12
　Trumpet newsreader file, obtaining, 96-97
funk music newsgroups, 189
fuzzy logic (computers) newsgroups, 268-269

G

game newsgroups, 227-228
　arcade/video, 225-226
　board, 224-225
　computer, 217-220
　fantasy/role-playing, 222-224

　multi-player, 220-222
　PBM (play-by-mail), 227
geological newsgroups, 288
GIF (Graphics Interchange Format) files, downloading, 54-57
Go game newsgroup, 225
golf newsgroups, 261
Gopher, 12
　FAQ lists, accessing, 26
　reading articles, 6-7, 48-49
Gopher services newsgroups, 305
graphics, downloading/decoding, 54-55
graphics software newsgroups, 274-275
Group Selection list (tin newsreader), 85-89
Group Selection screen (tin newsreader), 84-89
grouping newsgroups, 46
gun newsgroups, 231

H

ham radio newsgroups, 204-205
hardware newsgroups, 283-284
headers of articles, 5
health care newsgroups, 231
herpetology newsgroups, 287
hierarchies (USENET), 4-5, 14
　biz, advertising, 29
　news, newcomer newsgroups, 25
history (political) newsgroups, 239-240
hobby newsgroups, 215-216
hockey newsgroups, 258-259
holy wars, 37
homosexuality newsgroups, 245
human rights newsgroups, 231
humanist newsgroup, 246
humor (on USENET) newsgroups, 308
hydrology newsgroups, 288

I

IBM PC/clone newsgroups, 280-281
individualism newsgroups, 235
interactive spell check command, 93
international culture newsgroups, 245
international current events newsgroups, 234

Internet, 10-13
    culture, 34
    Delphi services, registering, 166
    netiquette, 23-31
    newsgroups, 302-305
    surfing, 38
    telephone trunk lines, 35
Internet encryption newsgroups, 230-231
Internet in a Box (Spry, Inc.), AIR, 111-122
Internet Press, 303
Internet Registration menu, Terms of Use command, 166
Internet Talk Radio service, 304-305
investment newsgroups, 195-198
IRC (Internet Relay Chat) services newsgroups, 307
ISDN (Integrated Services Digital Network) newsgroups, 270
Islamic newsgroups, 248

J-K-L

jargonauts, 34
jazz newsgroups, 189
job-hunting newsgroups, 198-200
JPEG (Joint Photographic Experts Group) files, downloading, 54-57

kill files (articles), 37

LAN (local area network) newsgroups, 271
Latin music newsgroups, 189
leftism politics newsgroups, 237-238
liberal politics newsgroups, 237-238
Libertarian party newsgroup, 235
libraries (Internet), newsgroups for accessing, 304
Limbaugh (Rush) newsgroup, 237
linguistics newsgroups, 297-298
literature newsgroups, 185-187
    science fiction, 192
logic newsgroups, 293
lurking, 24
    delurking, 36
lusers, 37

M

Macintosh
    games newsgroups, 219
    newsgroups, 281-282
    NewsWatcher newsreader, 135-142
magazine newsgroups, 186
mailing lists, 13
Malamud, Carl, 304-305
martial arts newsgroups, 262
mathematics newsgroups, 292-294
medical science newsgroups, 289-292
men's movement newsgroups, 252
mental-ailment support-group newsgroups, 244
meteorology newsgroups, 288-289
microbiology newsgroups, 287
MIDI (Musical Instrument Digital Interface) newsgroup, 272
miniatures (wargaming) newsgroups, 228
misc hierarchy (USENET), 4
modem technical support newsgroup, 270
moderators (newsgroups), 16, 37
movie newsgroups, 183-185
MUD (multi-user dimension/dungeon) newsgroups, 221-222
multi-player game newsgroups, 220-222
multimedia newsgroups, 271-272
music newsgroups, 187-190
Muslim newsgroups, 248

N

names, newsgroups, 15
NASA issues newsgroups, 298
net. (Internet prefix), 37
netiquette, 5-6, 23-31
    writing articles, 17-18
Netizen newsgroup, 304
Netrek newsgroup, 221
Netscape newsreader, 123-124
    articles
        posting, 133
        posting follow-up articles, 131-132
        printing, 131
        reading, 128-130
        saving, 131
    newsgroups, subscribing/unsubscribing, 126-128
    starting, 124-125
newbies, 24, 37
    newsgroup, 304
news hierarchy (USENET), 4
    newsgroups, 308-309
Newsgroup Browser, 113-117
Newsgroup Selection list (tin newsreader), 88-89
newsgroup-related newsgroups, 309-310
newsgroups, 4, 14
    advertising, 29
    amateur radio, 204-205
    articles, *see* articles
    artificial intelligence, 268-269
    asterisks (*), 46
    astronomy, 298-299
    audio, 202-203
    auto racing, 259-260
    baseball, 253-255
    basketball, 255-256
    beverage, 208
    biology, 286-287
    books, 185
    bowling, 260
    boxing, 260
    business, 194
    carpet bombs, 35
    charters, 59
    chemistry, 287-288
    children, 249
    civil liberties, 234-236
    classifieds, 198
    collectors, 205-207
    comic books, 186-187
    computer systems, 280-284
    consumer, 194-195
    cooking, 208-209
    crafts, 209-210
    creating, 57-62
    cricket (sports), 260-261
    current events, 230-234
    CFVs, 61
    data communications, 269-271
    Democrats, 237-238
    descriptions, displaying, 84
    earth science, 288-289
    education, 250
    entertainment, 179-192
    ethnic culture, 245
    finding
        AIR newsreader, 114-115
        America Online, 156-157

Index

CompuServe, 144-146
NewsWatcher
  newsreader, 137-138
fishing, 261
folklore, 251
food, 207, 208
football, 256-258
Frequently Asked Question
  (FAQ) lists, 25-26
games, 217-228
golf, 261
Gopher services, 305
graphics, downloading/
  decoding, 54-55
grouping, 46
hierarchies (USENET),
  4-5, 14
history (political), 239-240
hobbies, 215-216
hockey, 258-259
Internet, 302-305
investment, 195-198
IRC services, 307
job-hunting, 198-200
lurking, 24
magazines, 186
martial arts, 262
mathematics, 292-294
medical science, 289-292
men's movement, 252
moderators, 37
movies, 183-185
multimedia, 271-272
music, 187-190
names, 15
netiquette, 5-6
  writing articles, 17-18
newcomers, 25
operating systems, 276-280
pets, 210-212
philosophical, 245-246
physics, 294-296
politics, 240
psychology, 242-244
racquet sports, 264
reggae, 189
religion, 246-249
Republican, 236-237
RFDs, 58-61
running (sports), 262
satanism, 248-249
science, 299-300
science fiction, 191-192
selecting, 28-29
  NewsWatcher
    newsreader, 138
  tin newsreader, 84-89
sexuality, 244-245
skating, 262-263

skiing, 263
skydiving, 263
soccer, 263-264
social sciences, 296-298
software, 272-275
space, 298-299
spamming, 38
spewers, 38
sports, 265-266
Stanford Netnews Filtering
  Service, 7
subscribing, 7, 38
  AIR newsreader, 115-117
  America Online,
    157-161
  CompuServe, 147-150
  Delphi, 169-170
  Netscape newsreader,
    126-128
  newsreaders, 69-73
  tin newsreader, 85-89
  Trumpet newsreader,
    101-102
support groups, 242-244
television, 179-183
testing (newsreaders), 29-30
text editors, starting, 69-71
threads, 4, 20-21, 89
  reading (Delphi),
    171-172
  selecting (trn
    newsreader), 75-76
transportation, 212-215
triathlons, 264
unsubscribing, 85
  AIR newsreader, 115-117
  America Online,
    160-161
  CompuServe, 149-150
  Delphi, 175
  Netscape newsreader,
    126-128
  Trumpet newsreader,
    101-102
USENET-related, 307-310
video, 203-204
WAIS services, 305
war (historical), 238-239
water sports, 265
women's issues, 252
writers, 186
WWW services, 305-306
.newsrc files (newsreaders),
  69-73
  tin newsreader, 82-83
newsreader newsgroups, 310
newsreaders, 6-7, 15, 65-80
  AIR, 112-122
  articles, *see* articles

Delphi, 165-175
Netscape, 123-134
NewsWatcher, 135-142
rn, 66-79
testing, 29-30
tin, 81-94
trn, 66-79
Trumpet, 96-110
NewsWatcher newsreader
  articles
    posting, 141
    posting follow-up
      articles, 140-141
    printing, 140
    reading, 139-140
    saving, 140
  downloading, 136
  newsgroups
    finding, 137-138
    selecting, 138
  preferences, setting, 141
  starting, 136-137
non-smileys, 45
numerical analysis
  newsgroups, 293
nursing newsgroups, 291

O

ob- (newsgroup humor prefix),
  37
oceanography newsgroups,
  289
opera newsgroups, 189
operating systems newsgroups,
  276-280
operations research newsgroup
  (math), 294
optics newsgroups, 295
OS/2 operating system
  games newsgroups, 219
  OS/2 operating system
    newsgroups, 276-277

P

PBM (play-by-mail) game
  newsgroups, 227
PCs (personal computers)
  games newsgroups, 218
  PC/clone newsgroups,
    280-281
personality (psychology)
  newsgroups, 242
pet newsgroups, 210-212
philosophy newsgroups,
  245-246
physical-ailment support-
  group newsgroups, 243

315

physics newsgroups, 294-296
pictures, *see* graphics
play-by-mail (PBM) game newsgroups, 227
Pnews posting program, 79
political correctness newsgroups, 231
political newsgroups, 240
polymers newsgroups, 288
posting articles, 4, 15, 109-110
   AIR newsreader, 120-121
   America Online, 163-164
   anonymous postings, 50-52
   CompuServe, 153-154
   cross-posting, 28
   Delphi, 174-175
   e-mail, 50-52
   follow-up articles, *see* follow-up articles, posting
   netiquette, 26-30
   Netscape newsreader, 133
   newsreaders, 79
      testing, 29-30
   NewsWatcher newsreader, 141
   tin newsreader, 93-94
   without newsreaders, 7
postmodernist philosophy newsgroup, 246
PPP (Point-to-Point Protocol), 97
printing articles
   AIR newsreader, 119
   America Online, 162
   Netscape newsreader, 131
   NewsWatcher newsreader, 140
privacy newsgroups, 235-236
prompts, responses (rn/trn newsreaders), 67-68
protocols
   FTP (File Transfer Protocol), 11-12
   PPP (Point-to-Point Protocol), 97
   SLIP (Serial Line Interface Protocol), 97
psychology newsgroups, 242-244, 297

Q-R

Quayle (Dan) newsgroup, 237

racquet sports newsgroups, 264
raves, 40
reading articles
   AIR newsreader, 118-119
   America Online, 161-162

CompuServe, 150-151
Delphi, 170-172
Gopher, 6-7, 48-49
Netscape newsreader, 128-130
newsreaders, 74-78
NewsWatcher newsreader, 139-140
Trumpet newsreader, 102-104
rec hierarchy (USENET), 4
recording-artist fan club newsgroups, 190
reggae newsgroups, 189
registering Internet services (Delphi), 166
relationships newsgroups, 244-245
religion newsgroups, 246-249
replying to articles, 152-153
   e-mail, 78
   Trumpet newsreader, 108
Republican newsgroups, 236-237
RFDs (Requests for Discussion), 58-61
rightism politics newsgroups, 236-237
rn newsreader, 66
   articles
      posting, 79
      posting follow-up articles, 78
      reading, 76-78
      saving, 77-78
      selecting, 74-75
   newsgroups, subscribing, 69-73
   starting, 66-69
robotics newsgroups, 269
rock 'n' roll newsgroups, 188
role-playing games newsgroups, 222-224
rot13, encoding articles, 19
running newsgroups (sports), 262

S

satanism newsgroups, 248-249
saving articles, 119
   America Online, 162
   CompuServe, 152
   Delphi, 172
   Netscape newsreader, 131
   NewsWatcher newsreader, 140
   rn/trn newsreaders, 77-78

tin newsreader, 92-93
   to files, 107
sci hierarchy (USENET), 4
science fiction newsgroups, 191-192
science newsgroups, 299-300
searches
   newsgroups (AIR newsreader), 114-115
   regular expressions (tin newsreader), 86
selecting
   articles (rn/trn newsreaders), 74-75
   newsgroups, 28-29
   NewsWatcher newsreader, 138
   threads (trn newsreader), 75-76
self-improvement newsgroups, 242
selling-computers newsgroups, 283
Sevetz, Kevin, 303
sexuality newsgroups, 244-245
SGI (Silicon Graphics International) newsgroups, 282-283
shareware newsgroups, 275
shouting (articles), 27
sig quotes, 38
signal-to-noise ratio, 38
signature files (Delphi), 172-173
signatures (articles), 5
skating newsgroups, 262-263
skiing newsgroups, 263
skydiving newsgroups, 263
SLIP (Serial Line Interface Protocol), 97
smileys, 6, 43-44
SNFS (Stanford Netnews Filtering Service), 7, 52-54
soc hierarchy (USENET), 4
soccer newsgroups, 263-264
social (Internet) newsgroup, 304
social sciences newsgroups, 296-298
software (newsreaders), 6-7
software newsgroups, 272-275
space newsgroups, 298-299
spamming (newsgroups), 38
special characters (articles), 27
spewers (newsgroups), 38
sports newsgroups, 259-266
spreadsheet software newsgroups, 275
Spry, Inc.'s Internet In a Box, 112

Index

stamps newsgroups, 207
Stanford Netnews Filtering Service (SNFS), 7, 52-54
Star Trek newsgroups, 192
starting
    AIR newsreader, 112-113
    Delphi newsreader, 166-169
    Netscape newsreader, 124-125
    newsgroups, 57-62
    NewsWatcher newsreader, 136-137
    rn/trn newsreaders, 66-69
    tin newsreader, 82-84
    Trumpet newsreader, 97-101
statistics newsgroups, 294
stereo newsgroups, 202-203
strategy game newsgroups, 227
subject lines (articles), 28
subscribing to newsgroups, 7, 38
    AIR newsreader, 115-117
    America Online, 157-161
    CompuServe, 147-150
    Delphi, 169-170
    Netscape newsreader, 126-128
    newsreaders, 69-71, 71-73
    Trumpet newsreader, 101-102
    tin newsreader, 85-89
Sun Microsystems newsgroups, 283
support group newsgroups, 242-244
surfing (Internet), 38
symbolic algebra newsgroups, 293

T

talk hierarchy (USENET), 4
telephone trunk lines, 35
television newsgroups, 179-183
Telnet, 12
tennis newsgroups, 264
testing newsreaders, 29-30
text editors (newsgroups), subscribing, 69-71
text game newsgroups, 228
threads, 4, 20-21, 89
    reading (Delphi), 171-172
    selecting (trn newsreader), 75-76

tin newsreader, 81-94
    articles
        posting, 93-94
        posting follow-up articles, 93
        reading, 91-92
        saving, 92-93
        selecting, 89-91
    exiting, 94
    newsgroups, selecting, 84-89
    starting, 82-84
trading card newsgroups, 206
transportation newsgroups, 212-215
triathlon newsgroups, 264
trivia game newsgroups, 227
trn newsreader, 66
    articles
        posting, 79
        posting follow-up articles, 78
        reading, 76-78
        saving, 77-78
        selecting, 74-75
    newsgroups, subscribing, 69-73
    starting, 66-69
    threads, selecting, 75-76
trolling (articles), 38
Trumpet newsreader
    articles
        archiving, 105-107
        posting, 109-110
        posting follow-up articles, 107-108
        reading, 102-104
        replying via e-mail, 108
        saving, 107
    folders, deleting, 107
    newsgroups
        devoted, 100-101
        subscribing/unsubscribing, 101-102
    obtaining, 96-97
    starting, 97-101
    Winsock, 96
Truscott, Tom, 13

U

U.S current event newsgroups, 232-233
university newsgroups, 250
UNIX operating system newsgroups, 277-278

unsubscribing newsgroups, 72, 85
    AIR newsreader, 115-117
    America Online, 160-161
    CompuServe, 147-150
    Delphi, 175
    Netscape newsreader, 126-128
    Trumpet newsreader, 101-102
updating
    Newsgroup Browser list
        AIR newsreader, 113-117
USENET, 9-10
    articles, 16-21
    components, 13-15
    Frequently Asked Question (FAQ) lists, 3
    hierarchies, 4-5
    Internet, 10-13
    netiquette, 5-6
    newsgroup names, 15
USENET-related newsgroups, 307-310
uuencoders, decoding graphics, 55

V-Z

VGA Planets newsgroup, 221
video game newsgroups, 225-226
video newsgroups, 203-204
WAIS (Wide Area Information Server) services newsgroup, 305
war (historical) newsgroups, 238-239
wargaming-with-miniatures newsgroups, 228
water sport newsgroups, 265
Windows newsgroups, 279-280
Winsock software (Trumpet newsreader), 96
women's issues newsgroups, 252
world current event newsgroups, 234
writers newsgroups, 186
WWW (World Wide Web), 12
    services newsgroups, 305-306
xiangqi (Chinese chess) newsgroup, 224-225

317

GET CONNECTED
to the ultimate source of computer information!

The MCP Forum on CompuServe

Go online with the world's leading computer book publisher! Macmillan Computer Publishing offers everything you need for computer success!

Find the books that are right for you!
A complete online catalog, plus sample chapters and tables of contents give you an in-depth look at all our books. The best way to shop or browse!

➤ Get fast answers and technical support for MCP books and software

➤ Join discussion groups on major computer subjects

➤ Interact with our expert authors via e-mail and conferences

➤ Download software from our immense library:
  ▷ Source code from books
  ▷ Demos of hot software
  ▷ The best shareware and freeware
  ▷ Graphics files

Join now and get a free CompuServe Starter Kit!

To receive your free CompuServe Introductory Membership, call **1-800-848-8199** and ask for representative #597.

The Starter Kit includes:
➤ Personal ID number and password
➤ $15 credit on the system
➤ Subscription to *CompuServe Magazine*

Once on the CompuServe System, type:

GO MACMILLAN

for the most computer information anywhere!

MACMILLAN COMPUTER PUBLISHING

CompuServe

PLUG YOURSELF INTO...

THE MACMILLAN INFORMATION SUPERLIBRARY™

Free information and vast computer resources from the world's leading computer book publisher—online!

FIND THE BOOKS THAT ARE RIGHT FOR YOU!

A complete online catalog, plus sample chapters and tables of contents give you an in-depth look at *all* of our books, including hard-to-find titles. It's the best way to find the books you need!

- **STAY INFORMED** with the latest computer industry news through our online newsletter, press releases, and customized Information SuperLibrary Reports.
- **GET FAST ANSWERS** to your questions about MCP books and software.
- **VISIT** our online bookstore for the latest information and editions!
- **COMMUNICATE** with our expert authors through e-mail and conferences.
- **DOWNLOAD SOFTWARE** from the immense MCP library:
    - Source code and files from MCP books
    - The best shareware, freeware, and demos
- **DISCOVER HOT SPOTS** on other parts of the Internet.
- **WIN BOOKS** in ongoing contests and giveaways!

TO PLUG INTO MCP: ➤ **WORLD WIDE WEB: http://www.mcp.com**

GOPHER: gopher.mcp.com
FTP: ftp.mcp.com

Home Page | What's New | Bookstore | Reference Desk | Software Library | Macmillan Overview | Talk to Us

Who Cares What *YOU* Think?

WE DO!

alpha books

We're not complete idiots. We take our readers' opinions very personally. After all, you're the reason we publish these books! Without you, we'd be pretty bored.

alpha books

So please! Drop us a note or fax us a fax! We'd love to hear what you think about this book or others. A real person—not a computer—reads every letter we get and makes sure your comments get relayed to the appropriate people.

Not sure what to say? Here's some stuff we'd like to know:

- Who are you (age, occupation, hobbies, etc.)?
- Which book did you buy and where did you get it?
- Why did you pick this book instead of another one?
- What do you like best about this book?
- What could we have done better?
- What's your overall opinion of the book?
- What other topics would you like to purchase a book on?

Mail, e-mail, or fax your brilliant opinions to:

Faithe Wempen
Product Development Manager
Alpha Books
201 West 103rd Street
Indianapolis, IN 46290
FAX: (317) 581-4669

CompuServe: 75430,174
Internet: FWempen@alpha.mcp.com